The Endangered Human Animal

AN EXAMINATION OF THE REVOLUTIONARY
SURVIVAL IMPERATIVES

Kurt Dreifuss

Introduction by
John E. Burciaga

HM
108
.D73
1984
R0048094598

TO MY WIFE, BESSIE

Without her loving care of my daily medical and nutritional needs, I would never, but *never*, have brought this book to market.

Books by Kurt Dreifuss

The Other Side Of The Universe
A United Nations System Of Bicameral World Service Federation
What Debs Means To America
The Endangered Human Animal

Acknowledgement for invaluable Editing and Proof-reading of these books must go to two Paulines: Pauline Asher of Clearwater, Florida; and Pauline Frank of Cedarburg, Wisconsin.

Library of Congress Catalog Number 84-52235
ISBN 0-9614149-0-1

First WSF Edition December 1984

Manufactured in the United States of America by The Society for a World Service Federation. P.O. Box 1362, Dunedin, Florida. 34296

No part of this book may be reproduced, for any reason, by any means, without permission of the publisher.

Table of Contents

Introduction　　　　　　　　　　　　　　　　　　　vii
Author's Foreword　　　　　　　　　　　　　　　　　ix

Part 1
THE BIOLOGICAL IMPERATIVE OF NATURAL
SURVIVAL THROUGH HUMAN SELECTION

Chapter		*Page*
1	Point of Departure	3
2	Man, The Predator	11
3	Persistence Of The Social Darwinist Fallacy	20
4	Man, The Cooperator	25
5	Much Maligned Man, The Competitor	31
6	The Thinker Versus The Inventor	35
7	Adumbrations Of Man's Creative Destiny	49
8	Natural Survival Through Human Selection (a) Enlightened Frugality	56
9	Natural Survival Through Human Selection (b) Reverence of Life	61
10	The Soilbed Of Empirical Evidence	67
11	Our Kin In Unlike Form	79
12	Squaring Man's Debt With Our Unlike Kin	88
13	The Rationale Of Life Sustaining Criminology	97

Part 2
THE ECOLOGICAL IMPERATIVE OF SOCIETAL TRANSFORMATION

	Prefatory Comment	117
14	The Quiet Social Revolution In Sweden	119
15	Violent Revolution In Mexico	129
16	The Revolutions That Shook The World	141
17	The Russian Revolution	154
18	The Violence Syndrome And Social Revolution	175
19	The Marxist/Leninist Prelude In China	181
20	The Chinese Civil War That Was A Revolution	191
21	The People's Republic Of China	205
22	Proposal: A Peaceful Revolution In The USA	223
23	More On The Proposal	239
24	The Ultimate Imperative	262
	Reference Notes	287

Introduction

The best solutions to world problems come from the best people: those whose keen intelligence and vision are matched entirely by their humanity and compassion.

Such an enlightened document is this book, the *magnum opus* of a heart and mind engaged for more than eight decades in the living and struggling of the years that bring us to the incredible age in which we now live. That the author's own life fully spans the present century and measures both the past and the future with perception and clarity, is adequate recommendation of these contents.

We are herein reminded of our true human heritage, the biological imperative that courses our beings with the persistent message that, despite our social and cultural defects, we are built to survive.

With an eye on the great social and political revolutions of recent history, the author argues for the most civilized alternative for these perilous times—a peaceful transformation beginning with our domestic economy and culminating in a cooperative world community.

The following pages are existential because humanity has indeed endangered itself, and prophetic because ingenuity and cooperation, not despair and self-destructiveness, can and must be the result of our evolution through the eons.

There is no better antidote to social depression than knowledge, perspective and an incurable optimism. They are all at the heart of this book and deserve the attention of all who care to ensure the future of our world and of our kind.

The Rev. John E. Burciaga
Clearwater, Florida

Author's Foreword

The thesis of Natural Survival Through Human Selection, which is the core of this study, grew out of a chance conversation in the late 1960s with my friend and kindred spirit, Frank C. McCurdy, then Chairman of the Department of Natural Sciences at Central YMCA College in Chicago.

The argument underlying the NSHS idea took hold of me like a compulsive obsession, demanding that I cling to it tenaciously. Little did I dream that the ensuing struggle with it would hold me in captivity for years to come, until I had fully charted a survival course for the endangered human animal.

Once I had managed to draft a basic blueprint, with the aid of such ideological tools as were available at the time, I dug into the research necessary for its support. Finally, I had the feeling that the case would have to stand largely on its own merits.

Having said this, I must take cognizance of the fact that we now live in the 1980s. The endangered human animal is much closer to nuclear self-extermination than when I began to draft my plea for its survival some ten to fifteen years ago. For the reader, too, this flash-back reveals the rapidly worsening human condition, up to the present, and stresses the urgent need for remedial collective action.

PART 1

The Biological Imperative of Natural Survival Through Human Selection

1

Point of Departure

> Tell me not in mournful numbers
> Life is but an empty dream
> And the soul is dead that slumbers
> And things are not what they seem
>
> Life is real, life is earnest
> And the grave is not its goal
> Dust thou art to dust returnest
> Was not spoken of the soul.
>
> Longfellow

A hundred years ago, every school child was taught to memorize these lines of Longfellow's ode to life. If the words sound dated today, the thought is eternal. And the thought transforms itself at once into the question: What is man? What is life?

By whatever words the poet or philosopher might phrase the thought today, it breathes the mystery of Being that has refused man an answer through the ages and will probably continue to refuse one long into the immeasurable future. (We use the term "man" in its broad meaning as a human being, male or female, unless the reference is clearly to a member of the male sex.)

Perhaps the answer is not the important thing. Perhaps, the important thing is what man makes of the wondrous gift of life, what depth of reverence he (or she) learns to derive from it. The thought has particular relevance to our present-day emphasis on science and scientific truth.

Every age has its own composite of life-outlooks, reflective of a synthesis of past bio-cultural behavior patterns and the life-styles of the momentary present. Looking back, the individual can see only in fragmentary fashion the play of the past in the present. He sees it through the limited horizon of his own personal life experience, circumscribed still further by the incomplete and transitory value-system of the particular society in which he is submerged. The philosopher,

Emanuel Kant, extended the limitations of the individual to all mankind. Man can never see "the thing itself" (das Ding an sich), only its appearance as viewed through the narrow categories of the human understanding.

It is with an almost obsessive awareness of this small framework of human knowledge that we embark at this time (May 1969) upon a study of the projective implications of man's past and present behavior characteristics. But it is not a novel undertaking. Men and women have pondered the subject throughout all written history and no doubt long before, from the time Plato projected the perfect state in his *Republic*, to Thomas More's *Utopia* and Edward Bellamy's *Looking Backward*.

For more than a decade, there has been a great outpouring of futuristic appraisals of what man can or might do with the wondrous gift of life. Every well-catalogued library has scores of these present-day writings. Germane to our discussion are three schools of thought: the bio-sociological, heavily weighted with the Darwinian concept of evolution; the technoscientific, reciprocally nurturing and being nurtured by modern industrial society; the revolutionary, which rejects both the other rationales. As of this writing, all three are characteristically expressed, often with wide divergence within a kindred group, in such works as these: in the first category, Robert Ardrey's *African Genesis*, Konrad Lorenz' *On Aggression*, and Desmond Morris' *The Naked Ape*; in the second, Alvin Toffler's *Future Shock*, John Galbraith's *The Affluent Society*, Jean-Francoise Revel's *Without Marx or Jesus*; in the third, Herbert Marcuse' *Reason and Revolution*, Charles Reich's *The Greening of America*, and the collected works of Mao Tse-tung.

These and many similar works, written over the past few decades, encompass the analytical input of markedly different life-outlooks. Projection of their contending value-systems into the future is of quite a different order than the Utopias of the past, dreamed up by fiction writers with a philosophical and imaginative bent of mind. It is scientific projection, applied to all human endeavors, with a twofold purpose. One part is to enable practical people to project their personal undertakings into the short-range future with a return of precise knowledge; the other, to assist specialists in the various physical and social sciences, to make long-range projections in the specific fields of their competence.

With short-range projections, science has done marvels in the political field. We can watch TV on election day and find out who was elected after only a few votes are in. The miracle is performed by selecting key districts of the electorate and counting the first votes cast there. The computer does the rest in a few seconds. Merchants make similar accurate projections by test-marketing new products, as do other specialists, in budgeting their operations a number of years into the future.

Knowledge in the physical sciences has given man the ability to determine far into the future the movements of heavenly bodies, chart their course through cosmic space, launch man-made space craft into orbit around other planets, land them on designated spots, calculate precisely how long it will take them to reach their destination. It enables man to measure the amounts of natural resources like oil and tin deposited in the crust of the earth, predict how long they will last under controlled conditions for man's use, and make similarly accurate prognostications as to the size of the world's population in the year 2000.

But long-range futuristic projection in the broad societal affairs of man is an infinitely more difficult and elusive task. There are lacking those commonly accepted measuring sticks so conveniently available to mathematicians and physicists; there are only the widely divergent ideas as to what the future *should* be! Yet, it is a crucially important task, for on its findings may depend the very survival of the human species and much of all other existing life on this planet.

There is consensus among informed people today (the 1980s) that, had we had the foresight a hundred years ago to evaluate the future impact of the social and economic practices in vogue, we might have avoided some of the pitfalls into which our headlong rush for material wealth has led us. We might never have engaged in the massive campaign of wildlife decimation and environmental pollution so vividly described in Rachel Carson's *Silent Spring*. It will now require a vastly larger investment in human resources, inventivity, and sheer time, to restore nature's ecological balance than it took to destroy it.

We now return to the question posed at the outset of this paper. *How can man use to the full the wondrous gift of life?* A meaningful answer spans history. In our study of the three schools of thought, especially as they emanate from present western society and have, by the persuasive force of military and economic might, dominated world affairs for over two centuries, we are much more interested in the empirical data these schools offer for the future of mankind than in their explanations of past or even present human behavior patterns. The continuum of past, present and future is, to be sure, inseparable. What has been said and done in the past about sociobiological phenomena becomes of necessity a kind of launching pad for an assessment of what can be expected to happen in the future. And in that sense only, it serves as a point of departure for the conceptual base of the biological imperative of Natural Survival Through Human Selection (NSHS), which is the subject to be explored in this part of our study.

In order that we may proceed from a mutually acceptable number of pre-existing humanistic realities, we should state what we take to be axiomatic about them. This can be done briefly and broadly in the hope the reader will accord us at least tentative acceptance while deferring final judgment until the full NSHS case is in.

We start from the premise that *mankind is still in a primitive sociobiological stage of development*, a deduction to which we are led by the huge gap existing between those ethical, aesthetic and material standards all religions and philosophies set as prerequisites for the good life, and the actual practices by which man violates them. The facts are commonplace and require only a quick listing. They include such realities as these:

1. The most devastating and barbaric wars in all history, waged for more than half a century by western warrior nations bent on the age-old aspiration of power and the spoils of empire building.

2. The enormous accumulation of ill-gotten wealth and concentration of military power in the hands of these nations that comprise less than 20 percent of the world's population. The wide-spread poverty and malnutritional disease among the great majority of the people around the globe, whose food-bearing lands and other natural resources have been ravished by the invaders in concert with the native landowning elites.

3. The accelerating despoliation of the earth's life and food-giving environment by the unbridled techno-scientific industrial and military pursuits of contemporary primitive man.

4. The mounting waves of domestic crime, corruption, and violence in the political, economic and social life of nations.

5. The bizarre flow of cultural monstrosities issuing from the insane chase for material wealth. A few examples taken from human behavior in the rich warrior nations are necessary to illustrate this strange social phenomenon: the college-bred bomber pilot who sees his job and does it with little or no compunction as to its barbarity; the specialist expert, hugely busy as a fractionated human being in the tiny niche of his specialization, while having lost the ability to converse intelligently about anything outside his tiny specialist niche; the rank-and-file human robots in technologically automated production, who all but excel their scientifically trained counter-parts in the inability to

communicate knowledgeably about anything of common concern; the nuclear physicist who is eager and ready to sell his scientific expertise to the highest bidder in military connected enterprise; the virtuous citizen at every occupational level, who declaims piously, "I hate war as much as anyone!" then belies his declammation every time his heart-beat quickens to the thrill of the drum and bugle corps and the inevitable salute to arms, as he stands in reverence at each public display of these military symbols of the "patriotic" kill.

6. Finally, the signs of emerging forces for fundamental change which, if not still-born, will mark the end of a long era of primitive human society.

We in the affluent West, as the dubious beneficiaries of the spoils of war (and the accompanying "work ethic" which helps us make the most of it), are accustomed to picturing the material comforts and luxuries, the leisure-time enjoyment of literature and the arts among warrior nations, as a form of "higher" culture. We call it civilization. It is an ancient, spurious kind of civilization. The Babylonian, the Egyptian, the Assyrian warrior nations had it until they succumbed to the military power of the Persian Empire in the century between 600 to 500 B.C. The Persians lost it to the Greeks in the battles of Marathon (490 B.C.) and Thermopylae (480 B.C.). The Greeks flaunted it, especially in the "Golden Age" of Pericles, until they in turn were done in by the Spartans in the Peloponnesian War (431–404 B.C.) and the subsequent Black Plague. The Romans, the Spanish, the British—all basked briefly in the illusory glory of their respective pseudocivilizations. Now we Americans in the United States.

Reason would dictate that true civilization, if and when it can be attained, will be more survival oriented. Today's status-quo thinkers may argue—and they probably voice the opinion of the great majority of people in contemporary primitive society—that man as a civilized being is making much progress in the techno-scientifically advanced nations, East *or* West. But if history teaches us anything, it is that truth is seldom on the side of numbers or of the brightest status-quo thinkers.

The simple truth is, of course, that the primitive moral standards of contemporary industrial society did not emerge full-blown from recent technological developments; nor are they any more or less reprehensible intrinsically than those of the past. They are precisely the standards handed down to us by very old and deeply rooted culture-values, augmented and confounded by technological science, but unchanged, unimproved. In the judgment of many competent observers, they are the mark of regression rather than progress. The historian, Arnold

Toynbee, takes a dim view of things. On January 3, 1973, he had this to say:

> Civilization is manifestly beating a retreat.... The ultimate cause of this regression is, of course, the sinfulness of human nature, but the immediate cause is the availability of tools for doing the tempting sinful job. These tools have been placed in modern man's hands by his technological advance.... We can now see that the word 'civilization' has been changing in its meaning since it was first coined—and it was coined in the 18th century, before the Industrial Revolution. Originally the word stood for a social and ethical advance, and this is its proper meaning; but it now has come to stand for a technological advance, with the tacit immoral understanding that every technological means at man's disposal may be used by man legitimately to impose his will, regardless of the moral character of his objective.[1]

Although Toynbee's assessment implies a full line of retreat in all major fields of human endeavor, his severest single indictment is directed toward the immoral role played by the United States in the Vietnam war.

Prior to the war in Vietnam when, in July 1945, the United States dropped the atom bomb on Hiroshima and Nagasaki, the nuclear physicist, Harold Urey, is reported to have uttered in dismay: "There is nothing in cosmic law that requires the continued existence of the human race." Toynbee echoes this and the concern of all thoughtful people:

> "When one species thus makes itself a nuisance to the rest of nature, nature has ways and means of getting rid of it by inducing it to liquidate itself. In the past, nature has repeatedly taken this precautionary preventive action. Has man now become an intolerable nuisance to the rest of life? And is technology the weapon that nature has deftly placed in man's hands to enable man to commit suicide? A majority of the species of life that have come into existence to date are already extinct. Is man going to join this majority? Or is he going, before it is too late, to repent and make his peace with nature and with his own better self?"

There is, fortunately, a strong survival oriented answer, and it lies oddly enough in the paradoxical nature of the very technological weapon which possesses the finality of total annihilation yet, also, has an opposite beneficial potential. This is to say, it bodes destruction in one direction but reflects man's creative genius in the other, which can, if employed to foster life-sustaining ideals, generate the dynamics of revolutionary societal change and a will toward human survival. But, that creativity can no more make a thing of beauty out of the time-worn stuff of primitive culture-systems, here or abroad than, to use an old expression, one can make a silk purse out of a sow's ear. What has to happen was stated by one of America's respected elder statesmen, former Ambassador to the USSR, George F. Kennan, when he said in an address at Los Alamos, April 22, 1972:

> An American society which would be in harmony with its own natural habitat would look a great deal different from the one we have before us today, and the necessary changes are revolutionary in the effects they are bound to have on the character of our society. There will be things we have to submit to which we will not at all like; changes we will have to accept that will interfere with cherished and valued habits; practices we will have to embrace which will seem to us as steps backward in what we have been taught to see as progress of civilization.

Existing political parties, reflected Kennan, can not be expected to come up with the ideas for such a transformation nor the type of leadership in executing them that our environmental and societal predicament calls for. "That must come *from outside the system itself.* . . . This is the only way of achieving a drastic revolution of the technological, economic and social character of our society without replacing the ballot box with the bayonet as the ultimate sanction of political authority." We set the rest off in italics. *"And unless such a revolution is accomplished soon, the time left for our civilization has to be measured in decades and not in centuries or half centuries."*[2]

Kennan's call for fundamental societal change through peaceful collective action in the political arena—where the action has to be—underscores the strategy, if not the goals, of our own study of the endangered human animal's survival options. Our thesis calls for socio-political revolution, in order to achieve a human life-style founded on *Natural Survival Through Human Selection.*

In PART I of this study we shall look at the historical setting and amplify the meaning of NSHS. PART II will link the NSHS Biological tenets with those of the Ecological Imperative. Integrating the two parts enables us to join the wellbeing of all societal life-forms with that of contemporary primitive human society, and chart a way out of the wilderness of mankind's ancient and still thriving barbaric myths and practices.

A prefatory word about NSHS: The central idea holds that man is capable, in a finite sense, of sustaining life on a fully ethical and ecological scope for all life forms, including his own, by virtue of his uniquely endowed inventive genius. The idea, carried to its logical conclusion, has a clout that is far more powerful than may appear at this point in our discussion. We shall explain as we proceed.

The wide ecological and societal front on which the thrust of Natural Survival Through Human Selection must become operative, makes it impossible to confine our examination to anything less than a broadly integrated, sweeping exploration of many areas of human endeavor: Science, education, religion, industry, agriculture, philosophy and the arts, ecology, politics, for they are all inextricably interwoven. By the same token, it would be impossible to touch upon more than a few essentials in so all-inclusive a realm of societal affairs; nor can we do more than draw sparingly, almost at random, upon supportive documentation from literally tens of thousands of relevant scholarly books, articles, tracts and treatises poured out monthly by commercial and academic printing presses. In the final test, the NSHS idea must stand or fall largely on the strength of its own argument.

2

Man, The Predator

It is a truism that cherished old beliefs and practices die hard. If their supportive rationale is suddenly removed they strive, nonetheless, to live long beyond their time. Old superstitions have this strong survival capacity. We westerners still avoid walking under a ladder. Elevators in some high-rise apartment buildings and hotels still go from the 12th to the 14th floor, skipping number "13" because guests might feel uncomfortable sleeping on an unlucky numbered floor.

A more socially mischievous persistence of invalid beliefs is the notion that skin pigmentation has something to do with racial competence and virtue. European Caucasians are still struggling to rid themselves of the notion that white complexioned races are superior to black ones, and eastern Mongolian peoples color their mythological witches and evil spirits in white!

For centuries women have been denied the right to participate in political affairs, on the notion that only the male member of the species possesses the sophistication and intelligence necessary to deal with the complicated affairs of state. It was not until 1920 that women won the right to vote and hold public office in the United States; and the battle for women's liberation from other restraints to equal opportunity in all societal affairs, is still being fought today.

There are, indeed, some dramatic exceptions to this tenacity of absurd old ideas to outlive their time. This occurs, however, only in the strictly physical manifestations of ancient beliefs which must, perforce, expire the very moment a newly evolved truth makes them obsolete. When Columbus' ships did not fall over the edge of the Atlantic ocean in his mistaken discovery of a new route to the East Indies, and a few more such globe-encircling adventures proved his idea to be essentially correct, the Earth's shape suddenly ceased to conform to the ancient belief that it was flat as a table. The belief that God would have supplied man with wings had He intended man to be able to fly, came to a quick end when the Wright brothers invented their flying machine; and the companion notion that man could certainly never fly to the Moon has now met a similar sudden death.

But in the realm of socio-biological phenomena false ideas are not so easily dispatched. One of the oldest and most stubbornly resistant of these is the belief that nature's food scarcity makes inevitable a struggle of existence among all living things, in which some survive and others perish, because there is simply not enough sustenance for all. The experience and deduction extend throughout all recorded history, and they are abundantly evident today in the high mortality rate and wide-spread malnutritional disease afflicting two-thirds of the world's people still living in poverty. The demographer, Nigel Hey, sums up the well known statistics on this with these startling words:

> Today, in this single 24 hour period more than 10,000 people will starve to death.
>
> Diseases caused directly by malnutrition will kill 80,000 to 100,000 more human beings before the day is over.
>
> One half of the children alive today will not live to become adults.[1]

Yet, it is only the *belief* in the inevitability of nature's death dealing scarcity that remains today, not the belief's *validity in fact*. The entire NSHS thesis is built around the untenability of the outmoded assumption.

The events that began to erode the base of this ancient and doggedly persistent belief occurred in the nineteenth century, as a consequence of the Industrial Revolution, which brought into being a host of unsettling by-products in scientific inquiry and mechanical invention. This convergence of industrial development and its attendant new ideas had a profound effect on the thought and the whole way of life in Europe and the United States; and though the immediate effect was actually to preserve and reinforce the old *scarcity myth*, it ultimately destroyed the supportive base. But the belief, without its base, continues into the present, to bedevil human thoughts and behavior.

The man who gave forceful and far-reaching expression to both the preservative and revolutionary societal thrust to this paradoxical phenomenon was Charles Darwin, one of the most distinguished scientists of the time. Darwin advanced a startling theory of evolution that set off furious controversy throughout the western world. The now famous contribution he made to scientific thought bears a direct sequential relationship to the projective NSHS thesis. It is thus a good place at which to start our analysis of historical precedent.

When Charles Darwin came out with the *Origin of Species by Means of Natural Selection, Or the Preservation of Favoured Races in the Struggle for Life,* November 24, 1859, the blast of condemnation from the highest authorities of the Church was heard around the world. The edition of 1250 copies was sold out on the day of publication. "Perhaps no book in the whole history of civilization," says Ashley Montagu, "has made so immediate and enduring an impact upon the world of thought and action as the Origin of Species—with the exception, possibly, of the Bible."[2]

The heresy of Darwin's revolutionary thesis, attributing to nature the selective role of starting and evolving all species, including man, was construed by the Church as a frontal attack upon the revealed theological truth that man was created in the beginning by God, full-cast in his biological stature—a creature of frailty and sin but of divine origin, nonetheless.

As a distinguished scientist in a lineage of famous English scholars, Darwin was bound to arouse wide attention with his image-smashing theory of evolution. Knowing the great storm of protest it would arouse, he published it only after many years of extensive study of plant and animal life both in the wild and under domestication, and after prolonged and generous sharing of his findings with other scholars working on the subject. Much of his documentation was based on his observations of wildlife in the Galapagos Islands off the coast of South America. Finally, under the persuasion of fellow biologists, he put his conclusions on the line.

The theory of Natural Selection through a Struggle for Existence, stated in Darwin's own words, holds that:

> A struggle for existence inevitably follows from the high rate at which all organic beings tend to increase. Every being, which during its natural lifetime produces several eggs or seeds, must suffer destruction during some period of its life, and during some season or occasional year, otherwise, on the principle of geometrical increase, its numbers would quickly become so inordinately great that no country could support the product. Hence, as more individuals are produced than can possibly survive, there must in every case be a struggle for existence.[3]

Darwin explains with meticulous care and voluminous supportive evidence how species are gradually modified through individual variation and natural selection over long periods of geological time. He concedes that man has only fragmentary knowledge on this but many clear examples in the fossil remains of extinct organic forms and the appearance of new species.

"If then," he summarizes,"the geological record be as imperfect as many believe, and it may at least be asserted that the record cannot be proved to be much more perfect, the main objections to the theory of natural selection are greatly diminished or disappear. On the other hand, all the chief laws of palaeontolgy plainly proclaim, as it seems to me, that species have been produced by ordinary generation: old forms having been supplanted by new and improved forms of life, the products of Variation and the Survival of the Fittest."[4]

These two excerpts contain the core idea of the Origin of Species which, for its rich storehouse of intimate knowledge about plant and animal behavior, still makes fascinating reading today. Though it created a furore among ecclesiastics of Darwin's time, because it posed a threat to the Church as the sole depository of the answer to the origin of life, there was also present in this unorthodox postulate a powerful rationale for the preservation of things as they are—if not in the Church, certainly in areas of human endeavor other than those in religion. In a basic sense, however, it is the continuing presence of Darwin's rationale that man is, inherently, a contentious and predatory animal that requires our attention.

For purpose of clarity, we need to separate the two realms of Darwin's biological observations: human society and the world of all other organic beings. There is prevalent, today, a kind of worshipful assumption in "learned" circles that it was not Darwin, himself, but over-zealous early disciples like Herbert Spencer and Thomas Huxley, who placed undue emphasis on the applicability of natural selection to human affairs. It is an unwarranted assumption. Darwin not only saw his findings as universally valid but, and this is the main point to be stressed here, he derived them in the first place from the observations of students in the social sciences.

The man who had the most direct influence on Darwin's thinking was the British economist, Thomas Robert Malthus. More than fifty years before Darwin's work, Malthus published *An Essay On The Principles of Population*. Making his observations in a day when scarcity of food was a universal condition facing man and beast alike, Malthus contended that poverty and distress are inevitable, since population increases by geometric ratio and the means of subsistence, by arithmetical ratio. The natural checks on population growth, therefore, are war, famine, and disease. This became the commonly accepted Malthusian law of population control, the ideological point of departure for Darwin's later scientific findings on the struggle for existence.

Darwin acknowledges the influence of Malthus in both the Introduction and body of the Origin of Species. After stating in the Introduction that chapters one and two will deal with the variability of species under domestication and in a state of nature, he goes on to say:

> In the next chapter (the third), the Struggle for Existence amongst all organic beings throughout the world, which inevitably follows from the high geometrical ratio of their increase, will be considered. This is the doctrine of Malthus, applied to the whole animal and vegetable kingdom.[5]

Darwin then added:

> There is no exception to the rule that every organic being naturally increases at so high a rate, that, if not destroyed, the earth would soon be covered by the progeny of a single pair. Even slow-breeding man has doubled in twenty-five years, and at this rate, in less than a thousand years, there would literally not be standing-room for his progeny.[6]

Foremost among Darwin's disciples who stressed the applicability of the new theory to the human scene were, indeed, Herbert Spencer and Thomas Huxley. But this "social-Darwinism" was not their own invention, as we have just noted. They simply took hold of the part that fitted the behavior of human beings as both they and Darwin saw it; and they are by no means alone among scientists, then and now, who stress the "human side" of Darwinism. The distinguished zoologist, Ernst Haeckel (1834–1919), wrote:

> The theory of selection teaches that in human life, as in animal and plant life, everywhere and at all times, only a small and chosen minority can exist and flourish, while the enormous majority starve and perish miserably and more or less prematurely. . . . The cruel and merciless struggle for existence which rages throughout living nature, and in the course of nature *must* rage, this unceasing and inexorable competition of all living creatures is an incontestable fact.[7]

The well known British anthropologist, Sir Arthur Keith, had this to say in 1931:

> Nature throughout the past has demanded that a people who seeks independence as well as peace can obtain these privileges only in one way—by being prepared to sacrifice their blood to secure them. Nature keeps her human orchard healthy by pruning; war is her pruning-hook. We cannot dispence with her services.[8]

Progress in agriculture and food chemistry during the past decade has dampered somewhat this social-Darwinist cult among scientists, but it still flourishes, is in fact enjoying a popular resurgence. Dr. Thomas Thompson, of the Political Science Department of St. Petersburg Junior College at Clearwater, Florida, sees it as one of the major hang-ups among science teachers in high schools and colleges, who still inculcate their students with the Darwinist rationale for the "red in tooth and claw" struggle for existence on the human scene.[9] In business and politics, especially at the international level, it is all-pervasive. One striking example will illustrate this across the board:

Shortly after his election in 1968 to his first term as President of the United States, Richard M. Nixon began his victory address before the Joint Chiefs of Staff with these words, broadcast over television: "I stand before you here to address you as your President, when I should be sitting humbly at your feet." For the next four years he unleashed the most devastating aerial bombardment of Vietnamese civilians of the entire Vietnam war—men, women, and children, including their homes and rice paddies. Then, running for a second term in 1972, against the peace candidate, Senator George McGovern, he was reelected by a landslide vote of the American people. So unbounded is the public's adulation of its social-Darwinist heroes, McGovern, himself, had continually to assure his audiences that he, too, was a bomber pilot in World War II, to keep from being stoned as an enemy of the people!

But to return to the welcome reception of Darwinism by scientists and, especially, by men of practical affairs in Darwin's own time. The latter, whether or not they had ever heard of the new dictum of the survival of the fittest in the struggle for existence, could not have asked for a more perfect scientific blessing of the dog-eat-dog competition, spawned by the Industrial Revolution, had they ordered one ready-made. The social havoc created by the completely unregulated operations of the rising class of enterpreneurs in commerce, trade and manufacturing—the exploitation of child-labor, the wretched working conditions, the low wages and long hours in the factories of burgeoning industrial communities springing up all over England and western Europe—all is a matter of history.

According to the Malthus-Darwin formula, such social conditions for most people are inescapable, because the struggle for existence between individuals of the same species "will generally be more severe between them, if they come into competition with each other than between species of distinct genra."[10]

On this, the only solace for struggling, distraught mankind offered by the *Origin of Species,* is the following:

When we reflect on this struggle, we may console ourselves with the full belief, that the war of nature is not incessant, that no fear is felt, that death is generally prompt, and that the vigorous, the healthy, and the happy survive and multiply.[11]

Darwin who was a thoughtful and objective observer must surely have had some mental reservations about the full applicability of this statement to human affairs when he made it, for death is often preceded by prolonged pain and suffering; poverty brings its own pangs of hunger, sorrow and early death of loved ones; fear is rampant, especially in time of war; and man-made war unquestionably is and always has been the ugliest phenomenon on the face of the earth.

Malthus, Darwin, and their colleagues were well aware in their own day, of England's role in the war against the rebellious American colonies (1775-1783); the war of 1812 with the newly formed American Union; the wars with France, Portugal and Spain (1796-1814); the Crimean War (1853-56); the wars with Persia and China (1856); and the Indian rebellion and the frightful massacre at Cawnpore (1857-58). To be sure, Darwin's theory of natural selection had nothing to do with the causes of this unedifying spectacle of human conduct. What it did do was to give them the stamp of scientific validation as part of the inexorable workings of the Malthusian "law" of the survival of the fittest in human affairs. As Montagu puts it:

> Darwin was himself the mildest, the kindest, and the gentlest of men, but he grew up in an age during which war—violent suppression and exploitation of masses of human beings both at home and abroad, by his own people, and what is more, by the class to which he belonged—was the order of the day.[12]

Brilliant scholars that Malthus and Darwin were, they demonstrated that even great scientists can make big mistakes. And between them they made a colossal one. They pronounced what they thought they had discovered to be a universal and permanent law of nature when, in fact, they were making wholly unwarranted deductions from a body of evidence on scarcity that soon proved to be short lived in the case of man. As already stated, they lived and carried on their research in a day when scarcity of food was a condition facing man and beast alike; they assumed it to be a fundamental premise for all time.

But less than a hundred years after them, a great scientific and technological revolution transformed western society (the locus of their observations) from a society of transitory scarcity to one of spurious abundance. The output of automation had suddenly created a new problem for the industrial economies of the West, never before experienced by man: the power of overproduction! This fools' paradise of western created overabundance is as serious a hindrance to human well-being as is the Darwinist fallacy of nature's scarcity. Even so, it has already made a myth of the latter, and once we humans face up to the fact that science in production requires more than technology and the automated assembly line, man will never again have to face the spectre of Want—*if* he chooses to apply the life sustaining knowledge of his scientific discoveries.

Here we must take cognizance of objections from critical readers, to this emphasis on the obsolescence of nature's scarcity. They can, indeed, point to an overwhelming array of facts that would seem to contradict it. If human society since Darwin's time has been transformed from a society of scarcity to one of abundance, they will argue, the great majority of the world's population are still poor and hungry. The gap between their impoverishment and the affluence among a few rich nations is widening rather than lessening. Even in the rich nations there is emerging in these first years of the nineteen seventies an ominous proliferation of "scarcity" problems; ie, the energy crisis, food shortages, population explosion, environmental despoliation—all apparently stemming from, rather than being alleviated by, the scientfic discoveries of the past century.

How, then, can one speak of a transformation from past societies of scarcity to contemporary societies of abundance? The clue to an understanding of the actual transformation is in the conditional words, "if man chooses to apply the life-sustaining thrust of his discoveries." In that "if" lies an option that has never before been given to man in all recorded history. As recently as the first decades of this century *man had no choice*. Up to that time, so recent as to be within the memory of many older members of the present generation, nature's scarcity was real, at least in so far as the limitations of human knowledge made it so. The struggle for survival between human beings was as unavoidable as between members of other species.

In a sense, that situation has completely reversed itself today and man, not nature, has become the culprit in the current food and energy crisis. The transformation has happened so quickly we have not yet been able to adjust to it, and we still think in ancient thought patterns of nature's scarcity. The new discoveries of nature's generosity have not yet demolished the spectre of Want, and it lives on beyond its time. As a result, a few powerful warrior nations have been able to misuse the scientific techniques of production—and warfare—for their own enrichment, and to upset nature's entire ecosystem so irresponsibly as to endanger the very survival of the human family.

It is this *abuse* of the newly acquired knowledge to produce a sufficiency of food for all, that has brought about today's food and energy crisis. Nature had no hand in it. Our study will undertake the task, first, of marshalling the evidence and probing for the causes; then, of exploring two merging roads that can, if we will it, get us out of the human predicament. The Biological road of Natural Survival Through Human Selection will start us off, then lead us into the Ecological one of Societal Transformation.

3

Persistence of The Social Darwinist Fallacy

Increasing numbers of scholars and scientists now recognize that Darwin seriously impared his scientific objectivity by allowing himself to be influenced by Malthus' "law" of the struggle for existence; but many do not, nor does the great mass of the public. Malthus derived his findings from the barbaric behavior of the human animal in nineteenth century England. Darwin took the "law" as the starting point for his own studies of all animals, domesticated and in the wild. In his own words, he made it the basis for his assessment of what he saw. It was a disastrous bias, for it led him to assign an exaggerated importance in nature to the part played by tooth and claw, and to overlook the equally and possibly more lasting role played by mutualistic and symbiotic behavior among most predator animals.

The one error compounded itself into another. Stated in biological terms, it caused Darwin to equate the *intra*-species *competitive* behavior both he and Malthus beheld among human beings at a particular moment in history, with *inter*-species predation for food common to all flesh-eating animals. There is a fundamental difference between the two. Except for the strange case on the human scene, competition among members of the same species carefully avoids battle unto death. There is an abundance of evidence for this, which we shall have an opportunity to discuss in the present and next chapter.

On occasion Darwin himself supported this in the *Origin of Species* and, in doing so, was obliged to contradict his opposite finding that the struggle of existence between individuals of the same species "will generally be more severe between them, if they come into competition with each other, than between species of distinct genera." In contrasting the inter-species struggle of eating or being eaten, with competition of males of the same species for a desired female (than which there is no fiercer contest!), he makes the following observation on sexual selection among non-humans:

> This form of selection depends, not on a struggle for existence in relation to other organic beings or to external conditions, but on the struggle between individuals of one sex, generally the males, for possession of the other sex. The result is not death to the unsuccessful competitor, but few or no offspring. Sexual selection is, therefore, *less rigorous than natural selection.* . . .[1]

Sometimes, points out Darwin, it isn't even a matter of choosing the victor in physical combat:

> Among birds, the contest is often of a more peaceful character. All those who have attended to the subject, believe that there is the severest rivalry between males of many species to attract, by singing, the females. The rock-thrush of Guiana, birds of paradise, and some others, congregate; and successive males display with the most elaborate care, and show off in the best manner, their gorgeous plumage; they likewise perform strange antics before the females, which, standing by as spectators, at last choose the most attractive partner.[2]

There are many examples, too, of impressive sham battles, especially among feathered creatures, in which the combating males display their most brilliant war-colors and puff themselves up to their fullest size; but when the battle is over barely a feather has been shed by either combatant. The female may even decide in favor of the loser, for something else that attracts her more than physical prowess.

Battle to the death among animals in the higher life scales is rare, except in the case of man, whether it be for a mate, food, leadership of a pack or whatever. Konrad Lorenz describes the ritual of avoidance of fatal combat which nature seems to have built into animal behavior, as a face saving device for the loser and a restraint upon the victor.[3]

The systematic and organized practice of killing the members of one's own species in massive numbers is an oddity with man, not a rule of nature. One would look in vain through the whole plant and animal world for the premeditated cruelties human beings commit against each other, including such tortures as slowly pulling out the finger nails of captured enemies, or slowly burning the soles of their bare feet, or nailing live individuals to a cross-beam by their hands and feet, or cutting off their genitals.

Other species, it should be added, do not possess those faculties of the human understanding that enable man to put into laws governing "civilized" behavior, such preposterous rules as bestowing upon individual members perpetuity of title to portions of the Earth's food-bearing territory and other natural resources. This makes it possible for human progeny to mature and procreate without being subjected, under the requirements of social-Darwinism, to a struggle of existence for their fitness to survive!

Man's self-annihilating behavior would seem to be more a case of the inter-species kill for food gone amuck among human beings, in their competition with each other, than an example of competition among members of other animal species. Here Darwinists have created a problem of semantics rather than one of biology, by their loose use of the term *competition* for the strange display of human madness. They then further complicate the confusion by mistaking this human distortion of true competition among members of the *same* species as being analogous with the *inter-species* struggle of existence.

As for the supposedly ferocious and bloody struggle for food between predator and prey, Darwin's own words that death is quick and painless are more accurate than those of his most eloquent disciples—if applied to non-humans. The telescopic camera-lens confirms them, and TV documentaries make them common knowledge. Lions stalking and killing their prey are revealed as having quite a placid and business-like manner as they go about the routine task of cornering and eating their meal. Not too dissimilar a predatory behavior is this from that of the farmer's wife in the act of killing a chicken and preparing it for the family supper, or the worker in slaughter-house killing cattle and preparing the carcasses for the market. The housewife, while disposing of the chicken, may be thinking of the hem that has to be shortened on her daughter's dress for the dinner dance at church that evening; the slaughter-house worker may be preoccupied with humming a particularly difficult part of the barber shop quartet of which he is the esteemed basso. We are violating no law of nature by giving the lion credit for thinking of some distinctive lioness domestic chore, precisely as man does, while providing for the family meal.

In retrospect, we can now see what Darwin as a product of his own time could not see; namely, that the whole premise of his specific observations as a naturalist, rested on two socio-economic factors in human society that were quite extraneous to any strict definition of biology. These were the hard conditions of life for the great mass of the people in early nineteenth century England and Europe, stemming from a true scarcity of nature and the "law" of the survival of the fittest, which Thomas Malthus erroneously deduced from those purely transitory conditions.

Small wonder then that with the persistence of the myth of nature's scarcity and the astounding increase in man's violent societal behavior, derived from that myth, we should be experiencing a resurgence of social-Darwinism. It began in the 1960's when the whole world was shocked by the atrocities of the war in Indo-China, brought into every family living room by television. The resurgence was additionally fanned by the beginnings of public awareness that both war and massive industrial pollution of nature's environment were threatening man's habitat on planet Earth.

Among the chief proponents of neo-Darwinism today are the aforementioned American popular-science writer, Robert Ardrey, the Austrian biologist, Konrad Lorenz, and the British zoologist, Desmond Morris. So great an impact did the writings of these men make upon the public mind at the time of their publication during the past decade that they became available in every bookshop, drug store and super-mart, in cheap paperback editions to meet the heavy demand. Ardrey's views probably had the strongest influence on or, more correctly, affinity with popular thought. He accomplished this with very dramatic, if perhaps not the most scientific arguments.

In his work, *African Genesis,* Ardrey makes us privy to what he calls the silent, almost secret, revolution in the natural sciences that followed the discovery of a manlike ape that thrived some two million years ago. The discovery was made by the Australian anthropologist, Raymond Dart, while on an archaeological search in the Makapan valley of the Transvaal in South Africa. Dart unearthed the skeletal remains of a prehistoric primate, since given the name Australopithecus africanus, "four feet tall, erect in its carriage, bipedal, with the brain still the size of a gorilla's: an animal, in other words, half way between ape and man."[4]

This was in 1924 when, Ardrey says, scientists were still convinced that man had arisen in Asia from some missing link of peace-loving herbivores like the chimpanzee and baboon. In 1953 Dart published a paper, "The Predatory Transition from Ape to Man", explaining the implications of his discovery. He deduced from a study of the teeth, skull, posture and habitat of Australopithecus africanus, that the creature had been carnivorous and had led a hunting life. The ape man had been a transitional being possessing every significant human qualification other than Man's big brain. The discoverer, says Ardrey, pointed to Africa as the scene of human emergence.

Ardrey, having thus raised the curtain on man's killer-role in the drama of life and death, proceeds with great dramatic skill (for he is by profession first a playwright then a student of archaeology) to make an assessment of the Dart findings. He opens *African Genesis* with these words:

Not in innocence, and not in Asia, was mankind born. The home of our fathers was that African highland reaching north from the Cape to the Lakes of the Nile. Here we came about slowly—on the sky-swept savannah glowing with menace.

. . . Children of all animal kind, we inherited many a social nicety as well as the predator's way. But most significant of all our gifts, as things turned out, was the legacy bequeathed us by those killer-apes, our immediate forbears. Even in the first long days of our beginnings we held in our hand the weapon.[5]

His summary continues:

What Dart put forward in his piece was the simple thesis that man had emerged from the anthropoid background for one reason only: because he was a killer. Long ago, perhaps many million years ago, a line of killer apes branched off from the non-aggressive primate background. For reasons of environmental necessity, the line adopted the predatory way. For reasons of predatory necessity the line advanced. We learned to stand erect, in the first place, as a necessity of the hunting life. We learned to run in our pursuit of game across the yellowing African savannah. Our hands freed for the mauling and hauling, we had no further use for a snout; and so it retreated. And lacking the fighting teeth or claws, we took recourse by necessity to the weapon. A rock, a stick, a heavy bone—to our ancestral killer ape it meant the margin of survival. But the use of the weapon meant new and multiplying demands on the nervous system for coordination of muscle and touch and sight. And so at last came the enlarged brain; so, at last, came man.[6]

The deduction seems plausible, but we find a serious flaw in the Dart-Ardrey line of reasoning. Granted that the change to a hunting life did, in fact, demand greater brain power of the erstwhile herbivorous Australopithecus africanus apes, and development of a higher order of intelligence and body coordination, would it not be reasonable to assume that this same necessity for mind and body development should also have obtained for other prehistoric predators, particularly those mammals closest to man in their behavior characteristics—the fox, wolf, lion, and tiger, to name just a few having the most villainous reputations as killers? In point of logic, any one of them should have been a more likely predecessor to man by sheer force of habit and a long head-start than the more placid vegetarian apes of primordial times.

But it has not turned out this way. Instead, after millions of years of the presumed brain-enlarging effect of a hunting life, these carnivores and all others, except man, still trail non-predators like baboons, lemurs—and a lot of rank and file monkeys—in the scale of intelligent life!

4

Man, The Cooperator

It is said that people generally have one of two opposite kinds of life-outlooks. There are the realists or "hard-heads" and the idealists or "soft-heads." The distinction may not be precisely scientific, but it is a rather useful one in illustrating the interplay of those neuropsychological eccentricities that underlie all individual behavior patterns, and determine broadly what each of us makes of the gift of life. Take a look around at your friends, in any walk of life, and see what a nice handle it provides in understanding what their attitude is—indeed, in predicting what it will be on major issues of public concern.

Each of these antithetical attitudes gravitates quite naturally to the kind of authoritarian validation that fortifies its prior temperamental needs. The hard-heads align themselves with the Darwinist explanation of the survival of the fittest in a struggle for existence, in which man holds the center of the stage as an incurable predatory killer; the soft-heads espouse the counter thesis of symbiosis between and cooperation within species, to be discussed in this chapter; they contend it offers a more universal and hence a more pertinent answer to the survival of species.

The two opposite schools of thought put a very different stamp on the origin, nature and, presumably, the destiny of man, for the destiny of a supreme killer must surely be different from that of a beneficent cooperator. It is probably because of this direct clash between the two scientific explanations that they are best known and most widely discussed in lay circles. Yet, both theories taken together, do not quite come to grips with what might be called the ethical gut-question every thinking person asks himself; i.e. does man-kind have nothing more empirically sustaining to look forward to, as a base for deep human aspirations, than this external interplay of cooperation and the predatory kill?

Within the narrow confines of the controversy, our NSHS thesis goes along, as we shall see, with the protagonists of cooperation. But we are fellow travelers only up to a point, at which there is a fork in the road. Before we come to that fork it will profit us to take a quick look at the case of Man, the Cooperator. It constitutes an important historical back-drop for our projective study.

The naturalist who made the first comprehensive study of cooperation among plants and animals was the brilliant Russian philosophical anarchist, Petr Kropotkin (1842–1921). His pioneering work, *Mutual Aid*, published in 1902, was written as an answer to the prevailing Darwinian argument, and is still a classic in support of the cooperative thesis.

For our purposes we need to direct our attention mainly on the cooperative behavior of animal species at the higher intelligence levels, though its display among plants and animals at all life scales is noteworthy. Inter-species predation for food is characteristic only of flesh-eating animals, cooperation is universal. In many ways it plays the lead role for survival among those organisms that are the simplest in structure, the smallest, and individually the most frail.

"Go to the ant, thou sluggard, and be wise," was spoken of the carefree, individualistic grasshopper, in the hope he might profit from the lessons of cooperation to be learned from his tiny neighbors, the ants. The highly structured, cooperative society of bees was taught to us in our grade school primers.

It would appear, indeed, that nature has endowed all living things with an ability to function in simplistic unity, in direct proportion to the frailty and total vulnerability of the individual member of a species. A single locust is as nothing in the struggle to survive; but let countless millions of them descend en masse upon a countryside, and they will denude the area of every square inch of vegetation. The bacterial world presents the same awesome power through action in unism, including its threat to man. The Black Plague of 1348 A.D., decimated entire cities of western Europe.

Kropotkin found cooperation even among the lowly invertebrate forms of marine life, and relates a striking case of mutual assistance among horseshoe crabs at the Brighton Aquarium in England. One of these clumsy animals had fallen upon its back in a corner of the tank, and its heavy sauce-pan like carapace prevented it from returning to an upright position, the more so as there was in the corner an iron bar which rendered the task still more difficult. Its comrades took turn in pairs trying to free their fellow prisoner from beneath the iron bar. When Kropotkin left the Aquarium hours later the work of rescue was still going on.[1]

The zoologist, S.A. Barnett, tells the warming story about the Emperor Penguins that live under conditions one might think precluded survival. The temperature of their Antarctic habitat often falls below -35 C. There are blizzards of 80 miles an hour, in which a man without shelter would die quickly. But the Penguins have an exceptional capacity for standing still and huddling together, to conserve energy and reduce loss of heat while protecting themselves and their chicks against the ferocious climate of an Antarctic winter.[2]

Chimpanzees show the utmost tolerance and restraint in teaching their young. The young are permitted to pester their elders and even the older juveniles, when playing their boisterous games. An occasional cuff may be necessary to restrain them, but otherwise the young are pampered. They are sometimes fed by adults other than their parents. They ask for food by holding out a hand.

Cooperation among adult chimpanzees, says Barnett, is evident in many ways. In greeting, chimpanzees, like people, throw their arms around each other. Mutual grooming takes up a great deal of time. Two adults may spend hours going over each other's fur.[3]

Many elephant hunters have told how these animals try to come to the assistance of a wounded congener. Jacques Graven tells of an incident in which two elephants took their places at a wounded friend's right and left, with another pushing from behind, to help the wounded elephant to what they must have felt would be a place of safety and recovery. On another occasion a group of "stretcher-bearers" was seen to raise a wounded animal in this way along a steep bank to a height of almost 50 feet.[4]

Examples of intra-species cooperative behavior could be cited ad infinitum from popular magazines like *Wild Life*, the scholarly *National Geographic*, and again, from numerous TV documentaries.

Cooperation between members of different species, often referred to as symbiosis, may not be as common as that within a species, but it is equally unmistakable. Graven notes that the need among certain birds to devote themselves to others is so strong that they will even feed fish. He records the case of a cardinal that was observed one day feeding a goldfish. The bird was seen doing this several times, and it was possible to get photographs of it perched on the edge of a basin and holding in its beak a morsel, which it would then transfer to the mouth of the goldfish.[5]

Then there is the case of the indicator bird and the bear. This bird is very fond of honey but is afraid to confront bees. When it has found a hive, it seeks out a bear and goes into an extraordinary act, flying about and singing at the top of its lungs. What is even more amazing is that the bear seems to understand and readily takes off in the direction indicated by the bird. Once at the hive, the bear makes short work of getting at the honey without paying any attention to the stings, which scarcely penetrate his fur and hide. And the bird is quite content to pick up the crumbs of the feast.[6]

The sea offers its own illustrations of symbiosis. The late Conrad Limbaugh observed small brightly colored species of shrimp that wave their long antennae to gain the attention of large fish. Though shrimps are generally the prey of fish and avoid advertising their presence to predators, the species in point display themselves colorfully and fearlessly. The fish goes after the shrimps but does not bite, nor do the shrimps take any evasive action. Instead, they climb upon the fish and proceed to consume the many parasites and any loose and damaged tissue. The fish stays docilely still for this cleaning and first aid treatment, and obligingly opens its gill covers and even its mouth, for a shrimp to enter and seek more parasites.

Divers have seen fish actually queue up and wait their turn to be relieved of their parsites through the services of the busy (and well fed) shrimps. The same fish have been noted to return periodically to the same shrimp cleaning station, as man visits his favorite barber shop. Says Limbaugh: "From the standpoint of the philosophy of biology, the extent of cleaning behavior in the ocean emphasizes the role of cooperation in nature as opposed to the law of the tooth-and-claw struggle for existence."[7]

Cooperation to protect members of a close-knit group can rise to heroic proportions. In his characteristic vivid style, Ardrey describes the unequal battle between two adult male baboons and a leopard. The two baboons were on night sentry duty while the others slept in a cave in the Waterberg of Africa. At dusk one of their most feared enemies, the leopard, made his silent appearance from the bush, waiting for dark, when he would pounce on a sleeping member of the troop for his evening meal. But on this occasion the two baboons on guard saw their enemy and, moving cautiously along the ledge of an overhanging cliff, dropped on him. One bit at his spine, the other at his throat. The encounter was quick and fatal. The leopard disemboweled the one with his hind claws and crushed the other with his powerful jaws. But it was too late. The dying, disemboweled baboon had hung on just long enough and had reached the leopard's jugular vein with his canines. Death enveloped prey and predator alike. And in the hollow places in the rocky, looming krans, notes Ardrey, a society of animals settled down to sleep.[8]

In a happier account, Lorenz tells the delightful story of how a group of waddling geese bluff a fox out of his goose dinner. It was accomplished by some great Canada geese advancing in solid phalanx upon the fox, with much fearsome screeching, quacking, and flapping of wings. The fox, with ears laid back and a disgusted expression on his face, glanced over his shoulder at the trumpeting flock and trotted slowly—so as not to lose face—away from them.[9]

This kind of cooperative counter offensive of the prey against the predator, says Lorenz, is known as "mobbing" and is not uncommon among social animals. Crows and other birds have been known to "mob" a cat, or any other nocturnal predator, if they catch sight of it by day. Many birds will mob an owl, if they find one in the daytime, and will drive it so far away that it will hunt somewhere else the next night. Among the larger herbivorous animals, zebras have been known to drive off a leopard by this massed counter attack, and even domestic animals like cattle and pigs can frighten away a wolf in this manner.[10]

Birds know exactly when to assemble for their long flights to warmer climate in order to outwit extermination by the ice and snow of winter. Taking off in pointed formation to minimize atmospheric resistance during the arduous flight, the flock always arrives at its destination by a wit known only to birds. Every last bird may not make it to the end but the flock as a whole does, and that is the essence of survival through time.

In human affairs, the profuse and varied manifestations of cooperation need no formal scientific validation for anyone with two eyes and ears in his head and only a smattering knowledge of history. The farther back we delve into history, the more limited does man's ability, as an individual, appear to be in securing and controlling his food supply. The earliest hunting communities were communal (cooperative) in organization, to assure equal sharing in the fortunes of the hunt, whether that meant feast or famine for all. They had, furthermore, to be nomadic in habitat to avoid exhausting nature's limited food supply in any one place. Even after primitive man had developed the art of cultivating the soil, life remained precarious, partly because of the vicissitudes of the weather, and partly because the yield of hand and simple tool production was small and uncertain.

Under such conditions of scarcity, it is not surprising that early man relied heavily on intra-group cooperation. Montagu believes that if primitive man had not placed the highest priority on cooperation within the human family, there would be no human beings today, an appraisal that would appear to find little disagreement among anthropologists.

In today's world, every facet of man's societal behavior is part of a complex pattern of cooperation. Modern man willingly submits to the collective will as expressed in his group's mores, its government and laws. As a food gatherer, he accepts his part in a far-flung and continuous chain of cooperation extending from the farm to the grain elevator, the cannery, freight yard, slaughter house, wholesaler, retailer, and eventually to his own table. And the cooperative chain extends both vertically and horizontally across a labyrinth of allied occupations: mining, manufacturing, transportation, buying, selling, accounting, finance, research, planning, organization—to mention only a few catagories of an endless list. To be sure, these interrelated endeavors also entail keen competition on which we shall have more to say. But the full scope of cooperation with man becomes abundantly clear.

5

Much Maligned Man, The Competitor

We have scrutinized predation and cooperation as the behavioral dynamics in the origin and survival of plant and animal life, the first for many species, the second for all. Although we have found them to be impressive, whether viewed singly or together, they do not fully satisfy a total explanation, certainly not for man. And the phenomenon of Man is the subject of this essay.

The Darwinist, Thomas Huxley, once said: "To a person uninstructed in natural history, his countryside or seashore stroll is a walk through a gallery filled with wonderful works of art, nine tenths of which have their faces turned to the wall."[1]

Focusing exclusively on the faces of Man, the Predator and the Cooperator, is not turning nine tenths of his faces to the wall, but over half of them. The full countenance of Homo sapiens, expressing outwardly something of his deeper biological nature, reveals not two but many faces. Dominant are five—

> Man, the Predator
> Man, the Cooperator
> Man, the Competitor
> Man, the Thinker
> Man, the Inventor

The variegated interplay of these faces presents a far more intriguing picture of Man's place in the total scheme of things, so far as the limited understanding of human beings can fathom them, than does the distorted one obtained by trying to describe the whole of man by looking at only a part of him. The complete picture suggests a creative power from which can flow a fantastically exciting process of evolution, beautiful beyond anything that predation and cooperation alone have to offer.

Some readers will no doubt question the adequacy of our count. If we are going in for numbers, why stop at five? There is Man the Theologian, the Materialist, Moralist, Opportunist, etc. They too play a role in shaping human behavior.

True. And within this affective connotation of the multiple faces of man, it would be fatal for comprehensive thought to omit the face of Aesthetic Man, and it would be futile to try to define it, for it defies definition. It was Emerson who said:

> "If eyes were made for seeing
> Then beauty is its own excuse for being."

And Keats,

> "Beauty is truth, truth beauty,—that is all
> Ye know on earth, and all ye need to know."

Man's experience of the beautiful and the good in life is an indivisible, all-encompassing experience, from the overwhelming ecstacy of the sexual union of two lovers to the azure blue of a summer sky and the flaming sunset across a meadow. Aesthetic and Ethical Man would traverse through all the pages of this study even if we were not to mention them directly again.

But these are not the faces of activists, either as killers, cooperators, competitors, thinkers or investors, in the struggle for species survival. Their role is more meaningful if viewed as revealing facial nuances of man's aspirational drives in the quality of life than as weaponry in the struggle for existence. The line of demarcation is unquestionably a thin one. Aesthetic-Ethical Man will, for example, have a key role, perhaps the lead role, in the evolutionary drama of the future.

Statically, the face of man the competitor may be viewed as but one facet in the physical and spiritual mosaic of the total human being. Dynamically, however, it reveals itself as being more closely interlaced with the five dominant action-prone faces, yet as inseparable from all the faces as are the dimensions of time and space.

In this full setting, even in contemporary primitive society, competition among human beings plays a role that is far more vital to individual and collective well-being than its loose and faulty association with Malthus/Darwin's law of the struggle for existence gives it. The demonstrable facts are that, contrary to popular notion, competition is not antithetical to cooperation; rather, it is an integral part of cooperation. In the interacting relationship between the two, lies the distinctive human quality of competition, for even if we try to equate it with competitive behavior among the members of other primates, we discover how infinitely more prolific and diverse it is with us humans.

Competition in human society is the balanced interplay of contention and cooperation. It rests on ground rules, as we shall see, that, in effect, replace violence between contenders with mutually acceptable conditions for peaceful triumph of the victor. As with other species, perhaps even more willfully, it seeks neither to inflict bodily harm nor death upon the adversary. It is the very opposite of the killer motif. Let us get down to some examples.

A battle between two armies hell-bent on destroying each other is not competition; it is, as already stated, an intraspecies display of predation gone beserk with man. But a struggle between two bowling teams, two contending merchants, two suitors for a particular woman, two rival construction firms bidding for a contract, two track stars, two contending lawyers, two physicians urging opposite treatment of a disease—all this *is* competition.

The distinction is crucial: the legitimacy of the kill between individuals of the same species is abhorrent to competition among all societal animals, as we have noted. It holds with man, whether the ground rules are communistic, capitalistic, or ancient. To define competition as being a reflection or sublimation of predation for food, is to disregard the basic law of group survival and, with humans, to miss the very essence of individual desire for contention under mutually accepted (cooperative) conditions for peaceful encounter.

We all become thoroughly enmeshed in the competitive and cooperative activities of society: the childhood preoccupations of play, which are later channeled into the classroom and the athletic field; competition to win a place on the team and competition between teams to win championships; competition in adult life for a job, and then competition with fellow employees. Successful competitors win prizes in the form of academic honors, promotions, prestige, corporate profits, influence and power over others. Communist societies no less than private enterprise societies engage in this competitive striving between individuals, while their collective achievements in outer space, the Olympic games, and the struggle for Middle East oil, leave nothing to the imagination as to competitive cooperation in the communist world.

The interplay of cooperation and contention, in its true sense, is to the benefit of both loser and winner. A thousand aspiring young singers competing to appear as soloist with a famous symphony orchestra, are probably better singers after the event no matter how they fared in the contest. They and all the other participants—teachers, musicians, conductor, promoters, clerks, ushers, printers—all were engaged in a very complex cooperative undertaking. A group of structural engineers who lose out in their competitive proposal for a new village water system, may be better prepared from the experience for success in a more significant future project—and in both ventures the cooperative efforts of all members of the group, from file clerks, typists, draftsmen, accountants, to the various engineering specialists, are integral parts of the competitive enterprise. Beyond these random examples, but a moment's reflection on the many-faceted display of cooperation mentioned on pages 40–41 will further highlight the indivisibility of competition and cooperation.

This presence of competition as the inevitable counterpart of *intra-group* cooperative relationships in modern society, hardly makes it necessary to belabor the details again in our defense of much maligned man, the competitor. We pointed out earlier (pages 23–26) that the bad reputation of man as a competitor stems largely, and unjustly, from the confusion that must be laid at the door of social-Darwinists, including Darwin himself, who unwisely use the term as though it were synonymous with the *inter-species* killer behavior of predator animals other than man, instead of with the generally non-fatal competition between members of the same species, common to all societal organic beings.

As a matter of fact, true competition in human society is not only a constant companion of all cooperative human endeavors, but is forever being augmented, transformed, and redirected by man's uniquely endowed inventive genius, a developmental sequence that leads us directly into the next and final chapter on historical precedent.

6

The Thinker Versus The Inventor

If the full range of man's survival drives consisted only of predation, cooperation, and competition—the behaviors reflecting his closest kinship with other organisms—we would be without a base for our projective study. Even the addition of Man, the Thinker, would change little in what would still remain a static human identity with the non-creative behavior of other life-forms, for thinking differs only by degree from the survival instincts of other animals.

It may be surprising to some, but man's cerebral faculties, his role as a thinker, if allied only with the above three survival drives is, more often than not, in opposition to the singular human aspiration for creative change, possessed in significant manner only rarely by humans who have the genius of inventivity. It is Man, the *Inventor*, therefore, rather than Man, the Thinker, upon whom NSHS socio-biological change will rest most heavily.

The human being's thinking equipment is used, in the main, first, to advance one's own self interest and, second, that of so-called in-groups, roughly in the order of family, clan, tribe, class, nation. This self-centered allegiance strongly ties individual thoughts to the preservation of things as as they are, especially if one enjoys a favored social and economic status.

With but few exceptions it is the quick of mind, the bright and calculating, that have always acquired the material possessions, achieved the favored positions and prestige that are measured as success in all walks of life. They can hardly be expected to relinquish these blessings without a struggle. By and large, they can be counted on to resist change with all the mental acumen and resources at their command. Within this framework of success, they are intimately associated with and faithfully supported by the best authorities in business, government, education, the sciences, and when seriously threatened, by the persuasive force of the military.

This resistance to change by the "successful" throughout history, led Karl Marx to his theory of the class struggle between contending sub-groups of the human species—the "haves" against the "have-nots." Taken in the aggregate and up to a point, there is merit to the Marxist thesis. Marx welcomed Darwin's demonstration of nature's warfare, since it gave him a biological foundation for his conception of the warfare of the classes, and he even thought of dedicating *Das Kapital* to Darwin. Had he, like Darwin, known what we know today, he might also have wisely traced the "class struggle" to that old, deep-rooted attitudinal posture derived from the now obsolete law of the scarcity of nature, that once demanded fending for oneself and one's class in the struggle for survival.

But there are the exceptions—those rare and precious cases when the individual as thinker and inventor is at one, and challenges the societal status-quo. When that happens it can produce a Socrates, a Jesus, Copernicus, Lincoln, Lenin, Debs, Einstein, Ghandi, Malcolm X, King, and, indeed, a Marx and a Darwin. The reader will recall that all but one or two of these great innovative thinkers were put to death or imprisoned under due process of law, administered by the best legal minds of the time; or maligned for their dangerous ideas by men of influence and erudition, as well as by the general public.

How can one explain these infrequent instances of deviation from prevailing behavioristic norms, which throw all considerations of personal safety and comfort to the winds? The compelling dedication and courage displayed by such individual behavior may be compared to the all-consuming love of a mother for her child, for which she will gladly give her own life if need be. We believe it can be ascribed to a standard of moral judgement which only the most knowledgeable and fearless kind of person is capable of reaching. Run-of-the-mill morality has nothing to do with it. All people, including bigots, racists, slavish conformists, the uninformed and mentally lazy, would insist they live morally upright lives. It was the late Louis Brandeis, Chief Justice of the U.S. Supreme Court, who once said that the most dangerous kind of person is one who is motivated by the best of intentions without understanding.

But even informed thought, aided by the Ethical Man, is not enough for the dynamics of evolutionary change under NSHS, unless there is present also Man, the Inventor. With him we enter a realm of behavior, unique with the human species. Invention is the open sesame that will unlock the doors to the mystery of man's future—to those ultimate goals of the good life that constitute the focus of our study. And by man, the inventor, we do not mean just man—or woman!—the inventor of three dimensional gadgets, but the discoverer of new ideas, new processes, new ethical and philosophical horizons. It is this face of man that has time and again changed all the other faces, from that long forgotten day when man first invented the wheel, to the discovery of fire, electricity, the course of the earth and the stars; the invention of printing, the steam engine, electric light, telephone, airplane, automation and the atomic bomb; the philosophy of the first cave dweller to Plato, Kant, Hume, Marx, Gandhi . . .

Any doubt as to man's singular possession of the inventive drive can quickly be put to rest by the undisputed findings of both anthropologists and biologists. There is complete absence among all non-human life forms of anything like innovative behavior. Plants and animals must take nature as they find it; they have no ability to reconstitute or remold the particulars of their environment. Their simple achievements of using bits of nature for tools or shelter—a rock, a stick or shrubbery—are so rudimentary as to rank far below the achievement level of even Australopithecus africanus, that half-ape half-man that roamed the earth as man's predecessor some millions of years ago.

David Lack, the well-known British zoologist, notes the "remarkable" ability of the Woodpecker-Finch which excavates insects from the bark of trees by carrying a cactus spine or small twig, and poking it into the cracks, then dropping it to seize any insect that emerges. This astonishing practice, he says, is one of the few recorded cases of the use of tools by any animal other than man or the apes.[1] Sally Carrighar, twice recipient of Guggenheim Fellowships for her authentic and delightful stories of life in the wild, tells of the simple ingenuity of a female sea otter teaching its young pup how to extract seafood from the shell by placing a flat rock on her chest while swimming on her back. She lifts the shell over her head in both hands and brings it down on the rock with a crashing blow until it cracks open.[2]

Many similar examples could be cited, and the reader can no doubt add more from his own observations of the limited use of nature's ready-made tools by animals "other than man or the apes." As for today's simians, their most advanced practices were probably far surpassed by primordial man many millions of years ago, to say nothing of the presumed progress made by the Neanderthal man a million years after Australopithecus africanus.

Creative ability is possessed by man alone. It has not only altered continuously his predatory, competitive, cooperative and thinking roles; it has forever merged them into each other. As the binocular vision of our eyes gives us the wonders of a third dimension, so does the composite of man's five faces in its never ending transformation through man's inventive genius, give us the full image of man—and a precious clue to the future.

The enormity of the impact man, the inventor, has made upon societal practices and culture-values and, in the process, toward far-reaching change, can perhaps be best highlighted in a conclusive way by a chronological recording of some of the milestones of inventive achievements since the dawn of history. The reader may wish to scan only quickly the long yet very fragmentary list of major categories, as a refresher on the comprehensive and unique nature of the human being's inventive faculties.

Medicine

Creative Development Prior To The Twentieth Century

> Presumed absence in primordial time of any conscious control over the vicissitudes of health, accident or injury.
>
> Reliance on magic, superstitions, early religious beliefs in good and bad deities, and on religions of animism.
>
> Trial and error discovery of curative properties in nature: herbs, teas, berries.
>
> Beginnings of conscious search for causes, treatment and cure of ill health.
>
> Emergence and growth of a specialist class of medical practitioners: witch doctor, medicine man, modern general practitioner, specialist and researcher.
>
> Development of schools for professional medical training; hospitals, clinics, research centers.
>
> Discovery of bacterial and other miscroscopic organisms in the human body as proximate causes of disease and mal-functioning.
>
> Beginnings of surgery and invention of surgical instruments.
>
> Development of disinfectants and sanitized surgical instruments, materials, equipments.
>
> Early development of public and voluntary health services and education.

Twentieth Century Medical Sophistication

> Control, reduction, and in many instances, elimination of deadly diseases.
>
> Prolongation of life through new medical discoveries and treat-

ments: antibiotics, vaccines, dietetics, vitamin compounds, public sanitation and personal hygiene, etc.

Transplantation of healthy vital organs of deceased persons, to preserve life of living persons with fatally diseased or otherwise impaired organs.

Invention of mechanical aids for ill-functioning vital organs.

Proliferation of governmental and voluntary medical research in a wide range of physical and mental health areas, to conquer disease and prolong life.

Integration and expansion of health services at all levels of local, state, federal and voluntary endeavors.

Nutrition

Reliance on nature's wild fruits, berries, plants, nuts.

Reliance on hunting and fishing for additional food supply.

Discovery of the art of cultivating the soil.

Development of animal husbandry for increased control of meat supply, butter and eggs.

Discovery of fire; development of the art of cooking and baking and associated culinary arts.

Sophistication of Foods of the Twentieth Century

Electric refrigeration, dehydration, canning.

Discovery and research development of additives for enrichment in vitamins, proteins, color, flavor, etc; same, for synthetic foods.

Development of quality controls, sanitary and health specifications by governmental and voluntary agencies.

Public education in nutrition; science of dietetics.

Discovery and research development of methods of processing vegetables and grains to obtain new and diverse foods of high protein and milk-fat content.

Expansion of agricultural yield through mechanized and automated productive methods; also through increased knowledge of methods of fertilization of soil; hybridization for improved quality and greater resistance to disease.

Year-round availability of a wide range of foods from all parts of the world as a result of rapid air transportation, improved methods of refrigeration, dehydration, etc.

Transportation

Land-borne

    on foot.

    on horseback, camelback or as rider of other animals; hand or animal drawn carts; wagons, after discovery of wheel; railroad on track, after invention of steam engine; development of diverse fuels for greater power, gasoline engine, electric motor, diesel engine, invention of automobile.

Sea-borne

    on hollowed tree trunks, rafts, canoes and other simple hand powered carriers.

    small one occupant sail boats; large multi-rigged ships; animal drawn river boats and ships.

    steam powered ships; oil and electric powered ships.

Air-borne

    free-floating balloons.
    power-driven Zeppelin type balloons.
    heavier-than-air craft.

Communication

    Person-to-person by word of mouth.

    Smoke signals from high places, over longer distances.

    Runner or riders on horseback serving as messengers.

    Use of picture symbols.

    Development of alphabet.

    Writing on papyrus, stone, other suitable material.

    One-dimensional drawing.

    Ancient sculpture.

    Invention of printing press.

    Invention and development of modern communications media: town crier, newspaper, periodicals.

    Invention of photography.

    Development of postal delivery service from early systems to contemporary world-wide services.

    Invention of telegraph and telephone.

Twentieth Century Sophistication in Transportation and Communication

    Propeller driven airplanes.

    Jet-propelled airplanes.

    Invention of phonograph and tape recorder.

    Invention of radio and television.

    Invention and early development of nuclear powered transportation.

    Invention and development of submarine travel.

    Invention of outer space craft.

    Explorations on the moon and preparations to land on other planets.

    Invention of global satellite television.

Production

Primordial gathering of fruits, nuts, berries, wild grains, edible plants, roots, etc.

Fishing and hunting, first by hand, then through successive stages of tool and power equipment development.

Soil cultivation through the same stages of tool, equipment and power development:

    Invention of simple hand tools: hammer, saw, grinder, masher, scythe, plough, etc.; development from wooden and stone tools to metal ones, from manual to animal powered.

    Invention of tools and equipments powered by air, water, steam, gasoline, electricity; invention of water-wheel, windmill, mechanically powered cultivator, tractor, saw, etc.

Emergence of class of artisans divorced from direct soil cultivation:

    Carpenter, stone cutter, blacksmith, weaver, shoemaker, miller, wagon maker, harness maker, etc.

    Development of barter and exchange; evolution of a common currency of exchange.

    Beginnings of industry and commerce; development of employer-employee relationship in home manufacture; the itinerant trader; the local shop keeper.

    Rise of the business enterpreneur; early factory production; large scale production.

    Productive specialization—the "middle man", technical and professional specialist, importer, exporter, banker, broker, lawyer, researcher, wholesaler, jobber, retailer, transporter, etc.

Invention of the corporate "individual" in production.

Rise and growth of the agricultural and technical college to train specialists and carry on agricultural and industrial research.

Productive diversification at many levels: for necessities like food, clothing and shelter; for luxuries like jewelry, cosmetics, sportswear and accessories; art objects; prestige articles like mink coats, oversized motorboats, yachts and sailboats; assembly-line mass production, etc.—all evolving out of man's irrespressible genius for invention and discovery.

Twentieth Century Sophistication In Production

Acceleration of scientific methodology and equipments; cybernation and automation; progressive displacement of direct labor and shortening of work hours; increase of leisure-time.

Proliferation of industrial mergers: geographically, across national boundaries and toward international proportions; vertically, from the farm and the mine to the consumer; horizontally, merging different kinds of productive establishments under central ownership and controls.

Dominance of advertising and research; a vast spawning of twentieth century gadgetry in household appliances, recreation and sports.

Eruption of a scientific and technological revolution in productivity of capital and consumer goods, which has transformed societies experiencing the revolution, from societies of scarcity to societies of abundance—again, all of this, for good and for bad, from man's inventive genius.

Social Organization

Early Nomadic Groups

The Family (earliest and basic social unit)
The Clan (group of families and individuals under a common leader)
The Tribe (merger of neighboring clans)
The Tribal Confederation.

Settled-Land-Based Groups
(after introduction of agriculture)

    The Principality, Dukedom, Duchy, etc. (in the West), and their equivalents throughout the world.

    The Nation-State (merger of the above type of smaller political units—by conquest and/or voluntary consolidation against common external enemies.)

    Political Alliance (between nation-states having temporary common interests)

    Common Market (regional pooling of common economic interests by a number of nation-states)

Internal Group Organization

    Political: Oligarchy, Patriarchy, Caste Systems, Absolute Monarchy, Matriarchy, Limited Monarchy, Theocracy, Democracy.

    Economic: Labor Guilds and Unions, Employers Associations, Technical and Professional Organizations.

    Religious: Christianity, Judaism, Buddhism, Mohammedanism, etc., and their various sects.

    Cultural and Recreational: Sports, Music, Literature, Education, etc.

    Education: Nursery, Primary, Secondary; Private and Public; Vocational.

Religion

Animism (endowment of nature's phenomena—the elements, celestial bodies, plants and animals—with divine powers)

Pluralistic Dieties (good and bad Gods and Goddesses)

Beliefs in Magic and Superstition

Monotheism; Doctrinaire Religions (theologies and sects)

Political Theocracies

Power-Struggle between Church and State

Separation of Church and State (in West and modern industrial society)

Scientific Challenges to Established Religions

Theological Accommodation to Science

Contemporary Intra-Church Conflicts: metaphysical versus socially oriented theology.

Literature And The Arts

Literature

Early spoken tales of adventure and wonder—(parents to children; religious, moralistic and personal stories among adults)

Early Drama—(play-acting among children in imitation of their elders, animals and nature's phenomena)

Early Drama—(religious ceremonials, epic and heroic drama)

Poetry

The Novel

Short Story

Music

Simple tonal and rhythmic self-expression

Cries, chants, and intonations related to the dance; religious and war ceremonials

Folk songs and ballads

Early use of musical instruments—(tom toms, drums, reeds, lyre, etc.)

Early choral music related to dance, ceremonials, etc.; same for instrumental music

Invention of new and varied kinds of musical instruments; development of structured and sophisticated ensemble music for choral and instrumental groups; also for combined group and virtuoso music

Musical plays, operettas and operas

Atonal, polytonal and other experimental music

Painting and Sculpture

(See *Communication* for earliest forms)

Classical (ancient) architecture, sculpture, painting.

Ecclesiastical art and art restrictions.

Remaissance (in West) of broader scope and freedom in art expression.

Impact of science and changing socioeconomic conditions on creative art; abstract and non-objective painting, sculpture, impressionism, etc.

Fractional and over-simplified though this digest of man's past inventive achievements is, it is impressive nonetheless. Compared to the Woodpecker-Finch's use of a twig to extract insects from the bark of trees, it is man who is astonishing, not the Finch. The earliest cave dweller may have had only his primitive brain and brawn to fend for himself and family for survival. But what a change his progeny wrought over thousands and millions of years, through their inventive abilities—for good and for bad.

So vast a panoramic view of the accomplishments of creative thinkers throughout all history, and from all parts of the world, defies details. But, in defense of our case of man's unique inventive genius we must, indeed, list a few significant modern ones to bring the accomplishments down to their present techno-scientific explosion. It is a time in human history when we need desperately to assess their impact for good and bad, and take life-sustaining action upon them. Starting with an arbitrary date during the western-oriented but world encompassing renaissance, will suffice.

1543 Nicholas Copernicus published his famous treatise, *De revolutionibus orbium coelestium*, in which he described the sun as the center of a great solar system, with earth and other planets revolving around it. His discovery became the basis of modern astronomy.

1660 Robert Hooke discovers cells. (Microscopically small masses of protoplasm, the several parts of which are capable, alone or with other cells, of performing all the functions of life.)

1668 Fransesco Redi observes that maggots do not arise by spontaneous generation; i.e., from previously non-living matter.

1675 Anton van Leeuwenhoek discovers protozoa.

1677 Johann Ham discovers spermatazoa. (Male fecundating cells).

1680 Van Leeuwenhoek discovers yeast to be a microorganism; in 1683, discovers bacteria. (Microscopically small plants having round, rod-like or spiral shaped, single-celled or non-cellular bodies, living in soil, water, organic matter, or in the bodies of plants and animals, some capable of motion by means of flagella or elongated shoots).

1762 Jean Jacques Rousseau publishes *Le Contrat social,* and a novel on education, *Emile,* which set forth for the first time in modern history, the theory that "man is good by nature and corrupted by civilization", and that "equality between men disappeared with the introduction of property, agriculture, and industry. Laws were instituted to preserve the inequality of oppressor and oppressed." His innovative thinking greatly influenced the tactics employed by Maximilien Robespierre and other leaders of the French Revolution.

1781 Felice Fontana discovers cell nuclei. (Portion of the cell-protophasm essential to life phenomena and heredity, containing the heredity-determining chromosomes).

1809 Jean de Lamarck advances theory of evolution through inheritance of acquired characteristics.

1821 Georg Wilhelm Friedrich Hegel publishes *Phenomenology of Mind*, and *Philosophy of Right*, which introduce a new concept of dynamic reality that reveals itself throughout history in a never-ending struggle between opposing ideas striving for supremacy. (Hegel called the deominant "idea-reality", at any given time in history, the Thesis; the challenging one, the Anti-thesis; and the new idea born of the struggle, the Synthesis. The human learning-experience in the phenomenon, he conceived being the permanent Absolute from which flows human progress). Hegel's creative thinking inspired the great social scientist, Karl Marx, to translate his philosophy into a revolutionary social action program.

1827 Karl von Baer discovers mammalian ova. (Female gamete or mature germ-cell possessing the chromosome set capable of initiating formation of a new individual by fusion with a male gamete)

1829 Martin Rathke discovers mammalian embryo pass through a gilled stage.

1848 Karl Marx publishes the *Communist Manifesto*, in collaboration with Friedrish Engels, setting forth the basics of Marxian socialism; writes his monumental work, *Das Kapital* (Vol. I published in 1867, Vols. II and III, posthumously, edited by Engels, 1885–95). The two works make incalculable impact on human affairs up to the present.

1859 Charles Darwin writes *Origin of Species* in which he formulates theory of evolution through natural selection; his findings greatly influence not only scientific thought but political and economic practice.

1860 Louis Pasteur disproves theory of spontaneous generation of life; his experiments show that all life comes from previously existing life; in 1862 advances germ theory of disease.

1866 Gregor Mendel publishes his theories of heredity, derived mainly from systematic cross breeding of peas over several generations; discovers that separate unit characters are inherited independently of one another, some appearing dominant over others, some, recessive or non-appearing in given generations of the inheritance process.

1866 Ernest Haeckel theorizes that embryos recapitulate, during their development, the course of the evolution of the organism.

1869 Friedrich Miescher discovers nucleic acid (acids composed of a sugar or derivative of a sugar, phosphoric acid and a base, found especially in cell nuclei).

1879 Herman Fol first observes an ovum in the process of fertilization by a single spermatozoon.

1886 Hugo De Vries discovers evidence, from which he works out theory of evolution by mutation. (Mutation: a genetic variation, sudden change in the normal type of an organism caused by reorganization in genes, or in chromosomal number or structure)

1902 W.S. Sutton suggests that chromosomes control the inheritance of physical characteristics.

1905 Albert Einstein postulates light quanta or photons, comparable to energy quanta and, on these bases, his explanation of the photoelectric effect; the same year he sets forth his special theory of relativity on electrodynamics of moving bodies and equivalence of mass and mechanical energy. In 1911 he asserts the equivalence of gravitation and inertia and in 1916 completes the mathematical formulation of his general theory of relativity. (Like Karl Marx, his creative thinking has enormously influenced the course of history in all human endeavors)

1906 Sun Yat-sen formulates theory of democracy, national cohesion, and guaranteed livelihood for Chinese people, in *Three People's Principles*; heads successful revolution against the oppressive Ching Dynasty in 1911; accepts economic and military aid from Lenin in 1923 in return for working with Chinese Communists, which lays the ground work for the establishment of the People's Republic of China in 1949 under Mao Tse-tung.

1918 Emil Fischer works out method by which amino acids join together to form proteins. (Amino acids are thus the molecular "building blocks" of which the larger protein molecules are structured)

1947 Mahatma Gandhi develops methodical strategy of non-violent collective resistance against oppression, which enables the people of India to cast off the yoke of colonial rulership by Great Britain. (Gandhi's theory of non-violent collective resistance proved to be immensely successful for people around the world, especially minority groups, deprived of civil and economic rights, whether by domestic or foreign ruling elites)

1959 William M. Sinton produces strong spectroscopic evidence in favor of the existence of plant life on Mars.

1960 O. Struve plans radio telescope survey to detect life in other stellar systems.

1970 H.G. Khorans and associates create first man-made gene, a possible step toward correction of inherited diseases and perhaps genetic engineering of improved humans and animals.[3]

This mere listing of a few, by no means all or even most, significant scientific contributions made to human knowledge by creative thinkers over the ages, stops short of their contemporary proliferation in socioeconomic affairs, in the earth's biosphere and outer space. But it is not within the purview of this study, and certainly not the competence of the writer, to dwell on the manifold intricacies of the subject. Suffice it to express wonder, admiration, and anxiety over the consequences: the brainless computers, misnomered test-tube babies, wonder drugs, vital organ transplants, automated mass production, labor-saving household appliances, electronic gadgets, TV, radio, manned trips to the moon, unmanned ones to Saturn and Jupiter, outer-space real estate projects, strawberries in winter, food preservatives, additives, polluted lands and water, ozone advisories.

7

Adumbrations of Man's Creative Destiny

Up to this stage in our study, we have *asserted* in numerous ways that, in light of man's unique inventive accomplishments, "scarcity has become a myth," and the kill among us humans for possession of nature's food-bearing territories, is as unnecessary as it is barbaric. But we have not as yet supported the assertion empirically; thus, we need to give indisputable evidence that individuals will, by the force of increasing pain and suffering, be driven to abandon their still primitive way of life, or perish en masse.

We trust that when the full NSHS case is in, we shall have met this commitment to the satisfaction of our readers, irrespective of their nationality, culture or sex, and have aroused in them a strong desire to participate in peaceful collective social action for fundamental remedial change. Man has truly made great material progress in the wake of human inventivity, but most of the inventions have been narrowly man-centered and acquisitive in purpose. They have not lessened the struggle for possession of the fruits of hand and brain. In fact, they have made it more bitter. Greater productivity has resulted in more tense and subtle conflicts; greed and self-aggrandizement permeate all walks of life, and the successful contenders become ever more powerful, and they band together against the vanquished and the weak.

Unbounded covetousness possesses us and perverts our reasoning faculties. Like some strange, accursed disease, it blunts the mind and settles upon all nations, polluting the very wells of knowledge with its poison. Truth and evil become confounded, and principles of thievery are elevated and cloaked as an ideal for the common adoration, while false prophets brazenly condone the wickedness of things and hold full counsel with despoilers in high places.[1]

The agony of human beings on planet Earth is not yet unbearable, and no great vision lights the way out of the darkness. Here in the West, where self-seeking inventivity has been most prolific, the "warrior on horseback" still rides high. The public bows in reverence before the brass and brain-trusters of military science and business; manufacturers compete for lucrative "defense" contracts, and their workers relish the fat wages to be derived from them; and professionals in all fields grasp eagerly for the prestigious jobs spawned in time of war.

Even Man the Cooperator condones the ugly spectacle, and there is probably no more perfect example of competitive cooperation than when the members of two or more "enemy" groups are busily engaged in slaughtering each other.

Competition in healthy civilian sports is similarly perverted by veneration of the kill. Every major sports event must begin with the playing of the war-oriented national anthem, to link it with man's time-honored practice of killing his own kind. Within the obsolete moral perspectives of contemporary primitive society, people rationalize as moral their pursuit of all manner of cooperation and inventive objectives. Thieves cooperate as diligently to accomplish their ends as do workmen in building a house. Men compete as eagerly in warfare, for the decorations of honor for having killed the most human beings, as do medical researchers for saving life.

These Janus-faced moral traits are equally manifest in all five activist faces of man. Their atrocities, rooted as they are in the predominantly acquisitive inventive triumphs in science and technology, are warning signals to the endangered human animal. Whether or not they will be heeded is problematical, and the outlook is dismal. Still, there is hope, and it comes from a most unlikely direction, where wisdom is minimal but creativity enormous. Unorthodox things began to happen amidst all the societal iniquity, vague adumbrations of a new ethical consciousness capable of embracing the life-sustaining truth of natural survival through human selection.

It all started in the 1960s with a thoroughly unscientific phenomenon: a youth rebellion. The now well-known uprising came with the suddenness of a thunderbolt before a storm, to confound all prevailing occupations and presumptions. It swept across the world like a pandemic hurricane gathering momentum and fury as it went. Bewildering to most people, the social eruption became most violent in the richest, economically most stable and secure and militarily powerful country on earth—the United States. Let us take a quick retrospective look at what happened there and why.

From a socio-biological standpoint it might be said that the 1960s were the threshold of a first tiny breakthrough of the NSHS thrust that had long been building up with Man, to burst forth as a kind of societal mutant, inexplicable to the great mass of people, particularly the older ones. Remarkably enough, the match that set off the explosion was made of truly homely stuff, dating quite some years farther back than the 1960s; and it is, indeed, the little match that holds our interest, for it was nothing more than a novelty household gadget of the 1920s—the crystal radio set![2]

We now know, of course, that the mechanical offspring of the crystal radio set has evolved into the amazing TV communications system, which itself is still in its infancy; but most of us have forgotten the seemingly unimportant toy-gadget that was the forerunner of TV. Let us see how, in the United States, it also caused the youth rebellion of the 1960s.

The crystal set's progeny did not take off on their own until July 1, 1942, over station WNBT in New York City; and regular TV programming to the general public, not until after World War II. Furthermore, these beginnings were limited, technically, to simple animated cartoons, and for the next ten years, though greatly improved in technique, confined to nation-centered entertainment: light comedy, musicals, wild-west thrillers, foreign spy stories. Aside from an occasion travelogue to other lands, TV did little, during this period, to bring the daily affairs of mankind around the world into one's living room.

This was also a time when the United States began rapidly to emerge as the world's richest and most powerful nation, with military bases and vast holdings in rubber, tin, oil, etc., in all parts of the globe. It would have been out of harmony with the spirit of the time to portray, over TV, the contrasting poverty of great segments of the human family.

Up to the early 1950s television had not disturbed old nationalistic concepts of ethical behavior limited strictly to affairs within the nation-state. The everyday lives of peoples in other countries remained untouched by television; and so did the glorification of the kill in time of war between nations. The ancient myths of heroism on the battlefield were left intact by TV.

Then, strangely enough, television became the match that set off the explosion. TV producers hadn't the remotest desire to create social upheaval nor the foggiest notion that, when the first blasts went off, they had done it!

Faint tremors of what was to come began to be felt in 1964, when the United States escalated the war in Vietnam lost by the French in 1954 because, as the French claimed, the Americans had failed to supply them with sufficient military hardware. Be that as it may, up to this time the military machinations of the western Powers for control of the

Far and Middle East's natural resources, as well as those in other parts of the world, were well-kept military secrets with little public fanfare, and battlefields marked "off limits" to television.

Perhaps it was bad intelligence, perhaps just Yankee cocksureness that, once we went into Vietnam with all our military might, we could win a quick victory as we had always done. So reasoned the military brass. What a choice grandstand seat TV would offer to every victory-loving American! We would be witnessing the glorious advance of our victorious troops, while sitting comfortably in an armchair in the living room.

Consequently, for the first year or two of the stepped-up American military operation in Vietnam, television was remarkably free of censored broadcasts made direct from war-stricken areas and battlefields. It would all be over quickly in a great victory in the cause of democracy and freedom. And for the first time in the history of warfare, television would record the momentous events—and on prime time!

But—instead of an inspiring show of our military prowess, hundreds of millions of people were stunned by what they saw. Day in and day out they beheld, with their own eyes, the glastly scenes of dying Vietnamese babies with bloated bellies and heartbreakingly starved bodies of skin and bone; thousands of frightened old men, women and children fleeing bombarded areas that had been their homes only days or hours ago, or huddled together in refugee camps after their rice fields and other edible vegetation had been defoliated by poisonous chemicals "to starve out the enemy."

Oh, but that was far from all. They saw human corpses floating down rivers after the massacre of civilians who presumably had "aided the enemy"—their fathers, brothers or sons; search and destroy forays into simple little villages from which the fighting men had fled and only old men, women, children and babies remained to witness the systematic burning of their thatched roof dwellings—and sometimes to be mowed down by direct machine gun fire as dangerous accessories to their fighting men; horrible scenes that turned one's stomach, of boys and young men lined up side by side as each was individually stabbed or shot to death then pushed over backwards into a ditch for a quick unceremonious burial.

Soon it didn't matter at all to the viewers, who committed the atrocities—"our" side or the "enemy". What did matter was that a shocked world had witnessed, *for the first time in history*, the horrors of modern, scientific warfare. When the promised quick victory did not come, there was a mad rush at top Pentagon and governmental levels to clamp on a tight censorship. But it was too late.

Old and young were shaken alike. But there was a difference. The older population—those who were already in their twenties or older *back in the 1950s* when television was in its very beginnings and merely added new photographic dimensions to light entertainment—were caught between irreconcilable worlds: the domestic and the foreign. Their minds and emotional responses had been molded in childhood to a pattern of nation-centered morality (give me the child up to six and I will give you the man); they were immobilized for any effective counteraction against the revolting carnage. They could not grasp the idea of equating ethical concern for the well-being of members of one's own national culture-group, with that of members of the human family in distant parts of the planet Earth. More important, if they lived in the rich countries of the West, they had compelling material interests in preserving their affluent way of life which, alas, they knew from all their training, had to be achieved through victory in war, as well as through personal thrift.

Older people's mental and emotional blockings went beyond national boundaries. If they belonged to the so-called two percent landed gentry of Asia, Africa, or Latin America they valued, above all else, the oil, tin, and rubber royalties from western mining firms, and they prayed to their Gods for the defeat of the rebellious Vietnam peasants.

The Great Moral Uprising had thus to come from the millions of young people "under 30." They, and they alone, had been born into a global community made real to them in early childhood, by the advent of world embracing television. The unbelievable spectacle of mass-murder, financed and justified by the political and military leaders of their own country, aroused their unmitigated horror. No inner conflict of irreconcilable value-systems served to block their outrage over the savagery that TV had revealed to them. Indeed, the young of the 1960's had been taught from early childhood to love and be kind to others. To their elders, that may have meant to others living in the only world that had any relevance to them: their own sub-culture group within their nation-state. Not so to the TV oriented young.

When the President of the United States gave the official nod for the Pentagon to escalate the war in Vietnam, he lit the match that sparked the youth of high school, college and working age around the world, to rise up in an outcry of "stop the killing!" To the bewilderment of the older generation, youths' sense of shared guilt became the more acute if their parents were in the upper income brackets and the family derived its wealth from foreign possessions. Their ideals for the good life had not yet been compromised by the spoils of war as had their parents'.

To youth, then, must be credited the distinction of having been the catalytic agent for the first thrust toward fundamental change. But what happened was more than a rebellion of youth. It was, in fact, the beginning of a deep and profound social stirring, more far-reaching than what we normally associate with social revolution—the French, the American, the Russian or Chinese revolutions. It was not the result of scholarly research or the wisdom of public affairs leadership. On the contrary, it was self-generated from the bottom up, out of the huge morass of man-made wickedness, and it came upon the scene like a sudden beam of sunlight through a thick blanket of black clouds, to dazzle the eyes and frighten a nefariously busy people out of their wits.

Years later now, that youth rebellion may appear to some to have been a premature sprouting, destined to be still born in a barren social climate. Perhaps. But, though momentarily quiescent, we believe it will, if we read the historical signs correctly, resurface as sure as day follows night. For their early part in the epochal struggle, those relatively few courageous and clear-headed young who took the lead over a decade ago, can take heart. They may have had their heads clubbed, their names besmirched, and their freedom denied during those first critical years. But they will be remembered long after their detractors have been forgotten.

To be sure, the explosive sense of enragement among the youth of the 1960s, coming as it did over the Vietnam war atrocities, lacked the knowledge and experience of mature adults. It was bound to be confused, simplistic, elemental, and momentarily stilled, but really not still-born. The spirit, the adumbration of truth, was there. And there were the innovative few of the older generation, who understood and spoke up and are keeping the spirit alive.

The psychologist, Daniel Yankelovich, of New York University, credits the student movement in our colleges with having pointed the way toward a society founded on simple living and reverence of life, both implicit in the concept of enlightened frugality: "Our sons and daughters on campus are urging us to stop our frantic rush to bend nature to the human will and in its place to restore a vital, more harmonious—and more humble—balance with nature. . . . Before the decade of the 1970s has passed, the new naturalism will become a powerful force, nationwide in scope."[3]

Yankelovish attributes another basic idea to the campus movement of the 1960s: a sense of community in today's shrunken and interdependent world. "In our present culture, many of the human bonds of community, bonds seen as so necessary to the spirit as to be constitutive of all that is humanly natural, have come apart for us. We will not restore human decency, repose, and stability until we restore them."[4]

This one commentary could be multiplied with the fearless utterances of countless other defenders of the youth rebellion against an ungodly long era of primitive and barbaric pseudo civilization. In retrospect, however, the most significant thing revealed by the phenomenon was the insensitivity of the affluent public to its meaning, and the promptness and thoroughness with which the established authorities of the rich nations villified and crushed it. Finally, it added one more historical example of the tenacity with which wealthy peoples resist revolutionary societal change. We repeat Kennan's words that this transformation "must come from outside the system itself," and that "unless such a revolution is accomplished soon, the time left for our civilization has to be measured in decades and not in centuries." His outlook is in keeping with the ultimate time-factor of three or four more decades of maturization of today's "young under 30," of their children and their children's children, to accomplish the change.

And so, if a befuddled old generation can be kept from plunging humanity into a nuclear war, the future holds promise for the emergence of a wiser, planetary-oriented human animal. With this thought in mind, we come to the fork in the road for our journey into the future. The one way is clearly marked, "To the Survival of the Fittest Through Natural Selection," the other, "To Natural Survival Through Human Selection." The first leads to a dead-end; the second, to ever expanding vistas of adventure and new life experiences.

We now invite the reader to join us in exploring the journey down the second road.

8
Natural Survival Through Human Selection

(a) Enlightened Frugality

Natural survival through human selection is the *sine qua non* of the future. It rests on man's singular inventive ability to sustain life on a broad ecological scale.

We shall discover from a wealth of evidence that NSHS is as incontrovertibly practical as it is morally imperative. Let us put it this way: NSHS will evolve from the elemental ethical aspiration of the rebelling youth of the 1960s, into the more worldly-wise efforts of creative thinkers in the sciences, linked with those of leaders among the public at large, to achieve peaceful revolutionary societal change. We might add that before this can happen, a psychological battle must be won, reconciling the small ethics of man's historically demonstrated inventive genius with that greater ecological and Cosmic Ethic—call it God-directed if you will—which, alone, can save the human species from its own death-wish.

The meaning of NSHS can perhaps best be conveyed by describing the two-fold goal of this ethico-physical struggle: (1) a common lifestyle of *Enlightened Frugality* and (2) *Reverence of Life*, to the fullest extent of man's finite capabilities. Viewed anthropologically, genetically, politically, or ecclesiastically, the dual goal stands out above all else as the rock upon which the future of mankind must be built.

Clearly Man, as a thinking animal, would really have no future, were the laying of that foundation to be nullified by prevailing notions of his innate behavior as a supreme killer. There would remain only an eternity of carnage between species and individuals, and a mockery of reverence of life.

This, then, is the conceptual base of the NSHS evolutionary process of the future, if creative human beings are ever to find happiness. The time for its fulfillment may not be yet, but that it is fundamental to our deepest religious and philosophical aspirations, is becoming increasingly apparent to all thoughtful persons.

One might argue that the time-span is inconsequential, be it a hundred or a thousand years; everyone living at this moment, except a very few centenarians, will have been long dead at the end of either span. Yet most people would like the assurance that the NSHS goal is real and attainable, and that individual effort today and tomorrow constitutes the only dynamics by which it can be reached. To this must, however, be added the fact referred to earlier, that individual assurance and, indeed, effort, can only become socially effective through the activist role of individuals gathering collective momentum through time. And time, itself, is of the essence, for knowledgeable leaders in the sciences and public affairs are of a common mind that time is running out. Although their concern may stem more from the widely accepted myth of nature's scarcity and the urgency for restraint, than from a commitment to the yet unpublicized NSHS thesis, they are creative thinkers, and this makes them potential allies in the NSHS cause. Let us cite a few examples that come to mind at this beginning of the decade of the 1970s:

Former Secretary of the U.S. Department of Interior, Stewart Udall, urges "the development of dramatic new economic theories that would end a system that creates a fat life of empty affluence." The new economics, he adds, "must restrain technology as a servant of man and incorporate as an objective the leveling off of U.S. population." He concludes with a warning of economic disaster if the nation persists in eulogizing a system of unrestrained production and consumption.[1]

Restraint in the pursuit of extravagant life-styles in a world of presumed scarcity is the common plea. The ecologist, George A. Borgstrom, is impatient with the unwillingness of rich nations to curb wasteful spending: "Over 2 billion of the world's 3.5 billion people live lives dominated by extreme shortages of food and water and by inadequate resources in soils and water. In sharp contrast to their misery, a Luxury Club of at most 400 million people enjoys a rich and steadily more abundant diet as well as a high standard of living in most other respects."[2]

Harrison Brown, of the National Academy of Sciences, recently addressed a joint session of the House of Representatives Committee on Science and Aeronautics, and the Panel on Science and Technology. He pointed out that "Humanity is fissioning into two major groups—the culture of affluence and the culture of poverty." In urging that this dangerous imbalance be corrected through greater self-denial on the part of the affluent nations, he went on to say that—

> Government of the rich nations should transfer to the poor ones, as much capital each year as can be truly absorbed effectively. . . . I suspect that, unless this development takes place in the future at a rate which is considerably more rapid than at present, the poor countries in their misery will erupt and the rich countries in their stupidity will take sides.[3]

The economist, Kenneth Boulding, pleading the case of nature's limited resources, attacked the blithe assumption among Americans in the 1960s that science and technology can provide us with ever greater abundance. "Is Scarcity dead?" he asked. "Yes," was the answer, "scarcity is dead. Science and technology have produced the Age of Affluence. Let us drink and be merry, there is plenty for all. Between science, automation and systems engineering, we can produce all we need with a fraction of the labor force, and today not even the sky is the limit." To which Boulding, with a penchant for plain talk and firm belief in the scarcity thesis, replied: "Any economist who defends scarcity looks like a Prohibitionist at a country club."[4]

And so, the scarcity argument is echoed by a thousand voices of praiseworthy people in the affluent countries: the Barbara Wards, John Galbraiths, Barry Commoners, Maurice Strongs, Gunnar Myrdals, Rene Duboses, Paul Ehrlichs, George McGoverns, Margaret Meads, etc. Yet, the simple *reality* is that the scarcity case, misapplied to the profligate life-style of the Luxury Club, while millions of people are starving, can not put us on the road to a world society founded on human well-being where scarcity *is* dead. Even in contemporary primitive society, Mother Nature's larder is abundantly stocked and she offers her bounty with great generosity.

Thus, the generally astute Boulding in matters economic, has to turn his question around and ask: "Is Frugality dead?" And to that the answer must be, "It had better not be dead, for upon it rests the fate of the human species." The turnabout may not seem important, but it is. It brings us right back to the nub of the problem: the futility of looking for a life-style of genuine frugality among people obsessed by a mania for material wealth, unless that mania can be cured by some form of external shock treatment.

We shall point out as we proceed, that enlightened frugality is intrinsically as different from the material affluence of rich nations as it is from the economic plight of poor nations. It is a manner of life, yet to be born, of man's creative genius in socio-scientific inventivity, and a resurgence of that faith in simple living, displayed briefly by a courageous few among the enlightened young of the 1960s.

In its outward physical manifestations—leaving the inner spiritual side for the next chapter—enlightened frugality may be associated ecologically with a back-to-nature movement of man's habitat. An article on the *Criteria for an Optimum Human Environment*, prepared jointly by a group of educators in botany and anthropology at St. John's College, Cambridge England, and the University of Wisconsin, USA, puts this into words that warrant mention, since they pertain to the concept of Natural Survival Through Human Selection.

> At the present rate of advance in technology and agriculture, with an unabated expansion of population, it will be only a few years until all life, even in the atmosphere and the oceans, will be under the conscious dictates of man. While this general result must be accepted by all as inevitable, the methods leading to its control offer some flexibility. It is among these that we must weigh and reweigh the cost-benefit ratios, not only for the next 25 or 50 years, but for the next 25,000 years or more. The increasing scope of the threat to man's existence within this controlled environment demands radically new criteria for judging 'benefits to man' and 'optimum environments.'[5]

These scientists also stress the fact that man's unique inventive genius does not completely separate him from other animals and their natural environment:

> Unique as we may think we are, it seems likely that we are genetically programmed to a natural habitat of clean air and a varied green landscape, like any other mammal. To be relaxed and feel healthy usually means simply allowing our bodies to react as evolution has equipped them to do for 100 million years.[6]

This simple statement of the health-giving properties of man's natural earthly habitat, sets the ecological conditions implied in the NSHS thesis, and poses man's responsibility to create a social order founded on *enlightened frugality*, within the finite power of human creativity. It brings to mind one more thought expressed by Boulding in tacit support of enlightened frugality with bloated affluence for none. But, in quoting him, we take the liberty of deleting the word "scarcity" used by him and substituting (in italics) our words *enlightened frugality*, which we trust will be acceptable to him:

> A spaceship society does not preclude, I think, a certain affluence, in the sense that man will be able to maintain a physical state and

environment which will involve good health, creative activity, beautiful surrounding, love and joy, art, the pursuit of the life of the spirit, and so on. This affluence, however, will have to be combined with a curious parsimony. Far from enlightened frugality disappearing, it will be the most prominent aspect of the society. Every grain of sand will have to be treasured, and the waste and profligacy of our own day will seem so horrible that our descendants will hardly be able to bear to think about us, for we will appear as monsters in their eyes.[7]

How the revolutionary transformation is to be accomplished is another matter. We feel certain, for the reasons already noted, that it willl not come about in the rich nations without a bitter struggle. This does not gainsay the fact that public affairs leaders like Kennan feel strongly that it *must* come about in the United States, if we are to survive as a nation.

The Frenchman, Francois Revel, offers the happy formula that it *will* come about in the United States:

The revolution of the twentieth century will take place in the United States. It is only there that it can happen. It has already begun. Whether or not that revolution spreads to the rest of the world depends on whether or not it succeeds first in America.[8]

At first blush, on the basis of the position taken by our essay up to this point, one could say that Revel's prediction is taken right out of Alice In Wonderland. But if he makes it in the sense that Kennan sees the revolutionary imperative, and within our premise that the transformation can only happen if its proponents are able to win the struggle against the reigning American industrial/military elite and its status-quo followers, Revel may really be on target.

9

Natural Survival Through Human Selection

(b) Reverence of Life

This chapter focuses on the central thought of the whole NSHS thesis. It is an ancient thought expressed in the maxim: "Give me a man's philosophy and I will tell you what he eats for dinner." And it is with the kind of food man of the future will be eating that much of the rest of this essay will deal. But first—

Sustenance of life, in all its forms, is implicit in the evolutionary concept of natural survival through human selection. The question is not *what* forms human beings will decide to sustain, but to *what extent* finite human capabilities can accomplish it. Thus, the case for reverence of life, pleaded here, encompasses all organic beings on spaceship Earth; in the very near future it will also apply to man's role on other spaceships of the cosmos.

NSHS deals with fundamentals: specifically, with two of the oldest and most baffling of all human problems; first, the defeat of hunger for the great mass of the world's population and other sentient earthly creatures; second, the attainment of a measure of inner spiritual contentment for the human individual. As a life-sustaining theory of evolution, NSHS postulates vis-a-vis the awesome magnitude of ecological phenomena, the primacy of the need for food and species reproductive controls. It rests, furthermore, on man's ethical aspirations to achieve a transformation in human dietary habits, and those of other carnivores in the higher scales of intelligence as well, and replacing them, so far as human ingenuity can, with a non-killer pursuit of nourishment.

To avoid misunderstanding, we should define, at this juncture, what is meant by "the kill." The taking of a life, in the biological context in which we are using it, occurs when a flesh-eating animal obtains its food by hunting, stalking or otherwise killing another animal that also has a conscious or instinctive will to live. It is the unequal life and death struggle between a predator and his prey, the latter experiencing fear and awareness of the carnivore's murderous intent upon it when hungry.

How far down the life scale below the order of marine and terrestrial mammals, and perhaps fish and reptiles, man can eventually carry his avoidance of the kill, is pure conjecture at this pre-reality stage of NSHS. The same limitation may be said to hold for human ability to minimize predation among other carnivores living under nature's and, to a far lesser extent, man's controlled ecosystem.

It should be clear that this definition rules out the plucking of a tomato, the cutting of a head of lettuce or the harvesting of a field of grain, as an act of the kill. Experimental studies are, indeed, being made on plants as to their responses to physical stimuli threatening or terminating their life-span. Biologist Robert Parenti, of Kansas State Teachers College, has conducted experiments that detect electrochemical cell reactions by beans, when the pods or stems are cut.[1] But such studies reveal no demonstrable sensory factors of pain or fear as we humans are able to detect them in vertebrate animal species. Besides, it must be remembered well that man is but a finite creature, and his ethical revulsion against killing is only as inclusive as the tiny realm of the human understanding permits. There is no suggestion here that he try to play God.

Bearing this in mind, the relationship of a man's philosophy to his dinner table becomes more than mere rhetoric, and the planetary economics of enlightened frugality flows as a natural consequence of reverence of life. Stated simply, the cause and effect sequence means that reverence of life is to regard life with a profound respect and honor. It implies difference and tenderness of feeling. It means to hold sacred and holy with a great and unquestioning love.

One doesn't kill and eat an object for which one has a deep and compassionate love. It is not an aversion traceable to any shallow sentimentality but, perhaps, to the profoundest emotion experienced by the human individual. It is capable of generating an enormous power of Collective Will by which mankind can:

Relegate to a vestigial place our predator characteristics in an all-embracing thrust of natural survival through human selection. Man will no longer kill for food! As part of the potentially beneficent impact this can make on the earth's total ecosystem, man will be able to modify the environmental conditions for other flesh-eating animals at the high intelligence levels, and thus minimize predation among them also.

Tangent to this life-sustaining role that the human animal must play on a broad ecological scope, we can look to the speedy and total defeat of hunger on the human scene. The linkage is inherent in the ethics of enlightened frugality founded on reverence of life.

A visionary dream-world, you will say with a smile. True, if dreamed within the old dog-eat-dog culture values of contemporary primitive human society. But there is a hard, still below-the-surface, body of socio-biological evidence giving it solid foundation. If we add to this ethical groundswell the successful engineering of NSHS social revolution, with which we shall deal in part two of this study, the dream-world will indeed begin to materialize. And, in today's technologically accelerated time-continuum, it can happen sooner than you think.

Paradoxically enough, the projective outlook is as old as it is new; and, from an evolutionary standpoint, is based on exactly the same external evidence as is its opposite; i.e., the Malthus-Darwin theory of Nature's mechanistic, inscrutable way of "accomplishing" natural selection, in a life and death struggle of existence. The difference here lies not in the evidence itself, but rather in the attitudinal posture from which the evidence is viewed. We can say in all seriousness, therefore, that NSHS simply stands Darwinism right side up on its feet instead of on its head, where it now stands and sees the evidence upside down.

We come, then, to marshalling a body of evidence that is both existential and empirical. The existential factors pertain to the need for human beings to feel an identity with a power and significance infinitely greater than themselves. We have to examine it, lest its universal and timeless presence be overlooked in the search for empirical "facts."

Throughout all recorded history, and one need not stretch the imagination to conjecture long before that, man's presumed reverence of life has been at the heart of human religious and ethical experience, from the earliest known beliefs to the great religions and philosophies of today: Hinduism, Jainism, Buddhism, Confucianism, Taoism, Judaism, Islamism, Christianity. Zoroastrianism, Pantheism, Bahai'ism.

Associated with reverence and deification of life has always been some kind of belief in immortality, spiritual and corporeal. The Buddhists have their Nirvana, the Christians their Heaven. Ancient burial grounds contain those worldly possessions of the deceased thought to be necessary in the hereafter. The concept of immortality is nurtured by both fear and hope—fear of burning eternally in Hell for a scoundrelly life led here and now, hope of reward for a good life. The rich give liberally of their worldly goods to the Church of their faith, some in atonement for ill-gotten gains, some in gratitude for their good fortune. The poor and sick pray for deliverance to a better world after death. Though there is no assurance that the offerings or wishes will be honored, or the future be a blessed or better life—or that there *will* be a hereafter, there is no aspiration in the human heart more universal and timeless than this one.

But it is the veneration of animal and plant life, serving as the spiritual wellspring of Natural Survival Through Human Selection, that primarily concerns us. Historiographers of the world's religions find evidence of animal veneration in the archeological and skeletal remains of Neanderthalers, who roamed the earth in search of food one hundred thousand years ago. John B. Noss tells us that "Neanderthalers treated the cave bear with special reverence. They hunted him at great peril to themselves, and respected his spirit even after he was dead. They appear to have set aside certain cave bear skulls, without removing the brains, a great delicacy, and also certain long (or marrow) bones, and to have placed them, with special care, in their caves on elevated slabs of stone, on shelves, or in niches, probably in order to make them the center of some kind of ritual."[2]

The graves of the Cro-Magnons, a nomadic people of the stone age, reveal similar evidence of animal veneration, especially with reference to mammals like the reindeer and horse. From the fragmentary knowledge we have of them, Noss believes they were a more developed genus of homo sapiens and "that there may have been some recognition of a kinship and interaction of animal and human spirits."[3]

E. B. Tylor first used "animism" as a descriptive term in his famous work *Primitive Culture* (1872), setting forth the theory that primordial man attributed a soul or spirit to both living creatures and inanimate objects.[4] In retrospect, the thesis seems a bit like belaboring the obvious, because most of the great religions of today, including such ancient ones as Hinduism and Buddhism, have animal and plant veneration as a central religious tenet. Pre-historic and present day animistic religions observe the common practice of selecting a particular animal species as a special object of veneration, sometimes in deference to its magnificent prowess, its importance as food, or perhaps more fundamentally, out of a sense of the symbolic.

A wide range of animals around the world is accorded this high status in animistic reverence. In Africa it is the lion, in Malaya the tiger, in Greece and Egypt the bull, in Australia the kangaroo, in India, Scandinavia and, again, in Africa, the cow. Similarly, reverence has been paid to the goose, the dove, the snake. None of these animistic religious observances is more grossly misunderstood by rank-and-file adherents of the man-centered Judaic and Christian faiths than the protection of the cow as the most sacred of all animals in Hindu religion.

The great Indian statesman and philosopher, the late Mahatma Gandhi, himself a believer in the Hindu religion, considered "cow protection" as the central fact of Hinduism, the one concrete belief common to all Hindus, and he spoke of it in these memorable words:

> Cow-protection is to me one of the most wonderful phenomena in human evolution. It takes the human being beyond his species. The cow means to me the entire subhuman world. Man through the cow is enjoined to realize his identity with all that lives. . . . She is the mother to millions of Indian mankind. The cow is a poem of pity. Protection of the cow means protection of the whole dumb creation of God.[5]

Plant veneration, on the other hand, among the religions of the world, can be illustrated by one beautiful example cited, among many others, by Noss: "Survivals of such veneration in sophisticated societies are seen in the use of the Christmas tree and of the Maypole. It is said that in Europe, in the Upper Palatinate, woodmen still murmur a plea of forgiveness to a large tree before they cut it down."[6]

The significant thing, above all else, that animistic veneration has to tell, going back in time as far as the records of history have anything meaningful to reveal to us, is the deep human need to expiate the taking of a life even when this is done for self-preservation. The brief review of the evidence just made shows that prehistoric *and* modern man reveal this need in common. It also shows their frustration at being unable to do anything to nullify it and still survive. All the inventive achievements over the ages have not been sufficient to resolve the dilemma!

This existential attribute of human behavior goes a long way toward explaining the special reverence bestowed upon a single animal, or a select few animals, in a symbolic gesture of atonement, expressed in the face of having to continue killing for food. The most remarkable thing, however, about animistic veneration is its tenacious staying power, to the point that it induces great numbers of people to abstain completely from eating the flesh of a dead animal.

Our projective study is not a treatise on vegetarianism in the sense in which that term is generally used. But the vegetarian diet-patterns of many large and ancient culture-groups around the globe have a very important bearing, indeed, on the future of the NSHS thesis of evolution. When we stop to ponder the fact that entire nations in Asia, Latin America, and other parts of the world have for centuries lived mainly on a vegetarian diet, in conformity to the dictates of animal veneration; and that they steadfastly adhere to it, today, at the price of poverty, malnutrition, and a shortened life-span, for lack of adequate protein nourishment—then, this respect for the right to life "of the whole dumb creation of God" reveals its enormous motivational power.

No one knows how many of the world's population today abstain from eating meat because of reverence for sentient animal life. The theologian, Herbert Stroup, a student of India for the past twenty-five years, estimates there are 250 million Hindus in that country alone, most of whom adhere to a vegetarian diet for religious reasons.[7] With an estimated two-thirds of the world's people similarly conditioned by the precepts of animal veneration, the total number predisposed against meat-eating, may run well beyond a billion.

Although this supportive historical background on the basics of the NSHS case, is still not complete or definitive, it should help us put into clearer terms now, the direction our thesis is taking, than we may have succeeded in doing at the outset. Joined with the planetary economics of enlightened frugality, reverence of life provides the underlying dynamics capable of fulfilling the human aspiration of abandoning "the kill" as a means of survival. Still, the two provide but one-half of the full evidence for natural survival through human selection. They bring mankind closer to, but still short of, the desired goal. The other half is to be found in the twentieth century explosion of empirical discoveries by creative thinkers in the sciences. Merging the two, will enable us troubled humans to transform aspiration into fulfillment through the irresistible power of an informed and determined popular Will.

10

The Soilbed of NSHS Empirical Evidence

Natural survival through human selection is "a many splendored thing." If, in the next thirty to fifty years, the matured young of the world can generate the collective will needed to bring this splendor into being, the achievement will surpass anything to which man has aspired since the dawn of history.

The empirical evidence for NSHS is manifold, but so is the opposition. We have already stated, in a general way, why collective support for it can not be expected to come from the rich nations and, since the case for NSHS is being made in the heartland of material affluence, it is advisable that we identify the specific groups from which the *opposition* will emanate. We trust that the reader is not among them. In any case, it is well that we designate them in the thought that he or she engage in a bit of self-examination, as we proceed.

First in number and unalterable opposition is the vast army of status-quo seekers, who are eager to leave things as they are. Their motivations are variegated: favored social or economic position; temperamental aversion to change per se; or the sheer inability to project thinking beyond the present, because of basic neuro-psychological limitations. This group forms a roadblock around which it is sensible to make a detour. In all probability, such conditioned people into whose hands this study may have mistakenly fallen, have already removed themselves as readers by now, for it must all have seemed like idle day dreaming. But this is, unfortunately, *their* problem and we shall have to leave them with it.

Then there are the happy meat-eaters. The prospect of abandoning the kill for food is hardly an attractive one for them either. It certainly makes a shambles of their dinner table. We can hear the vigorous protests of the many thousands of sportsmen-hunters, all of them believers in the Darwinian Fallacy, whether or not they ever heard of Darwin: "Why do you try to deprive us of the pleasure of eating meat?

It is not only our favorite food, but we enjoy stalking our prey for the kill."

They are joined in their protest by an even larger contingent of non-sportsmen, quite content with getting their meat at the corner butcher shop. Meat eating, they would have us understand, is a very old custom of some millions of years standing among us humans. People in the polar regions of the earth live almost exclusively on meat and fish, for that's all nature has to offer them, and they thrive on it. If there is a question of ethics involved in meat-eating, then God must have intended us to be meat eaters, for He has endowed no other food so richly with the life-sustaining amino acids as meat.

The arguments are valid up to a point, but they don't quite go to the heart of the matter. Meat-eating is, indeed, an old and for many a very enjoyable custom. The more significant fact is that "nature" accords to man an experience of pleasure in the performance of all his basic survival-acts—so long as they are necessary *for survival*—as though to make certain that he will carry them out faithfully, no matter what the obstacles: eating, for example; sleeping, exercising, and reproducing one's kind. When the act ceases to be vital to survival, the pleasure ceases. Note this, however: of these fundamental preoccupations, only one of them—meat-eating—and only for some people, requires an act of killing. All the others are life-giving.

Abandoning the kill does not necessarily mean depriving ourselves of an enjoyable diet, if man's inventive genius can provide all the essential nutrients in a varied menu of vegetarian and animal products. It is not the eating of an animal—human or other—that so greatly satisfies man's appetite, but the proteins, vitamins, fats, etc., that meat undeniably supplies, but with which a meatless diet can be fully enriched, without the necessity of killing and eating the animal itself. As for the sportsman hunter who sees the pleasure of the hunt, and the enjoyment of eating flesh, as innate and eternal with us all, it should not suprise him to be told that this is as much a mirage today as was once the obvious flatness of the earth.

We shall get to the hard scientific evidence shortly. For the record, however, three prefatory points need to be directed to the meat-eating opposition: (1) millions of people in Asia, and growing numbers in the West, to whom we have just referred in some detail, have deep reverence of life and a great aversion to killing; (2) many people in all parts of the world, especially urban dwellers, have lost the hunting desire and are "chicken hearted" when it comes to killing anything, whether for food or sport; and finally, most people have, in the short time of the immediate past and present, already become accustomed to disassociation from the need, personally, to hunt and kill for their daily food; they couldn't care less whence came their food, so long as it tastes good, looks good and provides them with a healthful diet. Most Americans get their ham in a can, their steak in a cellophane wrapper, and their hamburger in a bun—with piccalilli, mustard and catsup.

The plight of confirmed meat eaters is really only theoretical, since we must of necessity project the end of predation well beyond their time. But for their progeny, dedicated to reverence of life, the wonderful moment of fulfillment is even now discernable. Given the inventive spirit in the culinary arts and related sciences, we may soon be able to titillate the appetite of the most voracious carnivores, and vegetarians too, with a savory meatless diet. They will be eating steaks that have never known an animal, delectable dishes for the protein hungry eye; simulated "meat" of the future, created of plant and animal products, by the inventive genius of man; a synthetic steak, sizzling on the griddle as ever, salted and peppered to taste and flavored, perhaps, with a wee bit of garlic, or smothered in onions and served with one's favorite fruits, salad and green vegetables; then topped with a good drink and dessert!

Finally, we come to that amorphous mass of the silent majority—the great army of little and big conformists, run-of-the-mill careerists, family dedicated providers—all of them over-burdened, over-committed, overly exhausted from running so hard to promote their personal affairs. Not a part of the hard-core opposition to fundamental change in affluent society, that is represented by the other two groups, they are, nonetheless, difficult to distinguish pragmatically from them. Through a widespread cross pollination, they become a part of the total dead-weight which a small minority of creative minded revolutionaries has to dislodge from the dead-center of all three groups, to try to move them forward literally inch by inch.

This is not to allege that many of these people are not well intentioned or would not like to see social change, if it could be accomplished quickly within their own life-span and without too drastic a disruption of their accustomed preoccupation. In this, they are characteristic products of their time, endowed with a fair share of the common analytical abilities of Man the Thinker, but lacking in the rare qualities of Man the Inventor. They cannot project their personal affairs and ambitions creatively into the future. And so, they are unable to play a dynamic part in the unfolding of the drama of spiritual and social revolution, in which making human predation vestigial surely plays a lead role. These good people are destined, alas, to live out their days uncommitted to sustained collective action in behalf of

NSHS; unwittingly as often as not, they become allied in their negative posture to the status-quo thinkers in affluent, techno-scientific society.

The loss of so many potentially valuable thinking people to social transformation is a distressing but not a devastating one. It is in the nature of the whole problem under discussion. The fact remains that much important preliminary ground work is being laid even now: in the West by concerned individuals with whom the thinking and inventive faculties are at one; in large parts of the Orient and Africa, where the ethical climate is more favorable; by entire nations under revolutionary leadership.

Forging a new link between the life-sustaining spiritual values of the primordial past, to which the cultures of the far-east and south are still loyal, and the material contributions of contemporary science and technology in the west, can mark the end of a long era of primitive society. On this premise, we can begin to assemble the empirical data in behalf of the total NSHS objective: the defeat of hunger on an ecological scope.

In addressing ourselves to this awesome task, we must take cognizance of the important ongoing work agronomists and demographers are doing to secure a sufficiency of food for members of the human family itself, matched by effective population control. Theirs is a task of immediacy; ours, of ultimates. And yet, we believe that unless the two efforts converge in a profound transformation of human aspirations (a) to make human predation upon sentient animals vestigial and (b) to minimize predation among these animals themselves, the disjointed efforts are doomed to failure.

A common implementing strategy is, fortunately, the same for man and beast, as we shall see. Having to achieve a meatless diet for man, before it can be done for other mammals, is evidence of the human animal's own finite abilities and provides the learning experience by which its unique creative genius can be employed to sustain life among other finite creatures.

To this end, the NSHS tenet of enlightened frugality and reverence of life by man of the future, will demand an unswerving dedication to accomplish at least five inter-related—and to the true apostle of the status-quo, five impossible—creative endeavors. In specific terms, the objectives will have to meet five needs:

1. Development of a sufficiency of nutritious and palatable meatless food.

2. Achievement of environmental conservation, including preservation of domestic and wildlife, nature's mineral, metal, fossil, oil, and other resources.

3. Establishment of population balance in a total ecological sense.
4. Accomplishment of revolutionary socio-political change.
5. Exploration of cosmic space.

Progress in these fields cannot be assessed in any sequential way, because facets of each run concurrently. We shall, therefore, have to examine them throughout both the first and second parts of our study, to the extent that they bear on NSHS.

Food For The Human Family

Scientific research and development of a sufficiency of nutritious food for all members of the human family was highlighted at the 1963 international conference of the Ciba Foundation, attended by leaders in the biological and medical sciences. The conferees agreed that, based on well established laboratory tests, a nutritious diet must provide the proteins (amino acids), fats, carbohydrates, minerals, and vitamins, essential to survival.

The conference proceeded from the common scientific knowledge that all of these nutrients, especially the key proteins, without which life hangs by a thread, are abundantly provided by the flesh of dead animals. Nonetheless, the biologist, Colin Clark, declared that the findings of nutritionists show a broadly balanced vegetarian diet to contain all these nutrients. His report was based on an accumulation of data subsequently drawn together by the Food and Agricultural Organization (FAO) indicating that predatory human beings, even now, secure only 15 percent of the vitally needed proteins from animal flesh. The rest come from other foods in the following percentages:

Cereals	48%
Grain legumes, oilseeds and nuts	12
Starchy roots, vegetables and fruits	12
Milk (from animals)	11
Eggs	02
TOTAL	85%[1]

Realizing that most of the conference participants were western meat eaters, Clark hastened to add, "Let us not, however, talk as if we were trying to force the whole of mankind on to a cereal diet. Even if it is not physiologically necessary, we enjoy a diet of meat and dairy products." To which the late J.B.S. Haldane replied, "I would like to quarrel with Clark's remark that the vegetarian diet (of Southern India) is dull and uninteresting. In my opinion there are three centres of the culinary art in the world; one in France and Italy, of which we are at the margin; one in South China, and one in South India. The latter cuisine is the only one which is mainly vegetarian, and you cannot appreciate it until you have had no meat and fish for a month or two, when you begin to see that these people are getting at aesthetically. It is, in fact, far from dull and uninteresting."[2]

While this conversational by-play points up the consensus among nutritional specialists, greatly strengthened since 1963, that all the essentials of an adequate food supply for bodily growth and health are provided by a diet of both animal and plant products *without meat*, it also poses the two larger problems going beyond securing an adequate meatless diet: (1) satisfying the gustatory eccentricities of different culture groups, especially those accustomed to meat eating; (2) extending the techno-scientific knowledge and economic resources of the affluent industrial nations, now used to produce food in overabundance for themselves, and coordinating these with the rapidly growing agricultural research by organized blocs of poor nations, having a common interest in wiping out hunger among their own people.

Already there are signs that creatively motivated food merchants are thinking of the merits of producing more than just synthetic steak—a most welcome manifestation of the inventive genius in the commercial field. Note this syndicated news story that appeared in many Sunday newspaper editions, April 23, 1972, across the country:

> If world population increases outstrip our global meat resources, scientific and farming technology will combine to offer other resources of high protein food material. One of the most important of these is soybean, a crop that can be grown throughout the world.
>
> A new process reduces the soybean to its basic protein and then spins it into a high nutritious food base. . . . Fritzche, Dodge and Olcott, Inc., in New York, creates flavors for spun soybean that make it taste like chicken, ham, corned beef, turkey, liver, bacon, bologna. And these flavors are not derived from any animal, but from the lab.
>
> How would you like your soybeans? Well-done or rare?
>
> Currently, too, there are appearing on the shelves of supemarkets meatless "ham" and "pork sausage" put out by Miles Laboratory under the label Morning Star Farm. They are protein-rich, approximate the taste of real ham or sausage, and have the texture of pork. Of course, these initial efforts are far from "the real thing". But give the innovative genius of the human animal a bit more time!

As of this writing (July, 1973), soaring meat prices in the United States are giving housewives doing the family shopping a strong incentive to buy less expensive food, while imaginative food processors like the above, strive to improve and increase the variety and palatability of nutritious vegetable products. An unexpected pinch in the American habit of "living high on the hog" illustrates the versatility of human beings to adjust their tastes to changing conditions and pressing necessity.

On the more critical front of fighting hunger, biochemists and agronomists are making exciting discoveries in the new strategy of soil cultivation. They are finding that plant products can be processed into protein-rich food and, combined with animal products like milk, butter, eggs, and cheese, provide not only a balanced diet containing all the essential amino acids, vitamins, minerals, and fats, but offer the prospect of tripling and quadrupling the world's total food supply, at costs far below those of raising and slaughtering live-stock.

The 1969 FAO report on agricultural development points out that for normal physical growth and maintenance, the human body requires a daily minimum intake of proteins in which at least 8 amino acids—the essential amino acids—must be present in certain quantities, because these 8 amino acids cannot be synthesized by the human body. Plants, on the other hand, can synthesize all 20 (known) amino acids, so that animals and man ultimately rely on *plant proteins for life*.[3]

Although the amino acid pattern in most animal proteins, resembles that in human protein more closely than does the pattern found in any one single plant species, it is possible by mixing plant products, in which amino acid patterns supplement one another, to produce protein foods that have a biological value similar to that of animal proteins.

The infant science is making encouraging progress. In traditionally poor countries, creative thinkers are struggling against great odds to defeat hunger and malnutrition through the development of high protein multiple-plant foods. In the meat-eating West, creative commercial enterpreneurs are doing a flourishing business in the research and production of vegetable milk, butter, cream—and, as just mentioned, even a soybean substitute for sausage and hamburger!

Documentation of initial accomplishments is contained in a comprehensive report by Nigel Hey. It presents not just one man's view on the subject but an impressive body of data made available by more than thirty cooperating organizations in government, education and private industry. Included are the Brookhaven National Laboratory, Canada Department of Agriculture, Central Soya, Food and Agricultural Organization of the United States, Ford Foundation, Los Alamos Scientific Laboratory, General Mills, International Harvester Company, W.K. Kellog Foundation, Monsanto Company, National Plant Food Institute, Quaker Oats Company, Soybean Council of America, Swedish Informational Service, U.S. Soil Conservation Service, and other equally sophisticated organizations.

The documentation is wide-ranging and so directly supportive of the NSHS thesis, even though this is not its purpose, it warrants careful examination. We shall scrutinize a number of the more significant breakthroughs:[4]

Protein-rich Milk from Grain

As recently as the early 1960's, mortality among preschool children in Latin America was 10 to 40 times higher than in affluent North America. Children were literally starving to death for lack of protein in their meager, undifferentiated diet, derived mainly from corn. Within the limited resources at their command, agricultural specialists had long been trying to find an answer to this deplorable situation. In 1959 they found one. To quote from the report:

> Massachusetts Institute of Technology's N.S. Scrimshaw, and his colleagues at the Institute of Nutrition of Central American and Panama (INCAP), knew that all the necessary proteins and amino acids were available in grains and other plants, which are the raw materials used by animals that give us meat, eggs and milk. True, individual plants such as corn would not provide the right protein balance for proper nutrition. But what if different kinds of vegetable foods were mixed scientifically, so that *together* they contained essentially the same nutrients as animal protein?
>
> Dr. Scrimshaw and his INCAP team made up a list of reasonably low-priced vegetable products and compared their protein contents. They decided upon cottonseed flour, ground corn and sorghum grain as their basic ingredients. They blended these together as a flour and added small amounts of torula yeast, calcium carbonate and vitamin A, to provide the extra nutrients that would make the mixture equal in value to animal protein. The new product was named Incaparina, a word derived from INCAP and harina, the Spanish word for flour.[5]

Initial success left no doubt as to INCAP'S nutritional value. If it can also meet the test of palatability through time, the results may prove to be spectacular. For example: The children of Escuintla, Guatemala, were treated to the first batches of the new wonder food mixed with water. They liked it. Three times a day for sixteen weeks, a test group of children drank sweetened "milk-shakes" made from the powdered Incaparina and water. Each glass was nutritionally comparable to whole milk and contained more calories than three ounces of lean meat. After only sixteen weeks the children were noticeably healthier than when they began the experimental diet. Given the high stakes, the project raised high hopes.

After the success at Escuintla and neighboring communities, 12 retail stores near Guatemala City were supplied with individually wrapped supplies of Incaparina, each package containing enough protein to feed a young child for one day. By the end of four weeks, shoppers had snapped up 4,500 bags of the new wonder food. A local company was signed up as a manufacturer and distributor, and a second test in Guatemala City resulted in the sale of 350 *tons* of Incaparina in a seven-month period.

Other successes followed in Columbia. Not only was Incaparina a source of life-giving protein, but it was inexpensive. A 17½-pound bag cost the equivalent of only 10 U.S. cents. A Columbian housewife would have to pay nine times as much for powdered milk having the same amount of protein; five times as much for fresh milk, and three times as much for whole egg protein.[6]

Further study and wider testing of public acceptance is needed before passing final judgment on the use of Incaparina. That it is a versatile product has already been discovered. It can be used as a substitute for wheat flour, as an enriching agent in soups, puddings, cookies, precooked baby foods, and a host of other nutritious recipes. The basic ingredients can be varied, depending on local availability—rice, sorghum, soybean, corn—as long as it makes up 58 percent of the required formula.

Related Developments In Other Countries

Similar methods of mixing available plant flours into a single product, having the balanced protein composition that individual plants lack, are being successfully developed in other parts of the world.

In Mysore, India, researchers at the Central Food Research Institute have developed three new flours, by enriching wheat flour with various mixtures of peanut, tapioca, and semolina flours. U.S. Department of Agriculture scientists at Peoria, Illinois have developed a way of making the Indonesian food, *tempeh*—generally made by fermenting soybean—from a mixture of soybean and grains. The result is a new, tasty, vitamin-rich food. In Ethiopia, Swedish experts have developed their own "Incaparina" from chick peas and skimmed milk—a local cereal called *teff*. This porridge-like protein source costs 10 U.S. cents for a child's five-day supply.[7]

Israel is credited with making the first efforts to produce leaf protein food commercially. The Israelis use it as chicken food. Many of the green vegetables customarily a part of man's diet are rich in vitamins, minerals, and other essential nutrients, but contain only a small amount of protein per gram of dry weight. However, if mashed and pressed to remove all unwanted juices, *leaves of all kinds* can produce a product which is as much as 70 percent protein.[8]

The development of such concentrated leaf protein is still in its infancy. The results are not yet attractive enough to provide dishes for human consumption, but they are making available new sources of food for cattle and other livestock. Meanwhile, the initial Israeli experiments have stimulated interest in the potential of leaf protein as an added resource with which to solve the world's food problem. Nature's storehouse of leaf protein is vast, and many scientists are looking to the day when it will provide intriguing new foods from all presently unused parts of grain bearing plants; from grasses, alfalfa, beet tops, peanut leaves, and even the common weed.

Based on the remarkable, though little publicized, progress already being made by creative minded researchers and food processing companies, it takes little imagination to predict that these products will become standard parts of our diet in the very near future, and that they will taste as good as, and probably better than, the flesh of a dead animal—and perhaps be less dangerous to health. (Biochemical research is beginning to encounter some suspicious signs of toxic matter in the flesh of dead animals that may be the cause of cancer, and possibly other human ailments attributable to meat-eating!) In any case, the new agricultural methods of processing and making wise use of soil cultivation promise to reduce the wholesale slaughter of livestock, a subject on which we shall have more to say. Indeed, agronomists say that the day will come when more and more land will be devoted to vegetable crops, gradually decreasing the acreage available for raising food animals. They point out that animals are inefficient converters of food energy, that necessary nutrients *are* available in a properly balanced vegetable diet, and that animals sometimes consume or destroy food that humans otherwise would eat.

Hail the Soybean!

The soybean's fame as a prolific contributor of polyunsaturated margarines, shortening, and other nutritious foods, is already worldwide. The admittedly crude offerings on the shelves of your neighborhood supermart, today, are but fleeting examples of first inventive efforts, like the first tallow candle many centuries ago compared with the invention of modern electric lighting, or Watt's steam engine compared to atomic power, or the ox cart compared to the supersonic jet.

Food From Single-Celled Organisms

Perhaps the most far-reaching possibility in the development of an abundant food supply for *non-predator* man of the future, is being revealed by food produced from single-celled plants and animals. Commonly referred to as "single-celled protein" (SCP), it is derived from four classes of micro-organisms: fungi, yeasts, algae, and bacteria.

SCP food is not so fantastic an idea as it might seem to be at first thought. For centuries, the Chinese have been eating a kind of cake called *lan*, made from a blue-green algae. A pilot plant in France is now turning out a similar product.

In general, fungi are between 30 and 60 percent protein compared to 25.5 percent in milk. The potential yield from these microscopic plant organisms is incalculably enormous. Scientists who study fungi have named 75,000 species, and believe they could provide protein, as food additives, to feed many times the number of people presently constituting the world's population. William Gray, of Ohio State University, compares the yield of corn fed to livestock with the yield from the same amount of corn used as substrata for growing fungi. The fungus protein plus the protein extracted from the corn, serving as the "animal" provider, is seven times that produced by cattle!

Yeasts are among man's oldest cultivated plants. They contain the enzymes (from the Greek words meaning "of yeast") that break down sugar to form the carbon dioxide essential to rising bakery goods and the alcohol found in natural beers, wines and spirits. But as such, they are merely helpers in human nutrition; though they are about 50 percent protein, yeast cells, themselves, have not yet gained significant use as food products.

"The techniques of using the microorganisms that may hold the greatest promise of all," says Hey, "are still at the pioneering stage of development. Many technical problems must be overcome, but when they are, researchers are confident they'll have found the ultimate protein producers in bacteria. These microscopic plants or animals (scientists don't agree on just what they should be called) are tiny, compared to fungi or yeast, but they multiply at a rate that staggers the imagination. Researchers have found that bacteria can go through as many as 87 generations in a single day! One scientist has calculated that, if a single minute cell could be given limitless food and space, it could, in just 48 hours, generate a mass 4,000 times the weight of the earth!'"[9]

In all this we have not even mentioned the vast food resources of the oceans covering more than three fifth of the earth's surface. There are, for example, the great colonies of plankton and seaweed, rich in protein and vitamins. These tiny plant and animal organisms are the pasture grass upon which all the higher marine forms are dependent for survival. They offer a bonus food supply in addition to what man can derive from the soil.

And we have completely by-passed research focused on increasing the supply of meat, poultry and fish. Unquestionably, so long as food research emanates largely from the West, we can look for continued emphasis on eating the flesh of life-conscious animals. But to repeat for counter-emphasis, and by no means for the last time: once the NSHS ethical posture of *enlightened frugality* founded *in reverence of life* becomes increasingly dominant among the maturing young of the next three or four generations, predation by Homo sapiens will become gradually vestigial, certainly at the highest trophic levels.

The kill in search of food will become repugnant philosophically and unacceptable socially. A long way off in point of time? So was travel to the moon to the driver of an ox-cart a few anthropological moments ago.

11

Our Kin In Unlike Form

Man's First Steps to Non-Predation

We have presented the evidence of nature's bountiful storehouse of food from the soil, and touched upon man's ability to secure an adequate, healthful, and enticing supply of it, with or without animal by-products. We have shown, furthermore, that abandonment of the kill is not antithetical to human survival. Food from the soil is abundantly available to feed the hungry millions of the human family.

Having made this the premise of man's singularly innovative ability to grow life-sustaining food from the soil, and to combine that food with animal products, without recourse to the kill, we shall now direct our attention to the ensuing human desire to protect and enhance the right to life of *all* sentient creatures. We feel confident that creative thinkers in agriculture, nutrition, demography, and wildlife conservation will welcome this endeavor to curtail human predation to the fullest possible extent. They are already doing this in their own respective fields.

Of course, the NSHS dedication to reverence of life pushes us on to the supposedly more impossible next step; namely, to help carnivorous animals, *themselves*—wolves, lions, tigers, etc.—minimize predation for food. We don't have to worry about our closest kin, the herbivorous apes, chimpanzees, monkeys and other, generally, non-killer primates, except for their safety as prey for the carnivores. Since the latter, with the exception of man, kill only for food, it is reasonable to assume that if they can be assured of their keep through man's inventive genius, they will accept the gratuity in the same spirit of appreciation as domesticated dogs, cats, and other household pets do.

In the wild, carnivores (and omnivores) must now be predators because, like man, they cannot produce within their own bodies the amino acids essential to life, as herbivores do. Unlike man, they have neither the cognitive faculties that plague man's ethical sensitivities, nor the inventive ability to change their natural environment or animal nature, unless we help them do it. This takes us to the twofold, exploratory task of making human predation vestigial, and helping other animals minimize it among themselves, so far as finite human inventivity enables us to accomplish it.

Given the seeming impossibility and real complexity of the endeavor, we shall start by examining the ways toward abandoning human predation in areas we know best, and where we already have much practical knowledge; i.e., in the husbandry of livestock and care of household pets.

With respect to livestock, mutual benefits are well known. It takes no great clairvoyance to project some of the more important ones at this pre-action point in time. For humans the immediate economic gain will be the enormous savings derived from the reduction of countless numbers of livestock now raised for the slaughterhouse. A statistical tabulation of cattle, hogs, sheep, chickens, and fowl of all kinds, that man has to feed and fatten for the dinner-table, would approximate astronomical proportions: huge, also, is the cost of housing, transporting, slaughtering, refrigerating, processing and merchandising the meat.

The direct benefit accruing to mankind, in embarking on a nonpredation diet, is one of the remarkable consequences of abandoning the kill. Rather than entailing human sacrifice through a denial of full access to varied and nutritious food, it greatly enhances the prospect. And the aforementioned monetary savings to be gained, reveal only a small portion of the hidden social extravagance that goes with eating the flesh of a dead animal.

Before we explore the intriguing subject, perhaps we can add zest to the long dormant human aspiration, by further amplification of the benefits to us. We have seen in Chapter X how inefficient farm animals are in converting the plant food they eat, into meat for human consumption. They ingest three to four times more plant nutrients than they pass on to humans in the form of meat; some studies put it at five to seven times more.

In 1956 a group of biochemists and nutritionists, headed by James Benner, a geochemist at the California Institute of Technology, met to take stock of the world food situation. They concluded that "by utilizing the whole of the globe's vegetable resources, it would be possible to feed a world population five times larger than the current total."[1]

The study also pointed out that recent conquests of science and technology make practical the extraction of vegetable proteins, to replace or supplement insufficient animal proteins; also, the cultivation of protein-high vegetables that will be 100 percent edible; the farming of arid or saline soils, and, in the more distant but attainable future, the development of artificial synthesis of vitamins and proteins. And there are the millions of acres of arable land that will become available as a result of the reduction of great numbers of livestock. In England grass provides 60 percent of all nutrients for livestock; in India, an extreme case, 95 percent of the whole animal nutrients. It should, however, be added that man's competition with both domestic and wildlife is not all that encompassing in todays agrarian economies. Primates may need the same nutrients, minerals, vitamins, and salts that man must have, but they generally do not compete with man for the same types of food. They do not feed on the same portions of edible plants. Livestock eat the straw, the milling offals, the by-products of the oil-crushing industry, the tops of the pulp of sugar beet—these, and many other parts of plants not customarily used for human consumption.[2]

As we become imbued through the years with the NSHS life-sustaining tenets, it is reasonable to anticipate that we will adhere fervently to a policy of equalizing the amount of food grown and harvested, with a systematic return to the soil of the vital elements taken from it in the growing process: the nitrogen, potassium, phosphorous, calcium, water, etc., necessary for all plant and animal life.

The NSHS knowledge and techniques required to accomplish this are practicable, the chief obstacle to their optimum application being only the wasteful habits of over-production and over-consumption, indulged in by today's affluent warrior nations, hell-bent on preserving their profligate way of life. In contrast, the future NSHS life-style will continue to call on our agrarian kin in unlike form, to provide mankind with the milk, butter, eggs and cheese—all enjoyable parts of a meat-less diet. For this contribution to human survival, our generous kin are surely entitled to a fair share of nature's bounty; and this does not even credit them with their presence in the aesthetic completeness of the countryside.

With this finite but creative human role in mind, we can now venture on our next steps to marshal supportive evidence. It takes us into the domain of wildlife conservation, which offers us not only an overview of the important work of conservationists to protect flora and fauna of all kinds but, intentionally or not, also, a knowledge of some far-reaching side effects that lead straight to the NSHS objectives. This is actually a result of the fruitful cross-pollination of ideas among scientists in a wide range of life-sustaining research: medicine, biology, ecology, demography, wildlife conservation.

The ecologist, Joyce Joffe, defines conservation as "the reclamation of a dust-bowl, the control of pests, the saving of a single plant or animal from extinction, the declaring of a smokeless zone, or the development of new techniques of wheat-growing or sewage disposal. But whatever it is, it is all part of conservation planning for the future."[3]

The Vermont forester, George Perkins Marsh, is generally considered to be the father of the modern conservationist movement. In his now famous, *Man and Nature; or Physical Geography as Modified by Human Action* (1864), he set new perspectives in bio-sociological thinking. As a contemporary of Charles Darwin, he, like Kropotkin, did not become a proponent of the theory of species survival through natural selection. He once wrote in his youth that "the bubbling brook, the trees, the flowers, the wild animals were persons to me, not things." He was a true precursor of the emerging NSHS life-outlook.[4]

It should be said, however, that conservationists generally assume that the social-Darwinist acceptance of human predation upon animals is not antithetical to animal preservation. Although in this they are at cross purpose with the NSHS thesis, there is much to commend in their work of wildlife conservation and, perhaps in time, to align it with us. Writing for the World Wildlife Fund, Elizabeth Huxley describes the "Four Pillars of Conservation: the Ethical, Aesthetic, Scientific and Economic." She explains:

> The Ethical Pillar recognizes that man is a part of the natural world, that he cannot separate himself from it without losing an important part of his own heritage, and that every needless or avoidable destruction of his fellow creatures is in some sense a derogation from human dignity.
>
> The Aesthetic Pillar recognizes and accepts that natural beauty is no less a vital part of man's cultural heritage than man-made beauty, and that pleasure derived from hearing bird song in an English wood, or watching a herd of antelope galloping across an African savanna, is as important to human spiritual welfare as a Beethoven quartet, a pop song, a Rembrandt or a primitive.
>
> The Scientific Pillar recognizes that the natural world is the ultimate source and raw material of all human knowledge, and that to allow a species to become extinct before it has been studied and its potential contribution to scientific knowledge assessed, is both stupid and liable to deprive future generations of some vital part of their heritage.
>
> This last Pillar of modern conservation is an unfortunate departure

from the youthful dream of its founder, Marsh. So is the Economic Pillar:

> Wildlife constitutes an important human asset. The world would be a much richer place if the abounding wildlife resources that existed, for instance, on the North American continent, had been carefully conserved and *harvested* instead of being nearly wiped out, as happened with the bison, the fur seal and the otter, to name only a few.[5]

Thus, the prevailing conservationist philosophy finds human predation upon all animals not only necessary ecologically but virtuous and desirable as a preoccupation, provided only that the kill is carefully programmed to assure a full and continuing supply of healthy animals for our dinner table. It is almost impossible to pick up a book on wildlife preservation that does not stress the need for scientific programs of "harvesting" animal populations; and most treatises actually pay high tribute to the sportsman hunter for his dubious role in cropping "excessive" numbers of wildlife.

Relying on sportsmen-hunters for wildlife population control is like asking the fox to guard the chicken coop. Powerful hunter-lobby groups like the Gun and Rifle Clubs, annually secure local and state legislation supplying funds to *increase* rather than decrease excess animal populations. They make sure that the supply of wildlife is sufficient to satisfy the pleasures of the sportsman-hunter—and the commercial hunter, too.

Based on the ensuing data of our study, the argument that sportsmen-hunters perform a laudable conservationist service by cropping excess animal wildlife, is not only sterile status-quo thinking but a badly misplaced encomium. The ecologist, J.J. McCoy says, for example, that "mourning doves and bobwhite quail often have an annual mortality of 75 percent, regardless whether they are hunted or not."[6] And, it should be added that in parts of the world where the sportsman-hunter is a rare animal, nature, aided at times by the irreparable damage wrought by private commercial enterprise, accounts for closer to 100 percent of wildlife harvesting.

This must not blind us to the brighter and much more important side of contemporary animal conservation. But for its western man-centered aberration from life-sustaining concepts, conservationists are, nonetheless, setting the stage for the planetary, largely herbivorous man of the future.

In the hundred years since Marsh, perhaps the most dramatic development that slowly enabled conservationists to arouse public interest in wildlife preservation was the alarming rate at which commercial operators were decimating many well known animal species. The ecologist, Richard Fitter, reports that in the past two thousand years about a hundred different forms of animals have become extinct in various parts of the world. But in the last two hundred years commercial "harvesting" has increased the rate to at least one mammalian species every year, and he adds, "there are between 250 and 300 candidates for extinction in the wings, mammals officially regarded in serious danger of extinction by the International Union for Conservation of Nature."[7]

The conservationist, Bill Perry, tells the story of the extermination of the once incredibly abundant passenger pigeon. These pigeons were sociable birds, prolific breeders and, alas, good to eat. Larger than the mourning dove, they migrated in tremendous flocks. In the year 1810, the noted Ornithologist, Alexander Wilson, calculated that a flock he observed was more than a mile wide and over two hundred miles long, and contained more than *two billion* birds.[8]

Within a few decades large concentrations of these birds were wiped out. Farmers slaughtered them by the hundreds to feed their pigs. Merchants devised methods for wholesale slaughter. They used nets to ensnare hundreds at a time for shipment by the ton to city markets. By 1870, their numbers had become so reduced, ornithologists feared the extermination of the passenger pigeon. Their fears were well founded.

The last positive record of a wild pigeon was a bird shot in Wisconsin in 1899. A few captive passenger pigeons lived on in Milwaukee, Chicago and Cincinnati during the first decade of the 1900's. But in 1910 the last male died in the Cincinnati zoo, leaving behind the sole survivor of the species, Martha (named after Martha Washington). With her death in September 1, 1914, the passenger pigeon disappeared from the face of the earth. But you can see Martha mounted on exhibition in a glass case in the U.S. National Museum in Washington, D.C.

It was not until the early 1900s that conservationists were first able to mount an effective campaign of wildlife protection. In the case of birdlife it resulted in saving some of the most beautiful birds on the American continent: whooping cranes, egrets, spoonbills, and many other colorful and gorgeously plumed birds from what seemed certain extermination by commercial and sportsmen hunters. Literally millions of these feathered creatures were being shot down every year. For more than a decade the mounting slaughter had been going on without protest; and it had no more important purpose than to satisfy the fashion needs for bright colored plumage and small stuffed birds to adorn ladies' hats!

In 1892, according to reliable conservationist records, one feather merchant in Jacksonville, Florida, shipped 100,000 of these birds to New York. Over 40,000 terns were wiped out each season on Cape Cod, Massachusetts, and near one Long Island village in New York, 70,000 were taken in a single year. The bird-slaughter business boomed all over the country and the lucrative market for women's plumed hats quickly spread to Europe.[9]

It required the cold-blooded murder of a dedicated Audubon game warden, Guy Bradley, who was shot down in his skiff in Oyster Bay, Florida, one July morning in 1905, while trying to stop a gang of plume hunters, before any public notice was taken of this devastation of wildlife. The hunters were shooting birds in violation of an old unenforced law passed by the United States Congress to protect birds and other wildlife reserves then in existence, of which Oyster Bay was one. Two conservationists, Ann and Myron Sutton, tell what happened.

As Bradley rowed out into the Bay, the poachers fired a shot to warn their companions. By the time the warden arrived, a scowling phalanx of hard-bitten gunmen had lined up on the schooner, and when he called out to them that they were under arrest for violating the law, they gunned him down. Although the poachers were quickly apprehended and tried, they had to be freed in the absence of witnesses, and on their own word that they were fired upon first and only returned fire in self defense.

"It was only a local incident," write the Suttons—"the killing of an individual; but the story spread like fire in the sawgrass. Tempers flashed, and angry citizens, the more they thought of it, grew angrier still."[10] Conservationists at last had a *causa belli* and they made the most of it. With the help of an arounsed public, an organized campaign was launched by wildlife leagues, sportsmen's clubs, granges, garden clubs, and private citizens, for legislation to suppress the senseless killing of bird wildlife.[11]

The wanton slaughter of mammalian wildlife and, of course, domestic livestock, is an equally sordid story. In the meat-eating West, feasting on the flesh of dead mammals continues to take on daily orgiastic proportions. Several years ago the American TV celebrity, Jack Paar, toured the Nepal-Tibet region of the Himalayas. On his return he said on one of his TV shows: "We traveled a great deal by train. The Pullman accommodations were modern and comfortable and the food was delicious; but don't ask for meat. They eat very little meat except maybe some fish."

Emmet Dedmon, editor of the Chicago Sun-Times, made a similar observation about the Chinese diet habits on a TV broadcast, February 16, 1974, over educational channel WEDU, Tampa, Florida, following a visit to the Peoples Republic of China. Later, when a group of Chinese newspaper reporters visited the United States, one of the questions asked of them at the end of their visit was whether or not they had encountered any difficulties or hardships while here. Their answer, said Dedmon, was: "Yes, we had to eat so much meat. In China we are not accustomed to eating so much meat."

And so the "harvesting" of sentient mammals goes merrily on in the West. It is only because of the dedicated rescue work of wildlife conservationists that many species have been saved from extinction: the Blue Whale, largest animal that has ever lived; the Mediterranean Monk Seal, probably the second most endangered seal in the world; the American Bison, known to all Americans, whose great herds not so many years ago offered a seemingly inexhaustible supply of food. They were slaughtered indiscriminatingly, not just for food, but for the sheer primitive pleasure of the hunt and the kill.

Add to this list of endangered large mammals countless hundreds of small species, and you get the full picture of man's unbridled decimation of wildlife. The noted Swedish ecologist, Kai Curry Lindahl, sums it up as follows: "Within the span of a few centuries man's role in changing the natural environment, has been nothing less than cataclysmic. It has been said that the human species is a disease of the soil. I would like to expand the notion to include, in the areas of infection, other elements that form a living, flourishing landscape.

"Until clumsy man entered the scene, everything functioned in a rational way with optimum productivity in every kind of habitat.... Man not only ruined the soil, he burned and slashed the vegetation. Where he had not already drained the water, he polluted it. He exterminated animal life, forgetting that wildlife can flourish where domestic stock will perish. He substituted dead lands for living landscapes."[12]

Still, we take hope in the work of small groups of revolutionaries dedicated to the proposition that man's divinely endowed life-sustaining ability makes it possible for him not only to make human predation upon sentient animals vestigial, but to help them minimize predatory behavior among themselves. Many years ago a great but little remembered humanist stated it simply as a Credo of universal kinship with all living things:

> Universal Kinship means the kinship of all inhabitants of the planet earth. Whether they came into existence among the waters or among desert sands, in a hole in the earth, in the hollow of a tree, or

in a palace; whether they swim, fly, crawl, or ambulate; and whether they realize it or not, they are related physically, mentally, morally.[13]

Upon this Credo rests the fate of mankind.

12

Squaring Man's Debt With His Unlike Kin

There should be no doubt, at this point, of our confidence in man's ability to pay, at least, half of his debt to his kin in unlike form. Summed up in one sentence, it calls for wise use of nature's generous storehouse of food from the soil, and livestock's equally generous offering of milk, cheese, butter, eggs.

But how, you will declare in disbelief, can we square the other half of the account by means of so fantastic a job as helping non-human predators mend their predatory ways! A partial answer, at this NSHS pre-operational stage, has to be that the aforementioned creative thinkers in the natural and biological sciences and, indeed, also in the technological field, are already fabricating the tools to make it eminently practical.

To this, we must hasten to add that the tools are not yet being used in the life-sustaining interest of our animal kin, but rather to satisfy our own needs and desires at their expense.

We all know that, to-date, one of the human-centered uses of the tools pertains to the control of the population of livestock. Farmers have been successful in doing this, without recourse to the kill, long before the advent of modern science. They control the cohabitation of livestock, including the extent to which they allow these animals to engage in procreating their kind. They carry on large-scale scientific operations to prevent and cure death-taking diseases and infections that afflict livestock. They provide them with protein enriched food to preserve good health and maintain their population at desired levels, and, of course, to fatten them; all this, to prepare them for slaughter.

We spay female dogs and cats for removal of their ovaries, to control their population. Experimentation with reversible hormonal contraceptive drugs, for both male and female, enables them to return to normal reproductive functions upon discontinuance of the drug's use, if their keeper so desires.

At this point we come—at last!—to the strange phenomenon of innovative endeavors, sometimes bringing into being initially unnoticed results that are in direct opposition to their pupose. From the appalling amount of laboratory research and experimentation, carried on *annually* on countless millions of non-human mammals like monkeys, mice, dogs and cats, at great suffering and painful death to them, is emerging a body of knowledge on animal population control. It fits the survival interest of *our kin in unlike* form even more perfectly than it does our own! Carried on, at first, to test the safety and effectiveness of drugs, if taken by humans in the treatment of a host of ailments, the needless mass-murder of helpless animals then went on, to find ways of controlling *our own population* by contraceptive means. Paradoxically enough, the unconscionable brutality perpetrated upon our mammalian kin has come to a full turnabout.

At Last, The Benefits Can Go Two Ways!

Let us trace the remarkable development. By the middle of the twentieth century medical science had discovered birth-control methods that are now in wide use. Oral contraception and numerous other techniques are being used increasingly by married couples as well as single adults. In the West, old ecclesiastical objections are fast becoming obsolete. Among impoverished peoples in tradition-bound societies, aspirations for a better life are slowly beginning to create receptivity to the need for drastic reduction of population growth, despite ancient religious and cultural taboos against birth limitation. And it is again the adult young, the progeny bearers of the future, who will be most involved in the pursuit of ethically acceptable and scientifically safe methods of population control—for human as well as *non-human* mammals.

This unprecedented inter-species common survival linkage stems from the under-rated fact that safe *human* birth-control techniques were obtained in the first place from animal experimentation. Since every contraceptive pill to inhibit ovulation, every sterlization device for either sex, every method of contraceptive surgery, was first researched and tested out on different species of mammals until considered safe for humans, ipso facto: *if it works harmlessly for man and woman, it will certainly work harmlessly for other animals, who proved it to be so countless thousands of times with their own mutilated bodies and lives*. Their dearly paid contribution to the well-being of mankind mounts up the unpaid debt human beings owe to wildlife and domesticated animals, for which payment is long overdue.

As counsel for our mammalian kin in unlike form, we shall take our case to a knowledgeable and experienced judge for adjudication; namely, the practicing wildlife conservationist. As is well known, he is already using a pertinent technique of anesthetizing large wildlife mammals to facilitate their trans-location from habitats made unsafe by man. Since animals have long played the key role in developing successful contraceptive drugs, substituting such a drug for the tranquillizer poses no great problem. The practice of interchanging suitable drugs for similar, if varying situations, is really many-faceted, because no drug has yet been found that is 100 percent safe for human or non-humans, and this applies not only to contraception but to all manner of medical treatment and usage.

Let us cite a few examples: The major consideration dictating the use or rejection of any drug or surgery is a comparative one. We willingly use vaccines against typhoid or polio because of the low incidence of discernible ill effects, compared to the very high mortality rate if these diseases are left to take their toll unchecked. We are prepared to take a high risk of fatality in the performance of surgery or administration of a drug, if all experience indicates certain death without the use of some known medical aid, though it offers only an outside chance of success. The same striving for minimal risk applies to birth control efforts in behalf of any life-conscious animal.

We come to the significant correlationship as to the degree of safety in the use of contraceptive drugs and devices, all of it in favor of *non-human* mammals. According to comparative studies made by Celse-Ramon Garcia and Edward Wallach of the Department of Obstetrics and Gynecology at the University of Pennsylvania, the risk of death that women take by preventing ovulation through the use of oral steroids (the pill) "may be of the order of 3 per 100,000. Thus, if as these studies indicate, there is an association between the use of oral contraceptives and the thromboembolic complications, the risk is indeed small."[2]

The other side of this picture reveals the striking fact that contraceptive controls for domestic and wildlife animals, once these animals have validated the techniques, show a higher percentage of safety and effectiveness because (1) no contraceptive method or device, as already noted, is ever used by human beings until it has been found to be very safe when tested out on other animals and (2), in the transfer to human beings, the factors of safety and effectiveness lose some of their validity. The two points, especially #2, have a more pivotal bearing on the whole NSHS projection than may be evident at this juncture. This should become abundantly clear to most readers, and to some, no doubt, shockingly so in subsequent chapters dealing with some surprisingly little discussed aspects of demographic controls across the entire ecological life span. But, to continue—

Many ill effects experienced by women using oral contraceptives are due to the fact that the animals, on whom the drugs were first tested during the early hazardous stages of experimentation, do not have the same toxicity tolerance to birth control chemicals as do human beings. Even primates like monkeys and baboons, whose physiological and reproductive functions are most like those of human beings, vary greatly in this respect; so that errors creep in when a contraceptive drug found to be safe wtih non-human mammals is transferred for human use.

Carl Djerassi, Professor of Chemistry at Stanford University and President of Syntez Research Laboratories, cites some typical examples of the differences in response to chemical toxicity and in metabolic reactions as well, between human beings and other mammals. Studies in the use of one experimental drug revealed that man excreted 94 percent of the drug in the urine and 1 to 2 percent in the feces. In contrast to this are the following data as listed by Djerassi:

Species	Excretion Urine (percent)	Feses (percent)
Man	94	1–2
Rat	90	2
Dog	29	50
Guinea pig	90	5
Mini pig	86	1–2
Rhesus monkey	90	2
Capuchin monkey	45	54
Stump-tail monkey	86	1–2

Djerassi concludes from these differences in animal responses, *with no vision, alas, of the NSHS future*, that "nobody can argue with the requirement for animal toxicity data before administering a drug to humans, even in short-term clinical experiments dealing with only a few individuals. . . . the sole reason for selecting *any animal* is to provide a model for extrapolation to the human."[3]

He buttresses this prevailing position of scientists on the validity of animal research with the observation: "Unless all research is to be performed directly on a man—a suggestion that can hardly be entertained with completely new agents—*much more work needs to be done in developing useful animal models* that have some predictive bearing on man's biological responses to a given agent."[4]

It should not be too surprising to Djerassi if, in the light of the infinitely more attractive NSHS life-style, human beings will succeed in achieving a scientific value system in the next few generations that is the very opposite of his projection. It will be *research on man for man and on non-humans for non-humans*. To demonstrate its feasibility, we need to follow in the footsteps already being taken toward it by wildlife conservationists.

We have referred to the translocation of animals from unsafe habitats to protected wildlife refuges, national parks or zoo banks. From the beginning this proved to be a simple task for small and harmless animals. But it was no easy matter, as one conservationist put it, to get three tons of fighting rhino into a crate and aboard a truck for shipment. Sometimes the frightened animal had to pay with its life as a result of fatal injury in the struggle against its good samaritans.

In the early 1960's, however, an East African veterinary physiologist, Dr. A.M. Harthorn, began experiments to help men engaged in translocation work, to *anaesthetize* large animals like rhinos, bison, elephants, hippopotamuses, and even smaller but equally frightened ones like gazelles, giraffes, baboons. The idea was to insert any one of several kinds of drugs by means of darts that would paralyze an animal just long enough to enable man to capture and transport it.

The initial difficulty was to find a drug or dosage that would neither kill the animal nor leave serious ill effects. A satisfactory opiate mixture called M99 was finally developed. The new drug-laden darts were small and could be propelled at a safe distance with crossbows or special gas-powered guns usually aimed at the animal's rump. M99 could stop the largest rhino. The technique is so well advanced now that an animal can be tranquillized just enough to make it drowsy and docile yet able to remain on its feet and walk to a waiting truck. The Chief Conservator of Zululand, Ian Player, relates an incident in which a fully grown adult rhino was led docilely for two miles under the influence of M99 drug, much to the consternation of some tourists and other passers-by.[5] The development of drug darting since 1960 has made translocation one of the most important techniques for saving endangered species.

The deduction to be made from this, for purposes of wildlife population control without the kill, becomes self evident: use *contraceptive* darts instead of tranquillizers. Why the appeal of this rewarding idea has not challenged the inventive spirit of ecologists and conservationists is understandable, if we consider the fact that birth-control research, like most other related scientific inquiry, has been developed largely in western meat-eating societies. It is, moreover, our thought that, given their deep reverence of life, many conservationists will lend a sympathetic ear to emerging NSHS imperatives. They are accustomed to engaging in unorthodox, creative thinking. Many of them, like Kai Curry Lindahl, are painfully aware of the danger that, if the human animal persists in flouting biological survival imperatives such as this one, the mounting societal crises—to which we shall address ourselves in Part II of this paper, for they are inseparable from the biological one—may well be the logic of human self-extermination.

There is yet another promising source of potentially great scientific input toward implementing the life-sustaining control of animal population. Perhaps we will witness, in the near future, a significant body of contributions to wildlife contraception coming from predominantly vegetarian societies in Asia and South America, where reverence of life is more deeply rooted than in the West, and important participation in world affairs is on the rise.

This does not gainsay the value of much life-sustaining work being done by those small creative groups of western agronomists and agriculturalists discussed in earlier chapters. But the initial pragmatic techniques, designed to help wildlife carnivores minimize the need to stalk their prey for food, are supplied by conservationists. Accelerating progress on some already well known projects might include intensification of:

1. Annual population census, species by species, in major habitats; determination of net-count resulting from present ways of reducing annual population through the kill and other causes (human encroachment on animal habitats, environmental pollution and destruction, and nature's own ecosystemic phenomena connected with over-grazing, over-browsing, adverse climactic changes, disease, predator-prey imbalances).
2. A greater study of breeding characteristics of different species, their habitat range and food requirements; male-female cohabitation and procreative behavior.
3. Development of special birth control techniques suited to each species: drug-darting techniques and dosages; determination of variables in toxicity-tolerances of different mammals to which chemical contraceptives are administered; side-effects on other flora and fauna; possibilities for reversible and/or permanent steroids taken orally or by injection; surgical and other sterilization methods.
4. Modification of training programs for the new fertility control

programs: for professional, technical and field staffs; the same for educational programs for the general public and for volunteers.

5. Promotion of government and private financing; expansion of research and experimental facilities and staffs; securing strengthening of interstate and international cooperation. These ecologically exciting undertakings carry us to the borders of mankind's troubled societal affairs that call not only for revolutionary reform, in a survival sense, but, also, in a moral sense. That this inter-relationship rests on a solid moral base is a rarely discussed matter. It is a fitting subject with which to close this chapter of Part I of our study.

Nature's ecosystem requires that we make our assessment on the premise that if man is a mortal, life-conscious mammal, sensitive to pleasure and pain, and zealous above all else for self preservation, as all animals are, then there is logic in applying the same standards of population control for man as for all mammals that are mortal, life-conscious and sensitive to pleasure and pain. If killing surplus or otherwise unwanted wildlife is sound as a method of population control, then Hitler was right in methodically disposing of multi-millions of unwanted Jews in the Reich's gas chambers, to facilitate the Fuehrer's plans for German "survival"; ie, for Lebensraum and Deutsche Kultur!

If we apply the logic closer to home, then the incineration of thousands of Japanese non-combatant men, women and children in Hiroshima and Nagasaki, and of civilian Germans in Dresden, by the American army in World War II makes sense; then the slaughter of Vietnamese peasants, who are mortal, life-conscious and sensitive to pleasure and pain, even as you and I, also makes eminently good sense as an effective method of cropping human populations that endanger our own particular kind of national security and aspirations—for a global Pax Americana! The theorem is as "good" today as when Malthus first explained it in 1798 A.D.

This is not an odd notion emanating from the NSHS thesis. Joyce Joffe expresses the thought from an ecological point of view, adding the observation that Europeans and Americans, not so long ago, as anthropoligical time goes, engaged in the practice of harvesting black members of the species Homo sapiens, and shipping them from their natural African habitat to the United States.[6] There they were bought and sold over the block like horses, oxen, and other work animals; kept and husbanded—the latter often quite literally by copulation between the white male master and desirable black females.

Without belaboring ethical factors, suffice it to say only that modern science has made these practices as obsolete, wasteful and brutal as is the kill of sentient wildlife and domesticated animals. As for the role of the sportsman-hunter, this can hardly be classified today as a necessary food gathering endeavor. Hunting is already a vestigial predatory human characteristic, morally atrocious as a sport, and biologically meaningless even in contemporary primitive society, the defense of the sportsman-hunter by western conservationists notwithstanding.

Equating contemporary primitive man's horrendously unethical practice of liquidating "excess" human and non-human animal populations by means of the massive kill, for whatever purpose, is no statement of hyperbole. It runs parallel to the equally abhorrent one of the massive mutilation and slaughter of man's kin in unlike form, who are life-conscious and sensitive to pain, as is man.

No doubt, this whole complex of man's evil-doing makes millions of truly moral people wonder why the Almighty hasn't yet put this monstrosity of humankind out of the way—long before sensitive Arnold Toynbee wondered about it. The writer believes, parenthetically, that perhaps the stay of divine execution may have come because the small groups of creative thinkers, under discussion here, are moving in the direction of ending the human madness.

Looking beyond the first steps necessary to enable wildlife predators minimize the kill in their search for food, we see a thousand wildlife national parks in many parts of the world. The art of providing a protein-rich *meatless* diet to meet the special needs of carnivores, in these protected habitats, can readily be joined with similar food being developed for human consumption. It seems reasonable to suppose that, in the beginning, efforts will be directed primarily toward helping our closest mammalian kin whose behavior characteristics are best known; also, that making meatless food available will require the development of special techniques: use of helicopters, use of regular and appropriate feeding points and time schedules, separation of predators from their prey, etc.; for much of this there is already a well-advanced knowledge and operating experience.

Then, there is the other side of the picture: the adjustment of wildlife to this strange new feeding experience. Surely, this will call for much scientific study and experimentation, and checks against adverse ecological consequences, as well as for ways to expand the unorthodox life-sustaining human responsibility. Separation of predators from the prey they normally hunt should, however, pose no insurmmountable obstacles. It is already done in zoological gardens with moats and other physical barriers. The same things can be done *on a larger scale in national parks*, including construction of artificial lakes, streams, canyons, to mention just a few methods.

At this point some dedicated status-quo thinkers may well ask, "What will all this do to the animals themselves? Isn't it possible that, in the long run, it may have a bad mutational effect on their gene structure? Providing wildlife carnivores like tigers, lions, leopards, cougars, with a meatless diet, may result in profound biological changes in the future phenotypes of these present-day animals, that are impossible to predict." No doubt, it may. But there would be nothing particularly original about it. Man has been giving the treatment to household pets for thousands of years and, based on a lot of evidence available to anyone who likes cats and dogs, they seem to like it.

Man, himself, has been greatly changed over the long span of anthropological time, in some small measure at his own hands; more significantly, by natural selection, as have all nature's life forms. Whether or not this has gone deeply enough to have altered his hereditary gene-formula, remains an open question; evolutionists would say, yes; ecclesiasts, no. In any case, we would give heavy odds, if that were possible, that the human progeny two thousand or two million years from now would no more want to revert back to the primitive type of twentieth century man than we would want to return to the life of Australopithecus africanus or the Neanderthal man.

The thought gets us back to the fundamentals of creative NSHS societal transformation on an ecological scale: the collective practice of *enlightened frugality* and *reverence of life*. It is the only way man can win his case for the right to survive.

13

The Rationale of Life-Sustaining Criminology

Part One of the case for Natural Survival Through Human Selection is now in—almost, except for one question that we have left to the end. We have deferred an answer, not because the question is least germane to our study but, in a basic sense, most in need of a strong and *quick* answer to a major question raised by the study. It, also, poses the greatest difficulty in trying to find that answer.

The matter pertains to our earlier assertion that research and experimentation in the life-sustaining interest of the human mammal, must be carried on and performed on *humans*; and those in the interest of non-human mammals, on *non-humans*. As to how this can be done, in a manner acceptable to us humans, we have said nary a word.

Judging from the title of this chapter, you may already be thinking of the kind of answer we have in mind. Clearly, it pertains to the contemporary institution of criminology; but, not so clearly, to what we have in mind. We propose that every convicted "criminal", from one who is guilty of a petty misdemeanor to the perpetrator of a ghastly murder, *must* subject himself or herself to the performance of a category of life-sustaining penal service (LSPS), as demanded by the terms of sentence.

We have little doubt that, as of this writing in the summer of 1972, the proposal will clash so violently with cherished religious and moral values in contemporary primitive society that, if implemented, it will bring forth a storm of condemnation of its inhumanity, irrationality and impracticality. On that presumption, we ask you, the reader, to bear with us as we proceed with the specifics.

Let us start by taking a quick look at today's mounting crime wave in the United States versus our attempts to stop it. We shall then examine the revolutionary proposal of Life-Sustaining Criminology. The overview will focus on four important aspects: the prevailing concepts of criminology, the mounting crime wave, our prostrate system of penology, and the counteraction of Life-Sustaining Penal Service (LSPS).

Criminology

One can say without fear of contradiction that in every age and culture, the commission of a crime is defined as an act which, in small or large degree, endangers collective survival. Basically, it is an offense against the life of society. Suicide is legally a crime because it reduces, by one member, the survival strength of the entire human species.

Crime, thus, inevitably arouses a twofold collective response that pits punitive and rehabilitative measures against each other, the emphasis on the one or the other depending on the extent to which mitigating circumstances may or may not have contributed to the act of anti-social behavior. It is Society's way of protecting itself against repetition of the transgression, in part, by imposing punishment that will deter others and, in part, by rehabilitating the offender to productive life—after appropriate penalty has been exacted. The ethical and biological motivations for this dual social response seem hardly open to question; controversy centers more around the nature and method of suitable counter-action than around principle.

There is, of course, no universal code of human conduct by which one can differentiate an act of crime from accepted societal behavior. There are only sets of rules by which a given nation or other type of cultural in-group can, at a particular time and place, define its own criteria of what constitutes crime. The mass-murder of human beings, if they are the citizens of a so-called enemy nation, and the devastation of their habitat, does not (yet) come within the definition of criminal behavior. It does, however, make a powerful impact on domestic crime, as we shall have occasion to point out. Further comment on the conceptual base of criminology has to be deferred until we discuss the proposed system of Life-Sustaining Penal Service.

The Crime Wave

In these beginning days of the 1970s, in a supposedly civilized nation, one is no longer safe walking the streets, riding public transportation, or staying at home behind locked doors. It is a fear that permeates all levels of our society and all parts of our country. The underlying facts hardly need elaboration but, lest we fail to keep them vividly in mind, while analyzing the LSPS system, we had better cite a few examples to make sure they do remain vivid.

The 1967 report of the President's Commission on Law Enforcement and Administration makes this appraisal:

There is much crime in America, more than ever is reported, far more than ever is solved, far too much for the health of the nation. ... Crimes of violence are up in both the biggest and smallest cities, in suburbs as well as in the rural areas.

The report continues:

One third of a representative sample of all Americans say it is unsafe to walk alone at night in their own neighborhood. Slightly more than one-third say they keep firearms in the house for protection against criminals.... 43 percent say they stay off the streets at night because of their fear of crime; 35 percent say they do not speak to strangers anymore because of their fear of crime; 21 percent say they use cars and cabs at night because of their fear of crime.[1]

Newsweek magazine, citing specific cases, says that State Department officials in Washington set up a special guard system to protect women employees *within* the granite buildings of Foggy Bottom.[2] The crime students, Medford Stanton Evans and Margaret Moore, tell us the following in their study, *The Law Breakers*:

In New York, a group of Jewish men, fearing for the safety of their women folk and of their community in general, have formed a private association for self-defense purposes known as the "Maccabees"—named after the Hebrew fighting men of the Old Testament. "The whole thing is crazy", says Rabbi Samuel Schrage, "but it had to be done." Similar efforts at self-protection have been launched in other cities—Detroit, Orlando, Los Angeles, Chicago, Dallas, St. Louis. Says the manager of the gun department of a Dallas sporting goods store who is doing a booming business with people who want hand guns for self-protection: "People have sort of lost confidence in government to protect them."

Evans and Moore predict that, "as bad as the problem is, signs are that it is going to get worse." They conclude their observation with the statement that "the more our government suggests we are advancing toward utopia, the more we stumble backward toward the jungle.[3]

Students of crime, both here and abroad, find nothing in the way of crime in other countries that compares to what we in the United States are experiencing. This is not to say, however, that crime isn't a serious problem in all parts of the world. But why is it more rampant here? One might say that it acquires a greater momentum among us Americans than among other equally primitive peoples because we, as the leading world power, commit more violence on planet Earth than they do.

Our "leaders" in government and agri-industry, set an extra ordinarily convincing example for the perpetration of crime by our citizenry, old and young; they do it as shrewdly and perniciously in our domestic jungle as in the international one. And, since we have already discussed their barbaric behavior in civilian affairs at home, we need allude to only a few points that made the proposal of a system of LSPS as sound and, we assert in advance, as humane as it is mandatory.

The astute and sensitive public affairs commentator, Tom Wicker, puts the matter bluntly:

> In every major city in the United States you will find that two-thirds of the arrests take place among only about two-percent of the population. Where is that area in every city? Well, it's in the same place where infant mortality is four times higher than in the city as a whole; where life expectancy is ten years shorter; where common communicable diseases with the potential of physical and mental damage are six and eight and ten times more frequent; where alcoholism and drug addiction are prevalent to a degree far transcending that of the rest of the city; where education is the poorest, the oldest school buildings have the most crowded and turbulent schoolrooms, the fewest certified teachers, the highest rate of dropouts; where the average formal schooling is four to six years less than for the city as a whole. Sixty percent of the children in Watts in 1965 lived with only one, or neither, of their parents.[4]

This is stating the cause in its bleakest aspects, the plight of the majority of America's blacks, the poorest of the poor. Wicker is simply reminding us that poverty, in all its forms of human deprivation, is the fountain head of crime.

But what about the crimes committed by the young in the wealthy big-city suburbs? They and their parents are not poor.[5] Ah, but this brings to the fore that other prolific breeding place of crime—the *international* jungle. To illustrate, we suggest that there is a mighty revulsion among our youth, today, akin to what fueled the youth rebellion of the 1960s. Many of our young of rich parents then, frustrated in their effort to persuade government—and their parents—to end the killing of helpless peasants in Vietnam and the napalming of their homes and rice paddies, bombed the plants of American world corporations that were manufacturing the poisonous gases. The experience set off an explosion of youth rebellion, as you will recall, that rocked society.

May it not be that we see again, today, among socially conscious members of suburbia's young, an unheeded outrage expressed in anti-social behavior (crime) against their elitist community's material affluence, while poverty surrounds them on all sides? The retaliatory conduct of youth may, furthermore, be intensified now, as it was then, by a sense of shared guilt for their own unearned and, probably, their parents' ill-gotten wealth, derived from what they see and hear in their immediate family circle about the dog-eat-dog practices their elders and associates carry on in the business world. On this score we can only mention, at this moment, the extent of *unprosecuted* "white-collar" crime in high places, that runs into the billions of dollars *annually*. We shall come back to it when detailing the provisions of LSPS.

Finally, the killer syndrome in international affairs, rationalized as a lofty service to one's country in time of war, poisons every last crevice of civilian life, even in time of peace. It merges its penchant for violence in the sharp practices of business, trade, and the professions; it so blurs the distinction between legitimate dealings between individuals and nations as to spawn not only the crime and corruption that have always been the hallmark of materially rich warrior nations but, also, the eventual collapse of those nations.

Our Prostrate System of Penology

The sad state of affairs in our prisons is known to everyone who reads the daily papers, listens to radio or watches TV: the unpardonable physical conditions and terrible overcrowding; the mistreatment by ill-qualified prison staffs; the shocking relationships among inmates, themselves; and the bloody prison riots. Most alarming of all, so far as the safety of the general public is concerned, is the high percentage of recidivism. Substantially more than one-half of all first offenders return to crime, often of a more serious nature, as a result of what they experienced and learned from "old-timers" while in prison. The late Dr. Ralph Banay, former chief psychiatrist at Sing Sing, sums it up in one paragraph:

> The prison, as it is now constituted, must go. The philosophy from which it sprang is obsolete; its basic concept is erroneous; its physical plant is an abomination; its personnel, usually inadequately trained and usually politically controlled, consists more often of perfunctory jobholders than men dedicated to their calling. The system we grace with the name of correction is a static machinery, a vestige of medievalism rooted in barren soil, devoid of the fertilizing potentiality of organic growth. We shall have to correct the institution before we can hope to correct man.[6]

If the prison system must go, we propose that the necessary way to replace it is—

Life-Sustaining Penal Service

Perhaps it will ease our task of explaining LSPS, if we start with its relatively non-controversial aspects. LSPS will be directed to solving society's two basic categories of crime: felonies and misdemeanors. The overall plan will retain the twofold purpose of "punishment" and "rehabilitation", along lines that should satisfy both the advocates of an eye-for-an eye and those for restoring the offender back to normal life, after serving his or her term behind bars, or on probation outside of prison.

Less non-controversial, as already indicated, will be the method of requiring every convicted offender, whether guilty of a petty misdemeanor or a serious felony, to perform life-sustaining penal service, in the *specific* manner delineated at time of sentence. *Very* controversial will be the drastic reordering of the treatment of crime as practiced by our penal institutions.

At this point we need to interject a word of caution to the reader, who may be inclined to see LSPS as a venture similar to so-called voluntary practices long in vogue in some penal institutions. Investigations by reputable criminologists reveal most of them to be crude, sporadic and unjust, and carried on by largely unqualified and little-supervised prison staffs. The inquirers discovered that the great majority of "volunteers" among the inmates, in some of the prisons, came from impoverished minority groups, and were generally not properly informed of the true nature of the experimental drugs they agreed to take in order to test their safety, if used by humans; nor were they fully advised of other hazardous research to which they submitted themselves. There was, moreover, no relationship between the *degree of hazard involved* and the *prisoner's offense*.[7]

There is, also, a quantitive side to such unethical practices. Aside from a few popularly known cases of felons, countable on the fingers of one hand, who genuinely volunteer to perform life-sustaining service, the impact that the whole phenomenon has on crime might be compared to trying to sweep back the ocean with a broom. No, any similarity between this and LSPS has to be one of non-existence.

Let us, then, proceed with our envisionment of the LSPS system. The controversial—we say the fundamental—part of the system entails making life-sustaining penal service an organic part of the multi-faceted field of medical, biochemical, and related life-preserving research and practice; all of it becomes a closely knit part of the functions of hospitals, clinics, research laboratories, wildlife and environmental conservation, and day-to-day business operations.

This illustrates, at the very outset, the magnitutude of the undertaking, which is, however, no greater in size or in cost, than the problem to be solved. For purposes of clarity, we shall describe the system under the following headings:

The Two Major Divisions of Crime
The Court System: Its Composition and Duties
A Few Thoughts on Other LSPS Fundamentals

The Two Divisions

The one will deal, almost exclusively, with felonies, the other with misdemeanors. We should begin by emphasizing that the *intent* of the new criminology, with respect to both Divisions, is definitely *not* to injure, cripple or kill perpetrators of a crime, no matter how serious the offense may be. Although LSPS will be required of all offenders, whether they have committed a felony or a misdemeanor, the fact is that services hazardous to life will be assigned to very few people.

To facilitate effective LSPS assignments to the prisoners in the two Divisions will, probably, necessitate constructing penal institutions near to, or as physical parts of, agencies connected with the new criminology—the clinics, hospitals, laboratories, nursing homes, and other organizations engaged in health and related social service work. A host of life-sustaining services to be performed for these agencies come readily to mind.

The LSPS Division For Misdemeanors

In the area of misdemeanors like disorderly conduct, petty larceny, disturbing the peace, assault and battery, etc., *non-hazardous* LSPS would be assigned. For example; offenders possessing office-related skills—typing, filing, stenography, secretarial work—would be required to perform such duties; the same practice would apply to skilled craftsmen and professionals like mechanics, lawyers, carpenters, plumbers, entertainers, engineers, to name but a few, as well as to unskilled workers.

Since most misdemeanor convictions would be for rather short terms, careful advance planning and coordinating by administrative and professional staffs of the penal institutions and the cooperating medical, social and commercial organizations, will be essential to the success of the system. More on this later. Such matters as payment for LSPS service and control of the prisoners' behavior while in and out of the penal institution, for minor offenders and felons alike, will also be deferred, to be considered under the foregoing heading of a few thoughts on LSPS fundamentals.

The LSPS Division for Felons

The life-sustaining services required of felons will cover the entire field of medical research and experimentation devoted to advancing the health and increasing the life-span of human beings. The specifics are familiar to everyone: research to combat cancer, diabetes, leukemia, and countless other diseases; to correct bodily malfunctionings, including cardio-vascular, respiratory, brain, and neurological disorders; to test new mechanical devices to aid malfunctioning organs of the human body like the heart, kidneys, and lungs; and, of course, to bring about optimum safety in the use of contraceptive devises, methods, drugs.

What would be more humane, therefore, yet appropriately exacting, so far as the felon is concerned, and satisfying at the same time, so far as society is concerned, than making life-sustaining service a mandatory part of the legally imposed restitution demanded of perpetrators of a capital crime? How much more sensible as basic social policy than the wasteful and barbaric one of the electric chair! How much more meaningful for the convict! His or her awareness of the self-sacrificing work required as repayment of the debt to society, can not but help restore a sense of personal worth and dignity.

This approach to criminology, we firmly believe, will go far toward reconciling the opposing views of those who consider capital punishment as necessary to deter the most ghastly kinds of crimes and those who do not. It will assuage both the emotional need felt by many for full punishment by death, and others who cannot square this with reverence of life.

A killer receiving the maximum sentence for life-sustaining service will, indeed, have to be ready for death, should the type of research imposed prove to be fatal. But in death, the convict will have made the supreme sacrifice to preserve life of others, in compensation for the life or lives he or she took.

A cowardly individual could be expected to shrink from a mortally dangerous assignment, unless skillfully counseled, motivated, stimulated (or tranquilized, if other methods fail), and watched; someone sentenced for a particularly brutal crime might well seek a way out through suicide.

The Court System

Given the unorthodoxy of LSPS as the modus vivendi of the new criminology, we shall limit ourselves to clarifying its conceptual base, leaving the administrative and operational functions to specialists whose training and experience gives them the competence to carry them out. So far as the courts are concerned, we shall focus chiefly on the changed and augmented role that they must play.

The new criminology can live with the prevailing American jury system, including the defendant's right, in certain situations, to have his case heard and decided by a judge only—except for some important overall modifications. These have to do with the court's responsibilities and the make-up of its key personnel; they are necessary, because the complexity of mandatory LSPS not only places much greater responsibility on the courts than heretofore, but calls for a wide range of professional expertise going well beyond the field of jurisprudence.

The changes will affect the adjudication of both misdemeanors and felonies, but since only persons found guilty of a felony will be sentenced to perform LSPS that may endanger their health or life, or both, we shall discuss the need for the modifications, primarily, in relation to serious crimes against the person or property.

Let us begin with what is involved in hearing the evidence on a variety of felonies that come before a criminal court: murder, rape, grand larceny, embezzlement, swindles, child abuse, hold-up with a gun, etc.. It is essential that judge, jury, and even the attorneys, themselves, possess and/or have quick access, during the hearings and decision-making stages, to a diversity of scientific data on current needs and practices in medical research and experimentation; also, on the known extent to which the prescribed LSPS required of the felon may endanger his or her life: on the convicted person's own mental, physical, or psychiatric illness, known before or established during the trial, that may have caused perpetration of the crime in the first place; and, finally, on the degree of hazardous LSPS to which a felon should be assigned, as determined by the presence or absence of mitigating circumstances, and the innate differences in felonies. The embezzlement of a thousand dollars is not quite the same as the murder of a human being.

It seems wise to propose that the responsibility for following through, broadly, on the nature of the life-sustaining service a guilty person must perform after incarceration, should rest with the court that heard the case and *set the terms* of sentence. The reasons for placing it there, rather than with the penal institution or the cooperating agencies, can be stated briefly: the court hearings are open to the public and the news media; the proceedings are carefully documented as public records, and the court's professional staff and jury collaborate in making the crucial judgment, on the basis of the evidence before them—and all this applies to misdemeanors as well as felonies.

How can the difficult task be accomplished in justice to the criminal, the victim(s), and society? The question takes us to the necessity of modifying the composition and duties of the court's functionaries, especially, the *members of the jury*. Given the enormity of our nation's crime wave, in terms of financial costs to the state and society, and suffering to the victims, the decision has to be unmistakeably clear: no halfway measures will stop it.

In the new criminology, the indivisibility of the convicted felon's life-sustaining penal service and the court's role of setting the terms of a just and effective sentence demands nothing less than an extensive reorganization of the court's functions. Taking our cue for this from the aforementioned reasons, we would say that the first change has to be in the composition of the jury.

A plan that suggests itself, immediately, is that seven members be selected in the traditional manner, from the general public; the other five, from reputable researchers and practitioners in the relevant sciences and other fields. For crimes against the person, the professionals might include criminologists, biochemists, medical researchers in hospitals and pharmaceutical laboratories, acceptable to the prosecution and defense lawyers; for crimes against property, specialists would be added in such fields as accounting, banking and finance, and other necessary economic enterprises. Agreement as to the required *areas* of professionals for a particular type of crime, before selecting individuals, might be arrived at in a private conference between the ranking attorney for the defense, the prosecution, and the judge, himself.

The second innovation pertains to the assessment of the seriousness of the crime, on the one hand, and the level of hazardous LSPS to be assigned to the convict, on the other. The best criteria will, no doubt, come from actual experience. For a beginning, it may be helpful if the jury will make a broadly comparative judgment of the inhumanity of the felony before the court, by designating it as being either *most serious* or *less serious*, leaving it to a joint, standing operations committee of the penal institution and specific cooperating research or social agency to make the initial LSPS assignment. Here, again, the court must make this decision a *formal part of the record*, a certified copy of which to be sent to the penitentiary on or about the time the convict is incarcerated.

Some Further Thoughts on LSPS Fundamentals

After the incarceration of a person found guilty of a felon—we by-pass, for the moment, one who committed a misdemeanor—comes the critical implementation of LSPS. In projecting our thinking on this, we shall adhere to our earlier statement to stay clear of the details of administering and operating so unprecedented a system of criminology as advocated in this treatise. There are, however, a number of predictable benefits, problems, and *musts* that cannot be by-passed, if we are to make our case as clear and strong as possible.

We begin with the benefits, because they probably are not only of great immediate importance to both the convict and the general public but, in a deep ethical sense, also to the abandonment of mankind's senseless slaughter of our closest animal kin, already dealt with at length.

All in all, the public will have much cause to rejoice. What could generate a more powerful force of crime deterrance than a humane system of LSPS? The experience of having to *live dangerously* while serving time for a major crime, provides its own restraint against a repeat performance. The very prospect of receiving a more exacting LSPS sentence, if convicted again, is hardly conducive toward motivating a criminal to make himself or herself more proficient in ways of crime while in jail. What could be more effective in reducing recidivism to a minimum—in all probability, to near extinction?

What will not be new, is the continuing need for maximum security prisons for dangerous criminals. There remains, too, the necessity to keep in *permanent custody*, disturbed psychotics with uncontrollable desires to torture and kill their victims, in order to satisfy their sexual or other emotional compulsions. Medical science still knows of no cure for this!

Can the new system become a magnet, drawing to it the necessary professional talents in physical medicine, psychiatry, psychology, biochemistry, criminology, counseling, therapy, social work? Banay observed, in his time, that although it may be difficult to recruit and train the high order of personnel essential to any scientifically advanced system of penology, he went on to say:

> This much we know. . . . There are already at work in a few progressive correctional institutions, in several parts of the country, many able men who have dedicated their lives to an earnest effort to rehabilitate offenders. Most of these find that their best endeavors are enervated or frustrated by the corrupting atmosphere of the prison, with its overtones of recrimination and its taint of political bumbling. Many others who have embarked upon such careers have abandoned them in desperation, because the prison evils negated their professional objective.[8]

He concluded, however, that "Once the program is underway, demonstrating its social value, (no reference to the LSPS idea, for it was not known then) the opportunities for careers of a new type would attract gifted personnel into the service."⁹

From Banay's assessment one can reiterate, in good logic, that the antidote to our prostrate penal system, faced with today's out-of-control crime-wave, is the very concept of mandatory life-sustaining penal service, carried out in the responsible and humane manner just outlined. Such a new base of criminology, we feel sure, will appeal to dedicated staffs of the highest calibre in the social and biological sciences, in fulfilling the elementary ethics of their professions, and in employing every scientific means at their command to minimize hazards to the life and health of a convict, including the most feared kind of murderer assigned to dangerous life-saving duties.

To this we must add something less attractive about the anticipated problems, and possible measures to overcome them. These, we assume, will pertain, largely, to the obstacles to be surmounted in establishing the LSPS system; namely, the enormous amount of financial underwriting required to develop and operate it, and the danger of the emergence of a whole new complex of malpractices inherent in the system, itself.

Penitentiaries, prisons, and jails, are the responsibilities of our federal, state, county, and municipal governments. Obviously, nothing can happen unless the necessary legislative and juridical action is taken to make the new criminology official throughout the land, or even as an experimental project to be tried in a designated place and manner. In short, a public demand for LSPS calls for the election of a large enough number of influential legislators capable of making it a reality in law.

The Cost Of The New Criminology

Before attempting to estimate the admittedly great cost of an LSPS plan, it will profit us to scan the horizon of the accumulated costs of crime to society over a long past, bequeathed to us by our still deeply cherished primitive culture-values. Those costs, coupled with our present penal system's waste of public funds, are colossal. In comparison, we feel confident that the LSPS investment, no matter how large, will be a modest and wise one.

Let us go back to the late 1960s when we began our research on the proposition of a new criminology. In 1966 President Johnson appointed a prestigious Crime Commission. It placed the *annual* dollar cost of crime in the United States at over $27 billion, a sheer monetary figure "as expressed in money stolen, embezzled and defrauded; loss of earnings by productive citizens through arson, homicide, vandalism, insurance costs; money spent to support police services, and the budgets of courts and correctional institutions."[10]

In the past decade the ever increasing crime rate and mounting inflation may easily have doubled or tripled that amount. To this must be added the cost of those hidden "white-collar" felonies that seldom come to trial and, if they do, are effectively transformed into misdemeanors by means of the legal subterfuge of plea bargaining. As one student of crime puts it, these dark crimes, like those of other undocumented offenses against society, constitute the *great bulk* of criminal activity. Educated guesses, based on numerous studies of the ratio between dark and documented crimes, place the annual monetary costs of major white-collar felonies at more than $40 billion for known crimes, and five times that figure for hidden ones, or more than $200 billion![11]

All this does not include the immeasurable cost of death, injury, and the all-pervasive suffering that white-collar felonies inevitably inflict upon society, especially upon the children, the ill and infirm of the impoverished segments of society.

These cost-estimates, compiled by reputable researchers in criminology, pertain to *ongoing* crimes. It would be impossible to draft meaningful cost projections for LSPS; they can only come out of the actual plans for setting up such a system, and the experience of developing and operating it. Major costs would, undoubtedly, have to be underwritten by initial investment capital for the construction of new and, where feasible, the remodeling and expansion of existing hospital, clinic, and laboratory research facilities and equipments. Similar investments would apply to existing and new penal institutions, the entire building program being part of an agreed upon integration into our penal system, of certified medical, biological, research, business, and social agencies. In this initial investment it will be well to include the training of eligible old staffs, as well as the augmenting and training of new ones, before all the construction work has been completed.

Though by-passing the cost of operations, we need to refer to it indirectly, in our closing comments about some other presently unknowable cost problems, and the danger of LSPS malpractices.

The Danger Of Malpractices

It must be said at this juncture in our advocacy of the new criminology, that we and, we imagine, you as well, have been cognizant from the very start, of a close linkage between the great danger of LSPS malpractices and the need for government and the public to play a vigilant role, as keen watch dogs, over the day-by-day operations of the system; and that this will have a great bearing on the costs incurred. Indefinable as these may be at this pre-existing time of the undertaking, we shall only enumerate, broadly again, some contingencies that must be watched and prevented from getting out of hand.

Undergirding the whole system is, of course, the federal legislative mandate, putting into clear legal terms the basic provisions of the new philosophy of life-sustaining penal servitude, supplemented by appropriate state and local laws. This statutory foundation will have to assure the strictest possible adherence to the LSPS objectives, by spelling out the more important regulatory precepts. Brought down to the administrative and operating level, we see the following imperatives:

1. No prisoners may be shifted, willingly or unwillingly, out of the life-sustaining category assigned under the terms of sentence.
2. No prisoner may be exempted from performing the LSPS imposed by the court, except for a well documented temporary disability or acute illness, certified to by a medical authority external to the penal system, upon termination of which the proper services must be resumed.

The purpose of these two statutory provisions is easy to illustrate. It will serve, on the one hand, to deter bribery of prison and cooperating agency staffs by a powerful crime syndicate, or independently wealthy and influential prisoners eager to pay their way out of doing hazardous LSPS, imposed for having committed a serious felony; on the other, it will protect less privileged prisoners, serving out a misdemeanor, from being forced to engage in LSPS in the felony category, as substitutes for illegally exempted felons.

To be effective, such an unorthodox complex of federal and state laws must have an enforcement bite. This could be accomplished by making the alleged violators subject to criminal prosecution by the accusing prisoner, through his attorney or a responsible agent, or by a citizen or government appointed investigatory body, to whom the prisoner may appeal for help. Liability should, moreover, extend not only to line personnel up to supervisory, administrative, and executive officers of the implicated penal institution, but, also, to those staff members of the affiliated agencies of the penal system, named in the criminal suit.

Having suggested these protective supports of the new criminology, we might venture into a few more thoughts on the ethical aspects. It would be foolhardy to assume that the sweeping changes entailed in transforming our socially wasteful prison system into one contributing to the common good, can be achieved without the aforementioned unceasing scrutiny through an inter-locking system of local and high-level governmental and citizen Investigatory Commissions, keeping a close eye on the LSPS policies and operating practices. Included would, no doubt, be periodic on-site studies of case-records and administrative control, to make sure that the programs are being carried out as prescribed by law.

It should not be too difficult to tie together the diverse state and local experiences under the new criminology, not only as to its problems but of equal, if not greater importance, the *successes*.

Perhaps the governors of a number of adjacent states could set up a joint *Regional Criminology Task Force* for their region, the members to be appointed by the participating governors for a staggered term of years. Much good could be derived from such task forces, should they be forthcoming across the nation. They might meet and consult with the legislative heads of criminology committees of the states within their region, as well as with trustworthy citizen watch-dog bodies. It takes no great imagination to envisage the benefits that would accrue from this, both in a given region and as the result of inter-regional conferences. The very nature of such coordinating efforts and the cross polination of new and better ideas, would reduce problems and improve techniques.

Finally, a few words are in order about the prisoner's monetary obligations to both the state and his or her victim(s), balanced by the prisoner's right to payment for the LSPS performed. For example, if the commission of a crime was to destroy a life, limb, reputation, or property, or even if it was only a misdemeanor, we believe that it should be the court's responsibility, at time of passing sentence, to affix the amount of damages, and to set the terms of payment. The damages ought, furthermore, to take precedence over all other existing, pending or future claims against a convict, except those of immediate family dependents, which the court can adjudicate equitably in cooperation with appropriate social agencies. The same priority claim by the victim(s) should apply to any financial or property assets that the prisoner may possess, and the court should have the power to enforce payment of the damages, whether from such assets or LSPS earnings or both.

In reverse direction, the officialdom of the new criminology has a strong obligation, itself, to help prisoners who have committed serious crimes, to build a new life, in return for the long overdue and exceedingly important life-sustaining work they have to do in payment of their debt to society. Manifold though the obligation is, we, on our part, shall but allude to the areas in which it has to be carried out.

Prisoners sentenced to an extended period of years will, obviously, have to perform hazardous LSPS for only the minimum number of hours needed to do the research work, and this might include assisting the regular laboratory staff in routine tasks that they can learn to do. In any case, the prisoners will have much time on their hands, which can be profitably spent in society's interest as well as their own. This is the point to which we want to address ourselves in these final few words.

1. Every human being is torn, in the course of a lifetime, by unfulfilled aspirations, and, surely, this is true of convicts. For them it is a time when, in compensation for their important LSPS assignments, the prison and allied agency authorities can marshall a powerful set of forces to help them achieve one or another of their useful ambitions. In this respect, some of our best penal institutions are already doing good work. Under the new criminology, the obligation becomes mandatory. Remember this: in a real sense, every felon is facing serious bodily injury or death, for you and me.

2. As part of the above, illiterate and unskilled prisoners must be given the schooling and training needed toward learning a skill that is within their ability. For all other prisoners, so far as it is practical within tight security regulations, those who have successfully completed the educational and training requirements toward a specific manual or technical skill, a profession, the fine arts, or business management, should be eligible for employment within the new penal system, at a fair rate of pay, while still having to serve out their prison term. If such employment continues until the prisoner is discharged, the security restrictions would automatically terminate at that point.

3. Every Regional Criminology office should have an *Employment and Counseling Division*, including a field staff of specialists qualified, (a) to study the records of prisoners about to be discharged or possibly paroled; to interview and counsel them, and (b) to keep in close touch with the job market and employers, both in and outside the region, for placement opportunities.

This concludes PART ONE of our treatise on the *Endangered Human Animal*. In making the transition to PART TWO, it is well to remind ourselves that until the peoples of the world—not only we Americans—are ready to abolish poverty and war, which are the *causes* of crime, the new criminology is, at least, a just and humane way of curbing crime. It may be a valid way for all time.

Our outline of the LSPS idea affords but the merest glimpse of the bizarre confluence of crime-breeding forces, in our country, that is so overwhelming as to reduce our law-enforcement agencies to a state of utter helplessness. And, yet, the most astounding thing is not the impotence of institutions of penalogy, nor the pandemic fear and hysteria that crime is arousing across the length and breadth of a nation of more than 200 million people; rather, it is the absence of a creative societal counter-thrust for fundamental change in our archaic value-systems of criminology.

PART
2

The Ecological Imperative of Societal Transformation

Prefatory Comment

In this second part of the treatise on the Endangered Human Animal, we shall review with strong feelings of compassion, the four social revolutions that erupted in the first half of the twentieth century and are still running their course. They occurred in Sweden, Mexico, Russia and China.

Prior to the revolutions, democracy was non-existent in those countries. Monarchs ruled by the divine right of kings; they abhorred the very concept of democracy. The aristocracies disdained work as being beneath their dignity. This left the great mass of impoverished peasants and of growing numbers of city workers with no way of redressing their grievances in a peaceful, democratic manner. For centuries, however, there had always been one other way: violent rebellions. These had always been ruthlessly crushed by the armies of the monarchs and their allied nobilities.

By the early 1900s, came a new kind of poor peoples' revolution, *theoretically* based and intensively organized, for a massive military insurrection. Our overview of it left us with two thoughts uppermost in mind: the oppression and great suffering endured for centuries by countless millions of the peoples in those countries; and, except for the initial years of the Mexican Revolution, the high scholarship and unswerving dedication of the revolutionaries, who led the people in their struggle for a better life. Unquestionably, the revolutions had some success in improving the lot in life of the common people.

In limiting our coverage to an analysis of the causes and historical settings that brought on these unprecedented kinds of social rebellion, we shall stop short of trying to make an appraisal of the ongoing confrontation between the four post-revolutionary socialist/communist nations and the opposing industrially advanced capitalist ones. For the past two or three decades, this bitter, often violent struggle has become so dangerous to the very survival of the human family, that it behooves thoughtful people in all countries, to find a way of abandoning it, in self-preservation.

Having said this, we should add a counter observation about the revolutions; namely, that, though based on just cause, and motivated by lofty ideals, they did not discover the underlying cause, nor cure, of the social inequities that have plagued humankind since the dawn of history. In short, the real and attainable answer to human wellbeing still awaits fulfillment.

And what *is* that real answer? In order to uncover it, we think it wise, first, to study the course of the four revolutions while, at the same time, searching our minds for the missing link. This should enable all of us to detect more readily the elusive cause of, and answer to, so much human misery among the peoples of our planet's badly misnomered civilized nations.

14

The Quiet Revolution In Sweden

This little nation of eight million people has been so successful in achieving material well-being in recent years, there has arisen the notion that it has always been so with the Swedish people. Quite the opposite is true. Present-day prosperity was preceded by a long history of poverty and oppression.

It is not necessary to delve deeply into Swedish history for the causative factors. Suffice it to say that the Swedes, well known as an adventuresome seafaring people, also have a long record of warfare, including short-lived moments of empire building. Their seafaring exploits, associated with piracy and wars of conquest, extend back into history for more than a thousand years. In the course of time, they and their Scandinavian neighbors, the Danes and Norwegians, "dominated trade routes to Constantinople, sailed the Mediterranean, and ventured throughout the Baltic and into the rivers of Russia where they (the Swedes) founded the Russian state."[1]

During the Middle Ages these Norsemen, also known as Vikings, ravaged the coasts of northwest Europe from the 8th to the 11th centuries. Their invasion of England and impact on English life are standard textbook history. Sweden's struggles, for power and territorial possessions, with its immediate neighbors and the German states across the Baltic were constant, except for a brief hiatus during the reign of peace-oriented King Gustave Eriksson Vasa (1521–1560). His concern over the stagnant domestic economy and impoverishment of the people, in the wake of constant warfare, led him to foster the development of mining, agriculture and trade. Small wonder that he is remembered by the Swedish people as their first national hero who was "well beloved by his subjects and left the country in a flourishing condition."[2]

It was a brief interlude, followed after his death by renewed warfare and efforts at empire building which culminated, collapsed, and brought to an end, once and for all, Sweden's aspirations for world

119

power during the war years of Charles XII (1682–1718). For another hundred years, wasteful power struggles between a succession of inept kings and rivals among the nobility, who dominated the Swedish Parliament (Riksdag), turned the country back to impoverishment. Both kings and nobles derived their privileged status and wealth through merciless exploitation of the peasants, who had no representation in the Riksdag, as they were without property. "It was a period of scandalous corruption with little or no regard for the plight of the common people," writes the historian Joseph B. Board.[3]

Our quick flight over 1000 years brings us to the causes of social revolution in modern Sweden; namely, the worsened conditions, heaped upon the old ones by a new breed of seekers after material wealth: the rising class of industrial enterpreneurs of the 18th and 19th centuries. The transformation that this mirrored in the way of life of much of Europe, from agriculture to manufacturing, is conventionally referred to as the *Industrial Revolution*.

We shall be wise to abstain from using this term as though it were somehow synonymous with social revolution, a usage that leads only to confused thinking, since most recent social uprisings have erupted in nations on the threshold of industrial development. Industrial revolution denotes the far-reaching functional or mechanistic changes that occurred in national economies, as a result of human inventiveness: the steam engine, railroad, tools and machines, airships. As a societal composite of man's unique creative genius in the animal world, it had no more and no less intrinsic relationship to social revolution in the 19th century than did the inventive transformation of nomadic into agricultural life some 5000 years ago, or the discovery, in more recent times, of nuclear energy, the invention of outer-space craft, the computer.

Social revolution does not erupt from these creative achievements, but rather from man's *misuse* of them. If we remember this, it will help avoid a lot of unnecessarily befuddled thinking in our review of contemporary social revolution in Sweden, as well as in the other three longtime impoverished nations.

How did the change-over from the farm to the factory take place in Sweden? Sweden has always been an agricultural nation, and remains largely rural even today. At the beginning of the nineteenth century only ten percent of the population lived in towns, and for a number of decades the proportion did not change. By mid-century, the first faint stirrings of the Industrial Revolution began to be felt. A few examples: forest industries were stimulated by the invention of the steam engine.

Instead of having to haul cut-wood over rugged countryside from sawmills located adjacent to inland water-power, the whole logs could be floated, conveniently—and profitably—down rivers to steam-powered sawmills located on the coast.[4]

The Bessemer steel-making technique, perfected by a Swedish engineer, made possible the production of high quality steel. Production of pig iron rose from 80,000 tons in 1820 to 145,000 tons in 1850 and 205,000 tons in 1865.[5]

As the Industrial Revolution went into full swing, it began to shift political and economic power from the ancient landed aristocracy to the rising new class of industrial entrepreneurs; and, in the process, the more sagacious members of the nobility itself, accompanied the shift; they had the wealth needed to invest in the new manufacturing enterprises and the training and habits for material acquisition. For Sweden's common people there was open only the shift from impoverishment as farm workers to impoverishment as factory workers. The poet C.J.L. Almquist wrote of the time: "In Sweden there is no question of *seeking* poverty. It is a dowry of nature. . . . and when Christ says, Blessed are the poor, the pronouncement is most especially addressed to the Swedes."[6]

It has often been said that Sweden, throughout much of her history, was little better than an impoverished wasteland, and this is how it seemed to the great mass of the people in the 1800's and well into the early decades of the twentieth century. Between 1860 and 1910 more than 1,000,000 Swedes left the country for the United States. Their testimony of the hard economic conditions and social plight in the homeland is poignant and sometimes bitter. "Mother Sweden", wrote one emigrant, "can be compared to a mother who has too many children; she is too poor to feed them. And another: "As for me, I have missed Sweden but little. I long realized the oppression of her less fortunate citizens, the undue power of the upper classes, the disregard and harshness with which they used to push down the poor. . . ."[7]

Fear of poverty and starvation coupled with that of the miserable working conditions in factories, the long working hours, meager food and low wages, was no doubt the prime reason for the massive exodus to other countries; but a powerful stimulus, too, was the arrogance with which the upper classes treated working people, in their contempt for physical labor and those who were engaged in it. Documentation of the recollections of Swedish emigrants for the period are voluminous and we shall cite but two more.

A woman who had come to the United States told this story: "I left home at the age of eighteen and worked as a servant for many fine families. They were army officers and employers and even noble by birth. But heavens, I could cry when I remember how it was. We servants were all like slaves, and were so happy when we weren't scolded. If we didn't bow as politely as they wanted, they glared at us as though they wanted to tear us apart. And they were fine people, educated people. . . ." From a male newcomer came this: "When in America you tell how in Sweden a servant had to hold his hat in his hand when he talked to his master; you can't even get an Irishman to believe you. . . ."[8]

But it was not the Swedes who left the country to escape the hardships and injustices there, that sounded the call to social revolution, a revolution that turned out to be one of the most undramatic and yet most revealing of all social uprisings in modern history. Before we scrutinize the reason for this, a comment made in 1968 by the noted journalist Wilfrid Fleisher, is in order: "There is in Sweden no destitution such as exists in so many other countries. There are no slums in the true sense of the word; no one has to sleep at night on a park bench or under a bridge; there is a high degree of security in employment; there are no beggars; there is a high standard of living for the people; and hospital and medical care is within the reach of everyone."[9]

What happened to bring about this remarkable transformation? And is it so completely happy a one as Fleisher's observation would seem to indicate? Are its conceptual premises such as will further progress toward the dual NSHS planetary goal? For people who are generally familiar with the European labor movement, this 3-way question raises yet another one: Was what happened in Sweden a social revolution or was it simply typical of the way economically deprived factory workers fought a running battle with their new industrial employers, for better wages and working conditions, not just in Sweden but in every European country experiencing the changeover from a predominantly agricultural to an increasingly industrial national economy?

The answer is that what happened in Sweden was not only a Social Revolution, but a revolution in the most heartening sense of the term. The illusory economic gains, on the other hand, being made by the people of industrial nations generally—in England, France, West Germany, Belgium, Italy, the United States, Japan—were not and still are not Social Revolution.

What happened in Sweden was singularly endowed with a bold new revolutionary concept not present, or at least not operative in those countries. Swedes were breaking ground in a long over-due national thrust toward an *international ethics* of *peaceful co-existence* among the peoples of the world, not before attained by governments. In Sweden there had become dominant an all-pervasive *repugnance* to international warfare that gave a transcendent quality, a universality, to immediate demands for domestic well-being. It was a collective world outlook that had never gone beyond mere rhetoric in other countries. It was the vital spark of the Swedish revolution.

To be sure, the Swedish people employed the organized strategy needed to improve their living standards, as did the working people in the neighboring industrial nations. Every wise member of the Swedish "proletariat" carried a membership card in his *union*, his *cooperative* and his *labor (socialist) party*. But there the similarity with the European mainland, the British Isles, and the United States stopped—though in the latter country even that strategy was minimal.

Only in Sweden had the anti-war commitment become deeply implanted in all segments of society. It was in the nature of a wisdom born of centuries of bitter experience with the domestic aftermath of war. Because of its great influence for good, extending to all nations around the world, this wisdom bears careful analysis in our study of Natural Survival Through Human Selection.

Swedes had refused to become entangled in any of Europe's wars for more than 160 years—ever since their participation in the Napoleonic wars of 1796 to 1815. And there have been many devastating wars since that one: the Crimean War (1853–56); the Franco-Prussian War (1870–71); The Russo-Turkish War (1877–78); The Boxer Rebellion (1900); the Boer War (1899–1902); The Russo-Japanese War (1904–05); and, of course, the two World Wars (1914–18 and 1939–45).

None of the European industrial nations had been able to follow the Swedish example of resisting the lure of conquest and the pressures of one or another of the big western Powers to join in their military ventures. Sweden's political and industrial leaders did not bring dishonor upon themselves and tragedy to the people of their nation and the nations of the world, by refusing to engage in these self-defeating wars. Sweden's dedication to international peace, alone, has remained steadfast.

Herein lies the difference in the whole complex of events that meant some success for social revolution in Sweden and failure in all the other industrially developed nations of the West, including the wealthiest and militarily most powerful ones, among which the United States and Great Britain have, oddly enough, become the most fragile, so far as their domestic well-being is concerned. This paradox is of the essence of today's "world crisis" in food and energy shortages, a subject that is as indivisible from social revolution as are the two sides of a page.

Social revolution implies substantive societal transformation and, if consummated, a permanence and stability of the goals sought.

Applying this test to the struggle against hunger and social injustice, waged futilely by the peoples of the world prior to the 1900s, we discover that the Swedish people did, indeed, begin to accomplish a singular measure of success in the latter third of their 160 years of unswerving renunciation of war. Inseparable, however, from this fundamental motivating wisdom was the aforementioned thrust by Sweden's working people for a just social order, expressed collectively by the labor unions, cooperative societies, and the Social Democratic party. From the linkage remarkable things began to happen, albeit not easily or rapidly, but only after deeply encrusted social and political obstacles had been overcome.

We have noted why a million impoverished Swedes fled to America from 1860 to 1910. For twenty years after that the economic plight of the common people in Sweden remained unchanged. The Social Democratic Party was not born until 1889 and the cooperatives, as a mass movement, not until the 1890s. Together, they and the labor unions could make little impact upon government to pass social legislation, improving the lot of poor people, because the right to vote was restricted to the wealthy property holding Four Estates: the nobility, clergy, agrarian landowners, and the rising class of industrial entrepreneurs.

During the first world war there was great suffering. Though Sweden remained neutral, the war did, in fact, bring prosperity to the business community. As for the common people, an old proverb very well summarizes the matter in one sentence: Prosperity did not filter down to the poor people. When the armistice was signed November 11, 1918, the whole nation was hit by an economic crisis. The sale of iron ore, steel, timber, etc., to the belligerents stopped suddenly. Unemployment rose, prices skyrocketed, and food shortages caused riots. Strikes swept across the nation. What was most frightening to the Four Estates was the effect that the Russian revolution of 1917 was having upon the radical elements of the population. Worker demonstrations in Stockholm and other cities demanded a general strike, establishment of workers' and soldiers' councils and a socialist republic modeled after the Soviet Union.

The threat of violent revolution coming from Russia struck home among the wealthy. Hjalmar Branting, leader of the social democrats, who was well known for his advocacy of peaceful change to socialism, saw his chance for sweeping reform of the electoral system, which was basic to getting any social legislation passed in the Riksdag. He mounted a strong campaign for universal suffrage. The capitulation of the Estates opened the doors to the quiet revolution in Sweden.

Now that the Social Democratic Party had secured the right to vote for the members of unions, cooperatives, and for the population at large, it grew rapidly to become the single largest political force in the nation, but still short of the majority needed to get its programs through the Riksdag. Meanwhile, the government spokesmen of the upper classes continued to tinker with economic and monetary superficialities for another decade, while living conditions of the great mass of the people worsened and social unrest mounted. Then, from the United States came the stockmarket crash of October 29, 1929, and in its wake the great depression that swept throughout Europe. In Sweden a coalition of desperation was quickly put together by the social democrats, supported by the traditionally conservative farm bloc, liberals, and even some communists. They rammed through the Riksdag a comprehensive program of food relief, unemployment insurance, medical care, and low-cost housing.

By 1932 Sweden was well on the road to a healthy economy, while the depression in the United States raged on for another seven years, and Germany, Great Britain, France and Italy, were diligently preparing for world war two as the way out of their troubles.

The Swedish social revolution is still in its early stages, but already it is providing food for thought among impoverished nations whose populations have been decimated for centuries by famine and the wars of native marauders and foreign conquerors. The quiet revolution in Sweden is revealing to the people a way to human betterment. Thus, one has to look underneath the overlay of western science and technology for the revolutionary posture the Swedish people of all classes have learned to take in their domestic affairs; i.e., the renunciation of violence in international problem-solving. Once the benefits of dedication to international peace had imbedded themselves in the collective consciousness, they carried over into domestic affairs as naturally as water running down hill.

Sweden's commitment to *non violent* problem-solving thus runs like a common thread through all accounts of its recent history. As a result of 160 years of peace, to quote the historian Board again, "Sweden has been content to be a minor power, devoting her energies to peaceful internal development. The result is a homogeneous population, a well-developed economy, domestic peace, no irredentist groups, no colonies, no outstanding territorial claims, and no claims on Swedish territory by other powers."[10]

Sweden's economic well-being is sometimes attributed to what is supposed to be a singular sense of Swedish practicality: "In Sweden practicality is king, and when there is a conflict between practicality and other values, the other values give way." Maybe so, but practicality, untempered by creative idealism, has a way as often as not of becoming opportunistic expediency. Practical Swedes, it must be remembered, have a long history as a warrior nation, enjoying neither peace with other nations nor peace and well-being among its own people.

More to the point is another of Board's deductions that "we cannot but be impressed by the long period of peace which has not always characterized Swedish history. . . . Life was not always so tranquil, and there is a certain irony in the pacific transformation of a country which produced a long line of venturesome warriors, from the Vikings to Charles XII. Once Sweden renounced great power politics, her energies were consummated on internal development. Few modern societies have developed in such nonviolent circumstances; in modern times Sweden has neither participated in foreign wars nor experienced domestic violence."[11]

It is frequently said, by Americans, that the Swedes are not nearly so idealistic a people as they are often represented as being. There is, no doubt, some truth to this. As a matter of fact, they did quite well by themselves in deciding to stay out of recent and contemporary wars. They did a very profitable business selling their wares to any and all of the warring nations. Speaking both practically and idealistically, however, one must add to this, that selling merchandise, be it chemicals, steel ingots, or dimensional lumber, is a normal and necessary function of commodity interchange to meet life-sustaining human needs around the world. If the buyer engaged in warfare chooses to use the chemicals to destroy food crops, or dimensional wood to make the handles of guns, and the steel ingots to make bullets, that's his problem not the seller's.

Of far greater importance than these side-appraisals of secondary psychological motivations, is the basic fact that the Swedish people have been able, through non-violent social revolution, to transform a country that was once called the "Fortified Poorhouse" of Europe, into a land where there is no hunger. This first concern coupled with that of providing adequate shelter and medical care for all the people, carried out under law, and subsidized by both the state and private enterprise, is tantamount, in the prevailing American point of view, to the creation of an undesirable Welfare State. American writers often refer to Sweden as being such a state. It should be noted, however, that Swedes are not at all unhappy with their Welfare State. Like most Europeans, they do not share the American aversion to universalizing freedom from hunger as a basic right, to be enforced by the state, rather than as an objective to be left to a competitive struggle between individuals, no matter how unequal the conditions for that struggle may be.

The economics of the post revolutionary Swedish "welfare state" are often described as an unorthodox synthesis of Socialism and Capitalism. As one economist says it: "Simplicistically put, the production of goods and services is largely left to the private market, while the state has considerable influence over their allocation and distribution." The writer, Piet Thoenes, summed it up ingeniously with the phrase that Sweden has been "blessed with the fruits of a happy marriage between Adam Smith and Beatrice Webb."[12]

More down-to-earth than Thoenes' idyllic description of the happy state of Sweden's domestic affairs is the fact that, on the one hand, the "people's coalition" (the labor unions, Social Democratic Party, and the cooperatives—Kooperativa Forbündet or Cooperative Union and Wholesale Society, popularly known as KF) keep a watchful eye on the marriage, while the business leaders and heads of government, on the other, bring to bear on it a wisdom for resolving domestic conflicts nonviolently, learned from many years of experience in settling international differences peaceably. By any definition of a just and civilized society, this collective determination that no one shall suffer from want or social injustice, commends itself as being of the highest order of human achievement.

Today, Swedes often refer to their country as "the People's Home" (Folk hemmet). In all candor, this new kind of love of country by the Swedish people has an unabashedly economic aspiration for survival, which only those who have long endured poverty and social deprivation can fully enter into. It is the rock-bottom base of a just society in an age when nature's scarcity has become a myth, if predicated on a collective quest for enlightened frugality founded in reverence of life. Within this frame of reference, we conclude the Case of Sweden with Fleisher's excellent summation:

> Swedes are entitled to a whole series of benefits from the cradle to the grave—what the Social Democrats call a program for security at all ages. These include prenatal care for expectant mothers, an allowance for a child at birth, an annual child subsidy, free dental care for children, free school books, free school lunches, loans for

students, scholarships for more promising students, protective measures for workers, unemployment insurance, recreation facilities, loans for young married couples to furnish their homes, benefits for families such as reduced rentals, "own your own home" building loans, free medical care, pensions for invalids and the disabled, free annual vacations for housewives and children, and old-age pensions. Most of these benefits are available to all.[13]

15

Violent Revolution In Mexico

To the student of comparative world history, the Mexican Revolution presents a confused and an unfinished picture of events that refuse to conform to ideological blueprints for social revolt. The unorthodoxy stems from a complex of conditions and forces that is distinctive to the Mexican experience. What is not generally recognized is that these very conditions and forces underlie both the painful frustrations of Mexican revolutionary aspirations to date, and their potential for ultimate success in the NSHS sense, a goal none of the revolutions has yet attained.

From the NSHS standpoint of unfinished revolutionary business, it will be helpful to think of what happened in Mexico in terms that are often implied by historians but never actually used by them. In an overall sense, we will be talking about The Mexican/U.S.A. Revolution in Mexico. The reason is that since the middle 1800s, large-scale "American" corporations in Mexico have eliminated most competing European companies. By the turn of the century they had secured ownership and control of the major part of the country's vast oil, tin, coal, minerals, silver and gold deposits, as well as immense tracts of cattle-grazing and food-bearing lands.[1]

When the great mass of impoverished Mexican peasants and city workers rose up in rebellion and overthrew the tyrannical, American supported, Porfirio Diaz, in 1910, they were confronted not only by the Mexican upper classes, but, also, the United States government, acting "in protection" of the Mexican property holdings of the American corporations.

What has happened in Mexico, up to the present, has been powerfully conditioned by this dual input of the domestic government and the big foreign one up north.

We shall observe standard terminology by referring to the social upheaval in Mexico as the Mexican Revolution, while keeping the longer title in mind, because it reflects more correctly the revolution's full dimension, including the inhibiting role played by the United States. On the more hopeful side, this on-going counter-struggle serves to stress the wisdom of linking the NSHS concentric planetary goals with the socio-economic problems that the peoples of *all* countries have to resolve together and to weave into the fabric of a peaceful future world society. In today's barbaric human society, however, the atrociously oppressed Mexican people had no alternative, in their desperation, but to plunge into one of the most bitter and violent rebellions in modern history.

For more than two decades after the ouster of Diaz, there was only disastrous in-fighting between dissident, frequently, self-seeking leaders, and suffering for the great mass of Mexico's poor. Some of the rebels were motivated by purely local or sectional objectives, some by sheer adventurism or as agent provocateurs for Diaz; and, in one crucial instance, by the United States. Most of them had but one motive, which was to get rid of the dictator. Very few of the leaders had any idea of what a social revolution with a common purpose meant, or that it could only succeed under unified leadership.

This miserable state of affairs during the early years of the revolution did not just happen. Mexican scholars concur that the causes go far back in Mexican history and that, without an awareness of those causes, it would be impossible to understand the course of events after 1910. They can be revivified by taking a quick look at them under two rather broad headings:

> Mexico's rugged terrestrial features, and the effect these had on the earliest known native (Indian) populations.

> The rich mineral deposits that have lured foreign conquerors and investors to Mexico through the centuries.

Terrestrial Features

The historian, Charles Cumberland, tells how Cortez after one of his plundering expeditions to the new Spain, described the country to Charles V. The adventuresome General crumpled a piece of paper to demonstrate the configuration of the Mexican landscape. He was describing Central Mexico which he knew from personal experience, but it fitted the physical appearance of most of the country.[2]

Four great mountain chains zig-zag throughout most of Mexico, the Sierra Madre Occidental and Sierra Oriental, extensions of the Rocky Mountains of Canada and the United States, entering Mexico in the north; the Sierra del Sur and Sierra Madre de Chiapas, often towering

12,000 feet above the valley of Chiapas in the south. Illustrative of the impassability of these southern ranges is the fact that even today only one road cuts the seven hundred miles through them, from the central highlands to the Pacific.

All the chains become ever more rugged as they join and mingle in their north-south direction, reaching their most imposing heights in the states of Pueblo and Hidalgo in Central Mexico. Mt. Orizaba, Popocateptl and Iztaccihuatl, soar more than half a mile higher than the tallest peaks of the United States. The mountains become so immense and forbidding as to leave few passes for lines of communication or transporation.

Interspersed among the mountain ranges are high table lands, the largest and most important of which are in Central Mexico, where nearly half of today's population is concentrated, and five of Mexico's largest cities, including Mexico City, are located. Many of these intermontaine basins are windswept, eroded and deprived of sufficient rainfall for normal agricultural purposes. It is estimated that 50 percent of the land suffers from a continuous scarcity of water while only 13 percent (as compared with 47 percent in the United States) has sufficient rainfall in all seasons; to make matters worse, much of the well-watered area is in the mountains, where agriculture is impossible. In places where the amount of rainfall is adequate for raising crops, its value is diminished because it comes spasmodically and torrentially.

Exacerbating these hard natural conditions are still-active volcanoes existing on the fringes of Central Mexico, in areas where climate is pleasant, rainfall suitable for agriculture—and population the most dense![3]

The Native Population

When the people of Mexico revolted against the Diaz dictatorship in 1910, they were not a homogeneous population around which the revolutionists could build a campaign of sustained common action. The country's rugged topography had created isolated pockets of human settlement in the scattered intermontane basins, shut off from each other by towering mountain chains, impassable to all but the most venturesome and hardy societal groups. As a result, there evolved, over an immeasurable span of pre-historic and recorded time, a mosaic of separate and dissimilar culture-systems: semi-nomadic hunting and warrior tribes, simple pastoral societies, and highly sophisticated societies possessing well structured political, economic, and religious institutions.

This lack of social cohesion proved to be a disruptive force not only for collective action against the country's domestic elites, but an insurmmountable barrier to the development of a common set of revolutionary ideals around which the people could be united on a continuing basis, as was the case in the other revolutions under review. The divisive heritage bedeviled the Mexican people's struggle for freedom throughout the centuries. It perpetuated an encrusted disunity, stemming in part from the unceasing intergroup warfare and, in part from the atrocities of pagan religious practices.

Long before the Spanish conquest, the cruel terms imposed by ancient warrior tribes upon conquered people, and the demands of a fearsome, often schizophrenic and sadistic, pagan priest-hood for liberal offerings of human sacrifices to appease their angry nature-gods, were amazingly interwoven. The noted student of Aztec and Maya culture, Alfred Sundel, describes a typical sacrificial orgy of the fifteenth century. In 1486 Ahuizotl and Nezahaulpilli, co-emperors of the Aztec nation, completed a new pyramid to the gods of sun, war, and rain. At the dedication rites, some twenty thousand prisoners from conquered groups were lined up in long columns for the sacrificial slaughter. The two empire lords cut the hearts from the first victims with carved stone knives, then the priests took over. When the mass sacrifice was concluded, the altars were so smeared with human blood and bodies of the dead, that it brought on a plague.[4]

Such atrocities, coupled with the oppressive rule of the ancient tribal aristocracies, left deep emotional cleavages and hatreds between indigenous groups, that could be readily fanned by ruling castes to pit one against the other and prevent any common uprising. These father-to-son inherited intergroup animosities need to be kept well in mind in making an assessment of the abortive years of the 1910 Revolution.

The Spanish Conquest (1521–1820)

It was at the height of the Aztec power over subject Mexican people that Hernando Cortez and his conquistadores made their appearance on the Gulf Coast and sailed into the harbor that is now Vera Cruz. When the foreign invaders declared themselves opposed to the barbarous religion of the Aztec state, they found themselves surrounded by allies from other tribes. But as soon as the Spaniards had subjugated the entire native population, they wasted no time making known their real motives and putting them into practice: seizure of land, accumulation of riches, including everything from the produce of the land, the private possessions of the tribal aristocracies—their homes, their art collections—and their women. The fact that the invaders brought along few if any women in the beginning, made concubinage, whether by acquiescence or rape, a prime right of the conquerors.

The invaders were never more than a tiny fraction of the population—by the end of the sixteenth century, about 63,000 out of an estimated twenty million indigenous Indians. This numerical weakness made necessary a rigid system of social control in which the Spanish-born *peninsulares*, or gachupines, as they were contemptuously referred to by the natives, held a tight grip on all political and military power. They created a social caste system scaled downward as follows: at the top were the peninsulares and members of the Catholic clergy, who accompanied them on the long journey from Spain to bring the faith to the heathen Indians. Then came the *creoles* (born in Mexico of European, primarily Spanish parentage), who sought in vain to break into the exalted top echelon of the peninsulares and their Spanish born high clergy, but had to settle for lesser social positions as minor functionaries in government, the Church, and trade.

The creoles thus hated the peninsulares, and were the first among the dissatisfied population to foment rebellion. After them, near the bottom, were the *mestizos* and other lowly *castas* (offspring of mixed native and European heritage—in the case of the castas including negroid ancestry). At the very bottom were the horrendously treated *Indians* who outnumbered all the others combined by more than 30 to 1.[5]

Colonials and crown officials in the homeland quickly agreed that the Indians could, by sheer force of numbers, mount a serious threat to Spanish rule; they had to be totally crushed to avoid rebellion. Indians were placed socially and legally into a class apart, as wards of the state. Law isolated them into ghettos in the urban areas and denied them the rights of citizenship. They were not allowed to use firearms or cattle branding irons or European dress. They were "lazy by nature", useful solely for hard labor on the land and in the silver mines, under the lash of a whip. Spaniards pretended that there never had existed a preconquest Indian culture, and that never had the Indians had their own sophisticated aristocracy among the Mayas, Aztecs, and other powerful Indian nations.

But in the overall pursuit of power and riches, the Spaniards spared no one whether Creole, Mestizo or Indian. They imposed a system of forced labor and a despotic local rulership, exercized by every wealthy peninsulare from his palatial estate or hacienda. The forced labor practices were so brutal, especially in the silver mines, that many of the conscripted workers died of malnutrition and exposure to the elements. Distances between the laborers' settlements and the great silver mines often meant traversing on foot over 200 miles of hard and dangerous mountain terrain. According to late seventeenth century travelers, skeletal remains of laborers who didn't quite make their destination outlined the roads to the mines.[6]

The Independence Struggle

The Spanish empire, like all empires, carried the seeds of its own destruction. Eventually through time, the hated gachupines became so soft physically and corrupt morally, from too much wealth and leisure, that they could be overthrown by the mere weight of an aroused and desperate people, disunited and unorganized though they were.

Giving courage to the indigenous Mexicans, says the historian, Daniel James, "were two explosive events that took place—outside Mexico—the American Revolution of 1776 and the French Revolution of 1789. Copies of the Declaration of Independence were translated into Spanish and smuggled into Mexico. . . . The writings of the great French thinkers Rousseau, Volaire, and Diderot, and the accounts of the revolutions they had inspired, also filtered into Mexico. All this revolutionary literature was avidly read by the criollos, who promptly absorbed the ideas they contained and began thinking of how they could be applied in Mexico."

The creoles became the natural advocates of insurrection. When the legendary hero of the independence movement, the creole priest, Father Miguel Hidalgo, sounded the call of "death to bad government, death to the gachupines," in his little church yard at Dolores, Central Mexico, on a Sunday morning, September 16, 1810, he opened the flood-gates of the pent-up fury unleashed by native Mexicans against the Spaniards.[7] Alas, with no leadership ability, no clear social program, and a torn population unprepared for any kind of collective response, Hidalgo only brought on bloody street fighting between the creole and peninsulare factions, and a senseless slaughter of thousands of civilians that tore the country apart for more than half a century.

The aimless killing and destruction was lulled at last, but only on the surface. First came the brief strong-armed rule of the Indian leader, Benito Juarez (1863–67), who is often called the father of Mexican Independence, in recognition of his incredible victory over the combined forces of the French, Spanish and British invaders, which helped to end all further European empire aspirations in Mexico.[8] Then came the infamous dictatorship of Porfirio Diaz (1877–80 and 1884–1911).

But even this torturous road to independence, and its eventual and seeming miraculous success, could not have been traversed without the aid, again, of the ever-present outside force, the now rapidly emerging United States as a rich and ambitious industrial nation. On December 2, 1823, the young "colossus of the north" served formal notice, through the Monroe Doctrine, that the Western Hemisphere, henceforth, was off limits to European empire building. The declaration was destined to become the decisive thrust, not only for the establishment of the Mexican state but also for its continued domination by a foreign power, running through all the years of the 1910 revolution.

It is common knowledge that by the 1880s the black lustre of coal, oil, iron, and a host of other basic raw materials in the Mexican mountains, had begun to tantalize the covetous eyes of the rising new business elite in the United States, exactly as the bright lustre of gold and silver had tantalized the Spaniards. What is not so well known, is the fact that only eighty years before the revolution, Spain ruled a Mexico that was substantially larger than the United States. In 1830 the United States occupied about 1,600,000 square miles; Mexico, over 1,900,000.[9]

While the fate of the Mexican "state" hung in the balance and the country lay prostrate from internal strife, the industrial barons of the United States maneuvered their government into making the Monroe Doctrine work for them. In 1838 the United States seized a big chunk of northeastern Mexico (269,970 sq. mi.) that is now Texas—the richest political subdivision in the world, with the possible exception of the Russian Ukraine. Then followed 1838 to '48, when the Americans sliced off another piece (870,000 sq. mi.), comprising the northern half of Mexico that now constitutes California, Utah, Nevada, Arizona, New Mexico, Oregon, and parts of Colorado and Wyoming; all of it, together, half of what was once Mexico.[10]

This paved the way for the great family fortunes and gigantic multinational corporations of the United States, illustrated by such names as the Hearsts, Rockefellers, Guggenheims, McCormicks, and, of course, the Dohenys of Teapot Dome "fame"; of Standard Oil, United States Steel, Anaconda Copper, and others. From the 1880's on, the Mexican dictator, Porfirio Diaz, who greatly admired the get-rich-quick spirit of the Americans, welcomed with open arms their bids for lucrative operating concessions. At the outbreak of the 1910 revolution American holdings in industrial properties were worth more than all other foreign investments combined, and exceeded the total capital owned by the Mexicans themselves. Included were three quarters of the mines and more than half the oil fields; along the American border, enormous cattle ranches."[11]

Diaz saw the burgeoning industrial economy of the United States as a boon to Mexico. It proved to be that, not only for the Americans but also for the tight little group of shrewd, upper-class Mexicans possessed of an unbounded greed for material wealth. Moreover, it brought a modicum of prosperity to a growing middle class of industry-appended urban shopkeepers, merchants, plant managers, salesmen, lawyers, and the usual crop of technicians and professionals. All together, the new middle class plus the native and, indeed, the only temporarily resident foreign elites, never comprised more than 10 to 15 percent of the population.

For the great mass of the Mexican people, poverty and deprivation remained. Mexico under Diaz, it was said, had become the mother of aliens and the stepmother of her own children. The appalling conditions under which the Mexican people lived just before the revolution, are revealed by a few documented accounts:

> In 1893, 439 of every thousand live-born children died before reaching the age of one.

> In 1895, 86 percent of the population was unable to read and write, and at the close of the Diaz regime four out of every five persons were still illiterate.

> The 1910 census classified 50 percent of all Mexican houses as *chozas*, virtually unfit for human habitation.

> Textile mill owners found that for many tasks a child could perform as well as an adult, and at considerably less wages. . . . A British traveler stated in some mills the children were so small that they had to stand on boxes to reach the spindles.[12]

At the opposite extreme—unceasing poverty in the rural areas—was the hacienda system:

> The great haciendas gave an aura of wealth and gracious living; the land owners determined economic policy, set the standards of social intercourse, graced the exclusive Jockey Club, entertained foreign emissaries, and talked learnedly on every subject. . . .

> It has been estimated that at the height of the Diaz era about 3,000 families owned over half the land of the entire country. . . . One (hacienda) in Coahuila covered an area greater than the state of Oaxaca. . . . One railroad line in the state of Hidalgo traversed over 80 miles of land belonging to one family. One estate in Durango

occupied more than a million acres, and one in Zacatecas nearly two.[13]

Below the surface, resentment among the poor was mounting, but Diaz felt he could keep it under control with his iron-clad system for maintaining law and order. He permitted no legal channels through which the people could seek redress of their grievances. He forbade any form of labor organization; government officials saw to it that agitators were kept under close watch, and that the Press printed nothing adverse to the government's policy for law and order. Particularly effective was Diaz' practice of conferring upon leaders of the ancient order of banditry, official status as his personal and generously compensated representatives on the rural and urban police forces.

The whole system greatly facilitated ferreting out local trouble makers, imprisoning unregenerated ones, and removing dangerous and influential ones by "shooting them in the back while trying to escape," and reporting such instances faithfully in the press!

The Revolution of 1910

After reading accounts, by reputable historians, of the tumultuous and incredibly violent first two decades of the Revolution, one comes away with the feeling that, unlike the upper-class independence struggle of creoles against Spanish-born peninsulares, this time the social uprising unleashed all the accumulated emotional and physical outrage stemming from the long-endured suffering of an entire people. The oppression under Diaz was but one more agonizing moment in 400 years of ruthless subjugation by the Spanish invaders, preceded by countless millenia of savage treatment at the hands of pagen warrior tribes within their native lands.

How to cast off this latest yoke of domestic and foreign oppression? How to find the leaders who can marshall resistance before they are murdered by Diaz' bandit/police force? And what direction can the resistance take?

A good many years have passed since the moderate reformer, Francisco Madero, fired the opening gun of the revolution. It set off an explosion that reverberated across the length and breadth of the country. To the great misfortune of the Mexican people, the resulting social upheaval, violence, destruction, and directionless purpose, brought none of the redeeming or lasting benefits that social revolution seeks to achieve.

"The overwhelming characteristic of the revolutionary era", says

Cumberland, "was utter chaos. . . . the years between 1910 and 1924 which wrecked the economy, may have cost as many as two million lives. . . . the mass of the population probably had less to eat than they had two decades earlier, their educational opportunities had improved not at all, and they had no greater political rights. In almost every sense their condition was dismal."[14]

Mexican history was exacting its terrible price. Sixteen months after Madero had been inaugurated as President, he was assassinated by hirelings of both the domestic and foreign elites, with the open connivance of the United States Ambassador, Henry Lane Wilson. They carried on ceaseless counter-revolution, justified and supported by Mexico's intellectuals and middle-class "who never had it so good"—a typical middle-class phenomenon that has proved itself to be standard in time of great social transformation—with rare *individual exceptions*. Paradoxically enough, a free-wheeling spirit of political democracy emerged, imported from the United States, and worshipped equally by Mexico's upper classes and revolutionist. From the top down, it facilitated optimum use of the age-old strategy of divide and rule; from the bottom up, it brought to the fore an assortment of zealous, generally well-intentioned but careerist revolutionary leaders representing all manner of political thought, self-seeking ambitions, and sectional particularism.

From the very beginning of the insurrection, while Madero's rebel army was storming Mexico City, finally forcing Diaz to resign, other revolutionaries with ideas of their own, were recruiting their armies and taking control of government in outlying areas of the country: Emiliano Zapata in the south, Francisco Villa in the north, to mention just two of the more prominent ones. They made it clear they had independent plans for revolution, with no commitments to the Madero movement. Only one backward looking motif was common to all the leaders: the aforementioned detestation of a return to the Diaz era.[15]

By the 1920's, however, a new kind of foreign social philosophy began to influence Mexican thinking: the Russian Revolution of October, 1917. Socialist ideas were being increasingly heard in the public utterances of leaders of the revolution. By 1938 they became the corner-stone of reforms instituted by President Lazaro Cardenas (1934–'40). Under his administration, generally considered to be the high watermark of the Mexican Revolution, the Congress adopted a revised constitutional article #3, on October 10, 1934:

> The education imparted by the state shall be socialistic and, in addition to excluding all religious doctrine, shall combat fanaticism

and prejudices by organizing its instruction and activities in a way that shall permit the creation in youth of an exact and rational concept of the universe and of social life.[16]

Cardenas launched an ambitious program of social reform, which included: redistribution of more than thirty million hectares of land to some two million landless peasants; expropriation of the major oil producing properties of American and other foreign corporations; restoration of full civil and political rights to the native Indian population; equal public education for boys and girls.

The programs were eminently sound but short-lived. In the words of one historical commentator, "the agents of social transformation may have been a bill of rights in 1934, but in 1940 (when the new President, Manuel Avila Comacho took office), it was still on paper." The obstacles were overwhelming. There was neither the prerequisite collective will among the people nor a willingness on the part of the powerful American and still numerous European investors, to permit such ideas to succeed. The prominent Mexican commentator, Jesus Silva Herzog, summed it up in 1949. He credited Cardenas for his heroic efforts, and for some progress toward wiping out the worst aspects of a lingering feudalism, and for broadening a sense of nationhood among the people. He took stock of the adverse socio-economic conditions that made Cardenas' declared programs impossible. His key observation merits restatement here:

> The big merchants, bankers, industrialists and big owners of urban properties suffered only to a small degree. Slowly they recovered lost ground. . . . The number of the old wealthy, growing more wealthy, increased gradually over the two decades from 1921–1940. . . . the growth of domestic capital and capitalists (continued) in several categories: generals and politicians who took part in the Revolution and who after its triumph, occupied high civil or military posts; bankers who were "broadminded" about investing depositors' money in questionable deals; business agents and curbstone brokers, old and new merchants, friends, relatives, and associates of high public officials, and favorites of these. . . .

And he concludes:

> This explains, at least in good part, the immorality both inside and outside governmental offices. Money becomes the supreme aspiration of everybody, because in a capitalist society it opens all doors and provides innumerable material benefits. . . . By the first half of the forties we had a millionaire president.[17]

But the worsening economic conditions of the Mexican people, themselves, led to the election of another socialist minded President: Luis Alvarez Echeverria (1970–'76). The troubles that confronted him were all those listed by Herzog. A TV broadcast over NBC channel 5, on August 24, 1974, cited a figure of 20 percent unemployment in Mexico, plus serious underemployment. The newscaster added that 500,000 Mexicans had entered the United States, illegally!, in search of work. "So great is poverty among the poor," said the report, "that they had to live on a minimal subsistence diet of beans, vegetables and no meat, because that 'next to nothing' buys food to enable the family to survive."

Depicting the suffering during those sad times, the well known student of Mexican history, Stanley R. Ross, edited a collection of writings by leading figures of the Mexican Revolution, under the caption of *Is The Mexican Revolution Dead*? Today, in the 1980s, one can say that the Mexican Revolution is not dead. It has not failed. It has not succeeded. More to the point, its fate is hanging in the balance. The difficult, uncharted road to success still lies ahead. Whatever direction it may take, in order to establish a just social order, the builders who are planning it must bear in mind that the traditional political and economic goals, by themselves, are not enough to steer it into fruitful territory.

The urgency of making these goals subordinate parts of the Biological Imperative has already been stressed in Part I of this study. You will recall that it demands adopting a life-style of enlightened frugality, founded on reverence of life. This applies, moreover, to all nations, not just to Mexico and the United States; and it must be practiced in a total ecological sense.

We shall be wise, if we look for progress toward this goal, while scrutinizing the remaining chapters of our study. Failure to do so, will seem as though we are incorporating within the covers of a single book, two very different and unrelated subjects—biology and politics—when, in truth, the continued existence of the endangered human animal depends on its ability and determination to merge them.

16

The Revolutions That Shook The World

When revolution broke out in Russia (1917–'20) and China (1927–'49), waged by more than one-fourth of the world's population, there was consternation among big industrialists and landowning elites around the world. The rebellions involved too many people, scattered over too vast a territory, to be subdued. More importantly, they had, for the first time in history, a powerful, socially scientific unifying force that motivated both leaders and followers; i.e., the Marxist thesis of human progress through a class struggle between oppressed working peoples and wealthy ruling upper classes. It was a thesis that also envisaged the inspiring goal of a classless socialist (communist) society.

This solidifying power enabled the Russian and Chinese people to ward off defeat. It provided an array of protective armor and a staying power against disruptive attacks, both during the early years of the revolutions and after the fledgeling socialist societies had been established.

The adverse side that must be added in this chapter is that it was the very strength of these subtle underlying factors that, ultimately, became a serious impediment to the collective well-being so ardently sought by the revolutionaries. In the course of decades, as the Russian and Chinese post-revolutionary domestic conditions improved, and their military strength, as well as economic and political relationships with the poorer nations around the world, greatly expanded, so did the anticommunist fears and hatreds among the dominant capitalist nations greatly expand. However, strange as it may seem, we shall find that even in the relationship between the newly founded Union Of Soviet Socialist Republics (USSR) and the People's Republic Of China (PRC), old conflicting national ambitions began to flair up as early as the 1960s, and border warfare soon followed. In the 1980s, incredible though it is, the PRC and the USA, not so long ago the bitterest of enemies, are negotiating for a peaceful settlement of their differences, and an improvement in cultural and trade relations, while the USSR and USA are preparing for a planetary destructive nuclear war, to destroy each other. Since the latter aspect goes well beyond our subject, we shall return to the business at hand.

The Historical Setting

On the eve of revolution, the people of Russia and China, so dissimilar in their cultural past, had been reduced to an undifferentiated state of poverty and social oppression. With unceasing brutality the "divinely ordained" agrarian dynasties of the two countries, in collusion with their landowning nobility, continued to rob upwards of 90 percent of the population—the landless peasants—of the fruits of their labor, and to live in splendor on that plunder. But now there had come upon the scene in Western Europe and the United States, new seekers of worldly wealth and power: the rising class of industrial tycoons and their servants, the industrial middle class of small property owners and well-paid professionals.

As this new system of capitalist (bourgeois) democracy began to penetrate Russia and China, poor peasants flocked to the cities, in the hope of improving their lot in life, only to discover that, as industrial workers, they were as impoverished economically and helpless politically as they had been on the land. Their miserable state was truly identical to what befell that other great mass of the poor in Mexico, when wealth and power began to shift to the industrial elites there.

If we were to repeat verbatim here, the worst conditions in health, housing, education, and poverty, described earlier about Mexico under Spanish rule, and the worst in repressive measures imposed upon the Mexican people by the Peninsulares, and were we to substitute Russian and Chinese names of places, governments, church and military officers, the appalling details would fit the pre-revolutionary Russian and Chinese picture to perfection.[1]

We shall find that these conditions, as already stated, coupled with the power of the socialist ideal did, in fact, prevent a revolutionary stillbirth and, in doing so, revealed why the revolutions had to occur when they did, and in the manner they did. Beyond that, they acquired a societal dimension that encompassed far more than the class struggles of their time and ours. The socialist ideal, itself, has generated a complex of forces throughout the world, destined to have a profound effect upon future generations.

Based on this historical premise, we believe that a meaningful assessment of the options open to successful revolution in the two countries, must take into account the three-way struggle between western capitalism pressing into Russia and China at the time, the defenders of agrarian feudalism living beyond its time, and the growing force of a socialist credo envisaging the end of both social systems. The collapse of the decadent feudalism in the struggle is well documented history. The challenge of the socialist idea to the strident and firmly entrenched capitalist economy needs careful scrutiny, because after that must come some light on how to accomplish true progress in the common interest of all peoples.

The first act of this human drama was laid in Russia, the second in China; the third act is being played now, actively by some of us, passively by too many of us. There is, also, a Prologue that laid the historical foundation of the ongoing struggle, for good and for bad on both sides.

The Prologue

It spans the time from 1848 to the abortive revolution of 1905* that followed a long period of economic and political oppression suffered by Russia's vast peasant population and the growing numbers of industrial workers.[2] The plight of the poor was exacerbated by the Tzar's senseless military venture into the far-east, to dislodge the Japanese from territories they both coveted. Russia's ignominious defeat within one year (1904–05) created utter chaos across the nation. Food shortages and famine in addition to the heavy casualties of the war took a frightful toll of life.

The resulting revolutionary eruption was not, however, the product of the socialist movement. It was actually a result of the great popular outcry from all segments of Russian society—the heads of large foreign-owned business enterprises, the respectable county welfare organizations—the Zemstvos—and even the better informed members of the nobility and professional groups; and the people who had been hit the hardest—the peasants and city workers. From all came a fervent appeal for political and economic reform. Educated liberals at every social and economic level, including doctors, lawyers, journalists, educators, demanded the right of free speech and assembly, and a free press; the heads and management staffs of large foreign owned industrial corporations called for public education and health services; the impoverished city workers, for the right to organize and hold open

---

*For specific dates we use the old Russian calendar which is 13 days behind the present Gregorian calendar.

meetings, to enable them to discuss their common problems and draw up petitions for better wages and working conditions; the great majority of peasants, for a more just distribution of the land and its harvest. Finally, from all segments of the population, except the tiny hard-core of the nobility headed by the Tzar, came the demand for a democratically elected Duma modelled after the Parliaments of Europe, to assure the realization of those basic political freedoms.[3]

To these pleas Nicholas II not ony lent a deaf ear but unleashed a merciless campaign of repression, imprisoning the chief advocates of political reform and banishing to remote Siberia others who failed to escape the net set for them by the secret police. With incredible insensitivity to the will of an entire nation, Nicholas, one of the least bright and most vindictive of Russia's Tzars, pursued this almost childishly willful and cruel policy, until it brought about his own undoing a decade later. His single most infamous imperial order was given on a Sunday afternoon, January 9, 1905, and it will be remembered forever by all Russians as Black Sunday.

On that day, after a religious procession, thousands of people led by a problematical priest, Gapon, filled the square before the Tzar's Winter Palace in St. Petersburg, "to see their Holy Father" and present to him a list of their needs. His answer was given by a squad of soldiers who appeared suddenly, fired several volleys into the densest part of the crowd, killing more than 500 and wounding 3000. "All and everybody knew: January 9th was the beginning of the Russian revolution."[4]

Socialists had long been driven into exile. To silence the other "agitators" for democratic reform, Nicholas called and dissolved one powerless Duma after another, while he had his secret police infiltrate the ranks of the would-be legislators, to harass the most vocal advocates of political change. As for the underground work carried on by the socialists, it was often said that by 1905 Russia's working class was the most educated body of socialists in the world. It was a shrewd observation even though few people, inside or outside Russia, including most of the revolutionaries themselves, fully sensed its validity.

Having said this about the abortive upheaval in 1905, does not gainsay the fact that Marxian socialists had been preparing for revolution since the 1860s, when the now famous *Collunist Manifesto*, written in 1848 by Karl Marx and Friedrich Engels, was smuggled into Russia. This remarkably powerful brochure was avidly read by thousands of Russians, young and old, eager for a strategy that offered a way to get rid of the tyrannical and outmoded Tzarist regime. Here was not only a convincing strategy for immediate action but an attractive ultimate goal.

By the turn of the century, socialist leaders who had escaped imprisonment lived in exile: Plekhanov, father of the Russian socialist movement; Lenin, Trotsky, Kamenev, Uritsky, and scores of others. They roamed from one foreign city to another—London, Paris, Geneva, even as far as New York, wherever they were granted asylum—to theorize and debate the timing of the Marxist guidelines for revolution, and last but not least, to raise funds from sympathetic people eager to see the downfall of the autocracy of the Russian Tzars. In 1898 Plekhanov founded the Russian Social Democratic Workers Party (SD), to which the urban proletariat responded enthusiastically. Two years later the peasant-oriented Social Revolutionary Party (SR) came into being.[5]

Despite the efforts of the Tzar's secret police to prevent it, the emigres kept a steady stream of literature flowing back to the homeland, to the peasants across the far-flung steppes of the Russian empire, and the workers in the fast growing industrial centers. It was upon this solid foundation of an aroused peasantry and proletariat, indoctrinated with the socialist ideal, that was built the idealized revolution of Russia and China; and much of this revolutionary fermentation continues to take place around the world as these lines are being written. Since the first attempt to translate the socialist dream into collective action occurred in Russia, we need to examine the thinking that fueled it long before the outbreak of revolution in Russia and, later, in China.

1848: Emergence Of The Socialist Credo

The ideological fountain-head, Karl Marx (1818–'83), a socially ostracised radical in his life-time, is a world renowned social philosopher now. As a young man Marx was greatly influenced by the German philosopher, Georg Wilhelm Friedrich Hegel (1770–1831), who conceived ultimate reality as being a struggle between contending ideas striving from ascendancy. He postulated an ever changing idea-reality of *being* and *becoming*, defined in terms of "thesis" (the prevailing idea); "antithesis" (the challenging idea); and "synthesis" (the new idea emerging from the struggle).[6]

This philosophical concept is popularly known as the Hegelian Dialectics. Marx brought it down to practical affairs. Hegel's thesis became the contemporary capitalist class; the antithesis, the working class; and the synthesis the emerging classless socialist society. Marx is said to have quipped in one of his lighter moments that he simply stood the Hegelian Dialectics on its feet instead of on its head.

This philosophical somersault would hardly have been enough, by itself, to bring the storm of condemnation upon Marx's head from the reigning elites, which it did; or the worshipful encomiums from the oppressed masses and their leaders. That came from the fact that, on the one hand, the Marxist thesis led to social action by creative thinkers and, in turn, by thoughtful people among the poor; on the other, it aroused vigorous opposition by the rising new capitalist class. The staying power of this unprecedented philosophical impact on social dynamics largely predetermined the initial flow of events in the 1917 revolution and those to follow.

First, Marx laid bare the old simplistic notion of history as a directionless mosaic of past wars, conquests, peace, prosperity, intrigue, good and bad rulers. He replaced it with the concept of continuing historical class struggles between the exploited many and the ruling and privileged few. This Marxist world outlook quickly spread and became known as the Materialistic Conception of History. The next thrust of the logic placed the cause of the historical class struggles on the institution of private property in productive lands, industries and other "socially necessary" properties.

Private ownership of the means of production, said Marx, enables small groups of individuals with an abiding lust for such ownership, to accumulate large holdings of socially necessary property and to exploit the propertyless workingclass (proletariat), for their own enrichment. So unjust a system has to be brought to an end by the great mass of impoverished people who are its victims. The time has come when they, the working class, must take over government and establish a classless socialist society.[7]

Marx amplified his thesis of social inequities and its anti-thesis, the socialist credo, in his major work, *Das Kapital*. It is a comprehensive critique of capitalism, the first part of which was published in 1867, the remaining parts posthumously by Engels, in 1893. Numerous popular treatises beginning with the *Communist Manifesto*, issued jointly with Engels, and a continuous flow of articles and correspondence with colleagues, sounded the call for socialist revolution. In all of them Marx laid down four prerequisites to success, which he and Engels discussed broadly in varying contexts. A few words on each will give us the clue to what they meant, and the questions they raised for the leaders of both the Russian and Chinese revolutions:

The Capitalist Base

Comparing the burgeoning nineteenth century capitalism with the earlier agrarian economies, the *Communist Manifesto* points out that—

> Our epoch, the epoch of the bourgeoisie, possesses, however, this distinctive feature: it has simplified the class antagonisms. Society as a whole is more and more splitting up into two great hostile camps, into two great classes directly facing each other: Bourgeoisie and Polletariat.[8]

With respect to capitalism's own survival problems, the Manifest goes on to say—

> The bourgeoisie finds itself involved in a constant battle. At first with the aristocracy; later on, with those portions of the bourgeoisie itself, whose interests have become antagonistic to the progress of industry; all at times, with the bourgeoisie of foreign countries. In all these battles it sees itself compelled to appeal to the proletariat, to ask for its help, and thus, to drag it into the political arena.[9]

> The bourgeoisie itself, therefore, supplies the proletariat with its own elements of political and general education; in other words, it furnishes the proletariat with weapons for fighting the bourgeoisie. . . . What the bourgeoisie, therefore, produces above all, is its own grave-diggers. Its fall and the victory of the proletariat are equally inevitable.[10]

The Role Of The Proletariat

> Of all classes that stand face to face with the bourgeoisie today, the proletariat alone is a really revolutionary class. The other classes decay and finally disappear in the face of Modern Industry; the proletariat is its special and essential product.[11]

The Dictatorship Of The Proletariat

"The first step in the revolution by the working class," wrote Marx and Engels, "is to raise the proletariat to the position of the ruling class." Having accomplished the seizure of the State,

> The proletariat will use its political supremacy to wrest, by degrees, all capital from the bourgeoisie, to centralize all instruments of production in the hands of the state, i.e., of the proletariat orga-

nized as the ruling class; and to increase the total productive forces as rapidly as possible.

Of course, in the beginning, this cannot be effected except by means of despotic inroads on the rights of property. . . .[12]

Between capitalist and communist society lies the period of revolutionary transformation of the one into the other. Corresponding to this is also a political *transition* period in which the state can be nothing but the revolutionary *dictatorship of the proletariat*.[13]

Marx was well aware of the historical precedent for this harsh political strategy in time of social revolution. It was equally valid in the earlier class struggle between the rising industrial bourgeoisie and landed nobility, that culminated in the French Revolution of 1789 and the establishment of the *dictatorship of the bourgeoisie*. The aristocratic heads that rolled from the guillotines during that dictatorship of the bourgeoisie, ushered in what Marx and Engels correctly described as the epoch of self-serving bourgeois democracy.

There is a tendency among some historians of the Russian revolution to minimize Marx's use of the dictatorship concept, thereby attaching a certain stigma upon Lenin's insistence on it, presumably to further his own personal power as the potential dictator. Nothing could be farther from the truth. Lenin was too dedicated a Marxist and a brilliant scholar himself, (graduated at the top of his university class), to have been guilty of this.[14]

As a matter of fact, Marx placed the highest priority on setting up a proletarian dictatorship during the transitional period of revolution. He expressed great disappointment, for example, over the failure of the leaders of an abortive pre-socialist type revolution that occurred in 1848, and was waged en masse by the industrial workers of France, Germany, Italy, Austria and Hungary. On September 14 of that year he wrote in *the Neue Rheinische Zeitung*, of which he was the publisher:

> After a revolution every provisional organization of the state requires a dictatorship and an energetic dictatorship at that. At the very beginning we have reproached Camphausen (the head of the German Ministry of the revolution after March 18) for not acting dictatorially, for not having immediately smashed up and eliminated the remnants of the old institutions.

Prior to this he criticized Herr Camphausen for "lulling himself with constitutional illusions, (while) the defeated party; i.e., the party of reaction, strengthened its position in the bureaucracy and in the army. . . ." And, he continued:

A constitutional assembly must first of all be an active, revolutionary-active assembly. The Frankfort Assembly, however, is busying itself with school exercises in parliamentarism while allowing the government to act. . . . But what is the use of the best possible agenda and the best possible constitution, if the German governments have in the meantime placed the bayonet on the agenda?

The National Assembly should have acted dictatorially against the reactionary attempts of the obsolete governments (referring to all the revolutions going down the drain), and thus gained for itself the power of public opinion against which all bayonets and the rifle butts would have been shattered.[15]

These few excerpts leave little, if any doubt as to where Marx stood on the subject of the Dictatorship Of The Proletariat. One has to bear this in mind when appraising the course of events in Russia from 1917 on, because it was the central issue of contention among the revolutionists themselves. A strong argument can be made that, but for Lenin's genius in master-minding his one man campaign in behalf of the badly misnomered though sound Marxian call for exclusive proletarian rulership in time of revolution, the Russian revolution, too, would have gone down the drain, as had all previous rebellions of the oppressed poor. And, indeed, in the absence of the Russian precendent of success, so would have the Chinese revolution.

The Role Of The Peasants

Mark and Engels denigrated the receptivity of the peasantry to socialist revolution because they saw correctly, in their time, that the individually isolated mode of life of the peasants, except for the poorest tenant farmers, inculcated a strong sense of private ownership of the land. By and large, peasants displayed the same ardent veneration of private property as did small shopkeepers, doctors, lawyers, and other members of the middle class or so-called petty bourgeoisie of the cities.

Only when modern industry penetrates the countryside to replace the old agrarian aristocracy with that of the impersonal and centralized ownership of the land by the bourgeoisie, does the individualistic peasant sink to the common level of the propertyless proletariat. A few excerpts from the works of Marx and Engels will illustrate:

The lower middle class, the small manufacturer, the shopkeeper, the artisan, the *peasant*, all these fight against the bourgeoisie, to save from extinction their existence as fractions of the middle class. They are therefore not revolutionary but conservative.

> The small-holding peasants form a vast mass, the members of which live in similar conditions but without entering into manifold relations with each other. Their mode of production isolates them from one another instead of bringing them into mutual intercourse. . . . Each individual peasant family is almost self-sufficient; it, itself, directly produces the major part of its consumption and thus acquires its means of life more through exchange with nature than in intercourse with society.

In reviewing the growth of industry in France, Marx notes the transformation of the life of the peasants:

> In the course of the nineteenth century the feudal lords were replaced by urban usurers; the feudal obligation that went with the land was replaced by the mortgage; aristocratic landed property was replaced by bourgeois capital. . . . Small-holding property, in this enslavement by capital to which its development inevitably pushes forward, has transformed the mass of the French nation into troglodytes. Sixteen million peasants (including women and children) dwell in hovels. . . .
>
> The interests of the peasants, therefore, are no longer, as under Napoleon, in accord with, but in opposition to, the interests of the bourgeoisie, to capital. Hence, the peasants find their natural ally and leader in the *urban proletariat*, whose task is the overthrow of the bourgeois order.[16]

Back To the Eve Of The Revolution

Historians sometimes deplore the endless debates over theoretical fine points, in which the Russian revolutionaries seemed to indulge in their underground congresses and committees while in exile. Actually, the differences went well beyond academic pedantry. The most influential leaders, men and women like Plekhanov, Lenin, Trotsky, Spiridonova, Kollontai, and a host of others, were indefatigable students of history and on-going world affairs. They, like sophisticated scholars generally, knew that the collapse of the obsolete Russian autocracy was imminent. Nobody could foresee the exact moment, but that the battle was close at hand they were sure. In this atmosphere of urgency they had to decide how to implement Marxism which, though realistic in its time, raised more questions than it answered.

When is a system of capitalism sufficiently advanced to make a successful socialist revolution possible? What are the organizational options (a) for successful revolution and (b) for the survival of a socialist society threatened by counterrevolution during and/or immediately after the revolution? Does the Marxist demand for a dictatorship of the proletariat rule out socialist participation in a revolutionary coalition government that includes representatives of the middle and upper classes?

Such pivotal questions were at the heart of the interminable debates that preoccupied the socialist co-conspirators more than a decade before the demise of the Romanov Dynasty, February 26, 1917. Differences on how to proceed, when the time came, had already split them into two camps: those who believed that, according to the teachings of Marx, capitalism was not yet ripe enough in Russia for socialist revolution, and urged collaboration with the advocates of democratic reform, to hasten the day when revolution could be successfully undertaken; and those who argued that capitalism was aready full-blown throughout Europe and the United States, and being spread rapidly into Russia; the epoch of capitalism was here and it was not necessary for Russia's working class to suffer through all the stages when these were well known and could be skipped.[17]

During these verbal battles, leadership among the exiles was being increasingly centered on one Vladimir Ilyich Ulyanov. He had just finished serving a 3-year sentence in Siberia, and while there married Krupskaya Nadezhda, who was also serving time and was to become his life-long comrade in planning the revolution. Like all the revolutionaries under constant surveillance by the police, Ilyich took on one of his many aliases, this time, Lenin, and in 1900 set out for Geneva, Switzerland, to sit at the feet of the famous elder socialist, Georgi Plekhanov. Life had been relatively free in the sparsely settled far-off steppes of his Siberian exile, and Ilyich spent his time, as always, in intensive study and writing. He had already translated Beatrice Webb's *History Of Trade Unionism*, and written his first major work, *The Development of Capitalism In Russia*.[18]

In Geneva, Lenin, Plekhanov, and two other emigres, Vera Zasulish and Paul Axelrod, began publishing *Iskra*, the socialist periodical that was sent throughout Russia to explain socialism and unite the masses under its banner. As time went on, however, the matter of tactics began to divide Lenin and Plekhanov. The latter believed that Russia would have to be industrialized to a greater extent than it was, before the proletariat could wrest power from the bourgeoisie. In this Plekhanov did, indeed, have Marx and Engels on his side, as we have seen from their earlier statements. He also had the leading Russian socialists with him, but *not* the masses, as the leaders were soon to learn.

In taking the opposite position, Lenin put forth the realistic argument that the *Russian Democratic Workers Party* must have a tightly centralized policy-making body before and during the revolution as a protection against counterrevolutionary infiltration into the party's leadership and the membership at large. Democratic discussion, he pointed out, was to be full and free on all issues, but once the party had adopted an official position, deviation from it would subject the offender to party censorship or, if serious, to expulsion. On this note was sounded Lenin's future alienation from his colleagues.[19]

In 1902 Lenin was joined by a brilliant young revolutionary by the name of Lev Davidovich Bronstein who had escaped from Siberia, aided by a native peasant who hid him in a load of produce on the long trek back to Russia; and from there the underground forces got him to London. Arriving in the middle of the night he went straight to the secret address of Lenin, whom he admired both as a theoretician and actionist. Lev had taken on the alias, Trotsky, which happened to be the name of one of his former jailers in Odessa.

Lenin was greatly impressed by the young man then only twenty-three years old, and together they began at once to round up support among the emigres for Lenin's unpopular thesis on revolutionary tactics. But as opposition against it grew, Trotsky tried unsuccessfully to mediate the differences between the two camps. Things came to a head at a congress held in Brussels in July of the following year and attended by some sixty impecunious delegates, who managed somehow to get there from all parts of Europe and, by way of the underground, from the homeland. The debates were bitter and loud and endless, until the authorities banned them, and the delegates took off for London, hopefully, to come to a decision of sorts. And such a one it proved to be when Lenin got a majority vote at a meeting attended by only a small number of the original delegation; but the vote stuck throughout the 1917 revolution and up to the present, identifying Lenin's majority (Bolshevik) and the minority (Menshevik) vote.[20]

The historical import of the entire controversy lies in the uncanny accuracy with which it foreshadowed the real struggle for control of the State, that began within hours after Tzar Nicholas was forced to abdicate. But for the next few years of these dress rehearsals, one after another of Lenin's own supporters abandoned him. Even Trotsky wavered and, when the 1905 Revolution broke out, he, like others among the "evolutionary" socialists, hurried back to Russia to help along the process of bourgeois democratic reform. A frustrated Lenin went into seclusion, to bury himself in further study while watching the developments.[21]

Trotsky's participation in the 1905 upheaval became an invaluable experience in his own growth and, as preparation for the crucial role he was destined to play in the years immediately following the Tzar's abdication. In 1905 he quickly rose to the leadership of the Petrograd Soviet, a working class political action body that became a model for the soviets that sprang up in 1917. When the 1905 revolution was crushed and Nicholas resumed his ruthless suppression of all political reform, the wealthy foreign industrialists collaborated in hounding the socialists and outlawing their political parties. Now Trotsky had second thoughts on the wisdom of relying on bourgeois democracy, allied with Russian autocracy. The lesson weighed heavily on his mind; it eventually drove him back to Lenin's intellectually rigid but tactically sound thesis. In the process, however, he was angering many colleagues by his weaving back and forth between Leninists and Mensheviks; by this, together with a sometimes biting tongue and abrasive manner toward people disagreeing with him, Trotsky made some enemies who in later years proved to be his nemesis, depriving him of a place of leadership in the revolution second only to Lenin.

After the verbal battles, Lenin, having fallen out with Plekhanov and the other Menshevik board members of Iskra, resigned. Ever the scholar, he took to his books, but not for long. Soon he founded Vperyed (Forward) with funds from Alexandra Kalmykova, owner of a bookshop, and other friends. The new organization met with immediate success. While in seclusion Lenin also wrote *What Is To Be Done?*, a manual for socialist revolutionaries. It, too, received wide acceptance, especially among the growing mass of rank-and-file socialists in Russia.[21]

Lenin's remarkable ability to read the mood of Russia's poor, yet explain the most complex problems, in clear and simple language, to scholars and common people alike, attracted a new group of adherents to his way of thinking. Among them were such powerful future leaders as Anatole Lunacharsky, Alexei Rykov; the young feminist, Alexandra Kollontai, Maxim Litvinov, Levi Kamenev, Grigori Zinoviev, Stalin (Josef Vissarionovich Djugasgvili), Alexander Bogdanov, V.M. Molotov (Viacheslav Scriabin). By the time world war one broke out in 1914, Lenin was the undisputed leader of the Marxian revolutionaries.[22]

With this summary of the Prologue to the two revolutions, we come to the First Act played in Russia.

17

The Russian Revolution

The war set the stage, much as the disastrous one against Japan had done in 1904. But this time Nicholas' total ineptness for leadership, his inability to comprehend the sufferings that war brings to the people, or what war is all about, brought him down. On February 26, 1917, pressured by a distraught nation and an alienated aristocracy, including members of his own Palace entourage, Tzar Nicholas II was forced to abdicate.

The Eight Crucial Months Of The Revolution

Within hours of the abdication, a group of Deputies to the old Duma set themselves up as the Emergency Committee of a *Provisional Government*. On March 2, they announced the "government's" cabinet. An incongruous assortment of individuals, it neither represented nor understood the elemental forces that drive a desperate people to social revolution. Its officers included:

Prime Minister: Prince Georgi Lvov, a mild mannered, ineffectual nobleman, head of the old county union of powerless Zemstvos; Foreign Minister, Pavel Milyukov, a professor of history and leader of the conservative Kadets; Minister of War, A. Guchkov, Chairman of the War Industries Committee: M. Tereschenko, a sugar magnet; Minister of Industry, Alexander Konovalov, a munitions maker; Minister of Justice, Alexander Kerensky, a Menshevik who supported upper class demands to continue the war, while people cried for peace and bread—a cabinet utterly incapable of leading a social revolution![1]

Simultaneously, while the Provisional Government's Emergency Committee met in one wing of the Tauride Palace, the socialist leaders of Petrograd met in another wing, to issue their amazing Order No. 1. Three days after the Tzar abdicated, it commanded all military and naval units to form rank-and-file soldiers and sailors Soviets, and to make plans for an *All Russian Conference of Soviets*. From now on, all weapons were to be under the control of soviets and, under no conditions, were they to be handed over to the officers, even at their demand. The old forms of saluting and address between the soldiers and officers were abolished. The regimental soviets were to settle any misunderstandings between the rank-and-file and commanders; and, henceforth, every military unit was subject to the *Petrograd Soviet* and to its soldiers' council.[2]

For a few weeks the two pseudo governments made half-hearted attempts to reconcile fundamental differences, but soon the real struggle for control of the State began. The major political arm of the Provisional Government was the *Party of the Constitutional Democrats (Kadets)*, subsequently also called the People's Freedom Party, favoring a constitutional monarchy or even, ultimately, a republic—a party of the progressive landlords, middle bourgeoisie, and bourgeois intelligentsia.

During those first few weeks the Provisional Government could, from a legal standpoint, claim a semblance of legitimacy, since it was formed by elected representatives of the only remaining part of the Tzarist government—the Duma. In fact, it had little popular support. Its only chance of survival rested on the ability of the commanding officers of the Kronstadt naval base of 55,000 sailors, and the regiments of the army numbering some 165,000 soldiers in Petrograd, and those at Moscow and other major cities, to stem the tide of revolution in collaboration with the civilian police. In the face of the massive wave of mutiny among soldiers and sailors alike, this would hardly have been enough without mighty financial and material aid from the Allies, with whom Russia was still committed to pursue the war against Germany. The domestic aid collapsed of its own weakness; the Allied help was too little and too late.

In contrast, the Soviets that sprang up quickly in Petrograd and across the nation had the determined support of the great mass of the people, including the soldiers; but they were torn by internal dissension on the very issues that had divided their leaders before the Revolution. The old cerebral differences were now put to the test of political action, which resulted in disastrous infighting instead of a unified revolutionary policy toward the socialist goal. The splinter parties that emerged included the *Menshevik Party*, which wavered between endorsing the Provisional Government's efforts to continue the war and the long-range plans to establish a democratic government, modelled after the British system. Soon many of the members broke away to form the *Left Menshevik Party*. They were troubled by the Provisional Government's failure to address itself to the nation's economic plight, as evidenced in food riots and general strikes in the cities, and starvation among the peasants. *The Social Revolutionary Party* represented the poorest and small-propertied peasants in their ambivalence toward collective ownership of the land. It too split into the *Right* and *Left* Social Revolutionaries.

The Bolshevik Party espoused Lenin's position that Russia is ready for a socialist revolution, to be waged by the proletariat, soldiers, and poorest peasants—in armed insurrection, if necessary. It had little support from the other socialist parties, and relied completely upon the receptivity of the great mass of the people.[3]

One can say that, without much dissent from historians generally, this dissipation of effort would have assured the rising industrial elite's accession to power, but for one obstacle: *Lenin*. He determined the outcome at three crucial moments:

1. His announcement of the now famous April Theses upon returning to Russia on April 3, after ten years of exile.
2. The domestic counter-revolution of the "July Days".
3. Lenin's call in October, for armed insurrection.

We shall touch on them briefly, then move on with the over-all assessment.

The April Theses

Word that Lenin would arrive at the capital's Finland station spread quickly throughout Petrograd's shops and factories. An immense, inspired throng of the city's working people were on hand to welcome him, as were also the perhaps not so enthusiastic members of the All Russian Central Executive Committee of the Petrograd Soviet of Workers and Sailors. All his bitterest opponents whom he had fought while in exile were there, from Nikolai Tcheidze, President of the Soviet, to the hundreds of other revolutionaries who had poured back into Russia before he had arrived.

Lenin knew that many of the 400 Deputies to the first convention of soviets, just held in Petrograd, were also present, and that they were Mensheviks and Social Revolutionaries, solidly anti Bolshevik. Only days before leaving Switzerland he had learned, via the underground, that the Executive Committee, swayed by the emotional appeal of the Provisional Government "to save the fatherland," had agreed to continue the war against the German invaders.

As Lenin now glanced about at those top soviet leaders, the reality was brought home to him that, aside from their nebulous goal of a futuristic socialism, they had more in common with upper-class leaders of evolutionary socialism in the Provisional Government than with the Bolsheviks. To be sure, the most prominent among them were, like himself, of comfortable middle class background but, unlike himself, had not shed it. Some of them, like Alexander Kerensky, M.I. Skobelev, and Iraklii, even served in both the Central Committee of the Petrograd Soviet and as Ministers of the Provisional Government.

But this was of only secondary interest in Lenin's thinking at the moment. His mind was on that other audience to which he wanted to address himself: the impoverished and weary masses of Russia who had avidly read his message over the years.

That message had told them that the time has come when they must take revolutionary action, a message that called upon the poorest peasants and workers to take the land from the rich landlords and the industries from the equally wealthy foreign capitalists, and to convert those properties into social ownership by the people of a classless socialist society.[4]

One can hardly hold it against Russia's people—or Lenin, for that matter—that the then unforeseeable but imminent thrust of dark societal forces leading to a total human survival crises, was destined to blast much of the goal out of existence. But in those agonizing days of a devastating war already in its fourth year, Russia's poor worshipped Lenin for the goal he set before them, and they eagerly awaited his word to follow him.

Now, Lenin was not one to seek public adulation. Even his severest critics among contemporaries and historians alike describe him as a selfless, generous, and personally undemanding individual; and withal, a brilliant scholar, masterful strategist, dedicated revolutionary Marxist with an unshakeable faith in the Marxist thesis. It should not, therefore, be surprising, viewed from Lenin's position as the most respected—and feared—theoretician of the revolution, that he clearly saw the wide gulf separating the do-nothing policy of the soviet's Central Committee and the pent-up desires of the common people. The committee members, by and large, could readily vote to continue the war and defer the socialist revolution without disturbing their relatively comfortable mode of life; not so, the peasants and workers whose young men made up almost totally the frontline fighting force of the Russian army; they alone suffered the frightful toll of death and maimed lives.

Whatever else may have been on Lenin's mind on this occasion of public acclaim (described vividly by those present), all these factors must surely have been a part of it. One can argue with good reason, and some historians do, that it decided him to administer a public lashing to his procrastinating colleagues in the soviet. And this he did that night, in a speech before the Deputies at the Kshesinskaia Palace, directed literally and figuratively *over* their heads, and to that great audience not present in the flesh; it shook the rafters and left the official audience dumbfounded.

The Menshevik, anti-Lenin journalist, Nikolai Sukharin, declared: "I will never forget that thunderlike speech.... I came out on the street feeling as though on that night I had been flogged over the head with a flail."[5] Some of Lenin's own adherents, including even Zinoviev who had just returned with him through Germany, were left aghast. The most charitable among them felt that poor Ilyich had been away from Russia too long and lost touch. Kerensky expressed his belief that Ilyich Lenin had, at last, unmasked his real self and was now harmless. Little did he dream that in a few months the speech would be the undoing of the Provisional Government and himself.

No recording was ever made of the two-hour speech, but excerpts of the flailing appeared at once in newspapers across the nation as Lenin's *April 4 Thesis*. Trotsky who had made his peace with Ilyich and was one of the few leading revolutionaries who praised the speech, had this to say:

The theses expressed simple thoughts in simple words comprehensible to all: The republic which has issued from the February revolution is not our republic, and the war which it is now waging is not our war. The task of the Bolsheviks is to overthrow the imperialist government. But this government rests upon the support of the Social Revolutionaries and Mensheviks...

We must teach the masses not to trust (these) Compromisers and defensists. We must patiently explain: (He quotes from Sukharnov's oft cited notes) We don't need any parliamentary republic. We don't need any government except the Soviet of workers', soldiers', and farmhands' deputies!...

The success of this policy, dictated by the whole existing situation, is assured, and it will bring us to the dictatorship of the proletariat, and so beyond the boundaries of the bourgeois regime. We will break absolutely with capital ... and summon the workers of the whole world to cast loose from the bourgeoisie and put an end to the war. We are beginning the international revolution. Only its success will confirm our success, and guarantee a transition to the socialist regime.[6]

Thus did Lenin declare war upon the government—upon the governments of the world—in the name of the proletariat and, in Trotsky's words again, "under the name of *Theses of April 4* which has become one of the most important documents of the revolution. At the same time, Lenin separated himself from the Soviet majority, tossing them over into the camp of the enemy. That alone was enough in those days to make his listeners dizzy."

Finally, to put the historic moment into its proper perspective, we should add these words written years later by the astute and sensitive scholar, Frederick L. Schuman:

> This voice crying in the wilderness had at first little effect on the Soviets nor even upon Lenin's Party. He stood alone. But he was also alone in having a firm and inflexible purpose, a correct analysis of the realities and a clear grasp of means to end.[7]

Counter Revolution, Insurrection And International Counter Revolution

We have dealt in some detail with the April Theses because they laid the foundation upon which was built not only the Marxist/Leninist Revolution of Russia but that of China as well, and the revolutions that are still erupting around the world. The rest of the story, so far as Russia and China are concerned, is about the resultant factual events which, to repeat, can only be skimmed over here, lest we lose sight of the underlying fact that social revolution, today and in the future, must assure the survival of the endangered human animal. We proceed, therefore, with a thumb-nail sketch of—

The July Days

Lenin had assessed the pro and con forces of the revolution correctly in his April 3 address. Exactly two months later, the first *All Russian Congress of Soviets of Workers and Soldiers* opened in Petrograd. Of the 677 deputies, 105 were Bolsheviks, compared to a handful at the hurriedly called one in March—19, according to a report at the time. Though still in the minority at this central political body, they had made even more impressive gains in the nation's economic and military sectors.

Acting swiftly, Lenin's tightly structured central policy-making organization had created a network of Factory Committees of rank-and-file workers in the large industrial cities, and of Soldiers Committees in the garrisons. The Bolshevik Party's Military Revolutionary Committee, headquartered in Petrograd, maintained the closest kind of relationships with the Factory and Soldiers' Committees, especially in cities like the Capital, Moscow, Kiev. Civilian "military" Red Guards were organized by factory and shop committees across the country. They trained the workers in the use of fire-arms, in cacheing military supplies and weaponry, in disrupting counter-revolutionary attack, and perhaps most important of all, in developing intimate rapport with local army and navy Committees, whose members, it must be remembered, were the fathers, sons and brothers of peasant and working class families.

Here was an organized revolutionary thrust of a rebelling people, drawn together by an elemental if unstudied purpose, unprecedented in history. Behind it was the small Bolshevik contingent of the Petrograd Soviet, and behind that was Lenin.[8]

The Ministers of the Provisional Government knew this meant trouble, and something had to be done. The new Premier, Kerensky, decided in a not altogether patriotic move of desperation, to launch an offensive against the Germans who had penetrated deeply into Russian territory. His immediate purpose was clearly to get the troublesome soldiers out of the Petrograd garrison and back to the fighting front. But the soldiers refused to go; thousands deserted; whole regiments mutinied and arrested their officers. The offensive turned into a disaster.

At this point the Bolshevik Military Organization, flushed with these momentary successes, made its own reckless move that all but cost it the revolution. On June 8, it called for an armed but peaceful demonstration, as a show of strength. For the workers, soldiers and peasants, however, the time for conferences and talk had long passed. The revolution now called for deeds. A half million workers and soldiers took over the streets of the Capital, carrying banners and passing out leaflets with the action slogans: "Down With The Provisional Government!" "All Power To The Soviets!" "Time To End The War!" "Bread! Peace! Freedom!" Inspired by the enthusiasm of sheer numbers, and without any plans, the Kronstadt sailors and soldiers of the Petrograd garrison began an unorganized insurrection. Loyalist troops were called in by Kerensky to quell the uprising, and even the Soviet joined in the appeal to halt the rebellion, but all to no avail. From June 8 to the end of the month, bedlam reigned in the capital.

It was not until Lenin himself, who was in Finland at the time of the outbreak, rushed back to Petrograd to raise his voice that this was not the way to win the revolution; finally, the Central Committee of the Soviet managed to restore order, but not until the street fighting between opposing troops had resulted in several hundred casualties—and the first blood of the revolution had been spilled. Daniels, among other historians, takes the view that "if Lenin had planned to overthrow the government at this point, nothing could have stopped him—but he was waiting for a better time, he told a friend, 'no later than fall!'" If true, this is precisely what Lenin's time-table called for and what came to pass.[9]

The panic-stricken Ministers had one final move left to stem the tide of revolution. It involved a scheme that might have succeeded but for the ineptitude of its strategists among the upper classes. The Kadets had persuaded Kerensky to make a sensational announcement: the government had come into possession of documentary proof linking the Bolsheviks, under Lenin, to a huge German spy-ring, to get Russia out of the war, and showing that the Social Democrat Workers' Party Of Russia was the political front for Lenin's subversive work in behalf of the German Reich. Lenin had supposedly been "allowed by the German government to return to Russia by way of Germany, as a ruse to hide his real work as German spy."

The "evidence" was so cleverly fabricated and blown up by a mixture of fact and fiction, that the nation was momentarily stunned. The newspapers broadcast the story throughout Russia and the world. The immediate effect upon Lenin's own followers was one of great shock, and the Bolshevik movement was suddenly in disarray.

It is an old, old story that nations at war engage in heavily financed subversive activities in the camp of the enemy, and the Germans were experts at it. It was an open secret too in Russia, both prior to and after the February revolution, that the Bolsheviks, always impecunious, had no qualms about seeking funds from any source, foreign or domestic. Lenin often said, "If the German capitalists are stupid enough to give money to the Party we will gladly accept it, not only to carry on the Revolution in Russia but to help the German socialists overthrow the bourgeoisie in their own country."

But now the Kadets urged Kerensky to follow up promptly with military action to liquidate the Bolshevik organization, once and for all. Troops raided the offices of the Leninist paper, *Pravda*, and drove the Bolsheviks out of their headquarters in the Kshesinskaya mansion. Trotsky, Kollontai, Lunacharksy, Kamenv, Antonov, and others were caught and imprisoned. Lenin and Zinoviev went into hiding again. Elitist newspapers like the conservative *Novoe Vremia (New Times)* were jubilant.[10]

The subsequent weeks have come to be known as "The July Days," associated with the first efforts at military Counter Revolution. On July 8 Kerensky appointed Lavr Georgievich Kornilov, a dedicated and not too bright General of the old Tzarist army, to march upon Petrograd, capture the chief trouble makers and hang Lenin. To accomplish this Kornilov demanded reenactment of capital punishment, to restore order among mutinous soldiers, and Kerensky readily complied. Promptly, the Soldiers' and Sailors' Committees passed the word to the rank-and-file troops of all military units.

Reinstatement of capital punishment by an old-line General like Kornilov needed no explanation. Its message was clear: a promise of mass executions and destruction of the revolution. The Military Revolutionary Committees had learned an important lesson at the unguided June insurrection. This time there would be no street demonstrations to announce what had to be done. Covertly and systematically, the civilian Red Guard and Soldiers' Committees organized jointly to defeat Kornilov before he got started. The historian, Robert Goldston, sums it up well:

> Kornilov was to be defeated by the revolution before he set foot in Petrograd—in fact, before his regiments even marched. . . . Railroad workers tore up tracks, diverted trains, and completely isolated Kornilov's divisions. Messages and telegrams were stopped at the telegraph office and handed over to Soviet representatives. . . . Trains would move in the wrong direction, supplies would be sent to the wrong stations, artillery would disappear down the lengths of the track, staff officers would find themselves out of touch with their men.[11]

Trotsky observed pointedly: "The (counter revolution) conspiracy was conducted by those circles who were not accustomed to do anything without the lower ranks. . . . without orderlies, servants, cooks, clerks, chauffeurs, messengers, laundresses, switchmen, telegraphers. But all these little human bolts and links, unnoticeable, innumerable, necessary, were for the soviet and against Kornilov. The revolution was omnipresent. It penetrated everywhere, coiling itself around the conspiracy."[12]

Kornilov's "army" consisting mostly of minor career officers, mercenaries and loyal divisions of the conservative Don Cossacks, whose own ranks by now were hopelessly infiltrated by Bolshevik soldiers of their own mountaineer tribes, collapsed without a shot having been fired by either side. Kornilov was arrested on August 30 and imprisoned in a monastery!

While this episode was unfolding, workers and peasants were also brought up sharply by the implications of the counter revolution. One prominent industrialist is said to have supplied the key, unwittingly, in a public address much publicized by the Kadets. Confident that the situation was well in hand at last, he declared that the rebellious workers and peasants would come around soon enough after hunger and starvation brought them back to their senses. That announcement helped enormously to bring them back to their senses. It was what the revolution was all about.

The October Insurrection

The Bolshevik seizure of the state, Marxist style, was the inexorable consequence. It was accomplished quickly, and it might, indeed, have been bloodless but for the civil war that followed, fomented and aided by the Allies, who were eager to crush the revolution and help the Provisional Government keep Russia in the war against the Central Powers.

On October 10 the All Russian Soviet's Central Committee in Petrograd voted to launch the insurrection. According to Trotsky, the resolution was written hastily by Lenin with the gnawed end of a pencil on a sheet of paper from a child's notebook. The reasons given for not delaying concerted action by even a day were based, in part, on the ill-founded belief that socialist revolution was about to erupt in Germany, and spread throughout the world, as evidenced by massive insurrection in the German fleet; also, in part, on the very real threat of a peace between the contending nations on both sides of the ongoing war, with the aim of strangling the revolution in Russia. Memoirs of the Russian revolutionaries attest to this misreading of the German sailors' revolt and the imminence of world revolution.

On the home front, records Trotsky, "there was the indubitable decision of the Russian bourgeoisie and Kerensky and Co. to surrender Petrograd to the Germans—all this in connection with the peasant insurrection (throughout Russia) and the swing of popular confidence in our party (the elections in Moscow), and finally the obvious preparation of a second Kornilov attack (the withdrawal of troops from Petersburg, the importation of Cossacks into Petersburg, the surrounding of Minsk with Cossacks)—all this places armed insurrection on the order of the day."[13]

Despite much wavering and argumentation among the Bolsheviks themselves, the insurrection began October 24 with a "siege" of the deposed Tzar's Winter Palace, where the Ministers of the Provisional Government, led by Kerensky, made their last stand. But as was characteristic of Russia's common people, its rank-and-file soldiers, sailors, workers and peasants—certainly *not* of its traditional military and aristocratic elites—the siege was marked more by a battle of words than of guns, and the memoirs of the participants read more like the denouement of a comic opera than of war. It was the one, and only one, bright spot in the long years of violence and suffering unleashed by the international counter-revolution immediately after the October triumph. A few more words on the October action, before we move on to the post-October crises,then the second act of the drama played in China; and finally, to the global act that is still on stage.

The Bolshevik attack on the Palace was under the command of the scholarly, near-sighted and bespectacled Antonov Ovseyenko who, let it be stressed nonetheless, had been tested over the years and found to be a trusted and capable leader. The guns of the old warship *Aurora*, anchored in the Neva off the Peter and Paul fortress, were trained on the Palace. When the beleaguered Ministers refused to surrender, a number of shots were fired, aimed deliberately for psychological reasons, to miss their target! On the streets to the Palace, Red Guard members of the factory and soldiers' committees were scurrying back and forth between their respective units and the Military Revolutionary Committee of the Petrograd Soviet, headquartered at Smolny Insitute, for instructions. Both the Kronstadt sailors and the Petrograd Garrison's soldiers had been thoroughly Bolshevized and had distributed literally tens of thousands of fire-arms among the shop and factory workers. The proletariat was ready to seize the state! At the same time the capital's trams were running, the movies and theaters were doing business as usual, as were also the casinos and gambling houses of the respectable middle and upper class elements of the city.

Inside the immense Winter Palace, with its labyrinth of ornate halls, conference and banquet rooms stretching in all directions, were the Ministers and their "soldierless" army of 200 inspired young women of the "bourgeoisie"; they had formed the Death Battalion to help save the fatherland and 1500 Junkers (similarly inspired officer trainees not yet out of their teens) ready to die for the Tzar. All of them were awaiting the arrival of the government's loyal army from the front—

but it never arrived for the same reasons that held up Kornilov's army, if, in fact, there still was such an army.[14]

With all the hubub created by participants on both sides, by members of foreign embassies and interested onlookers generally, there was a constant going and coming in and out of the Palace, in futile negotiations. At 2 A.M. on the 25th, some 200 vociferous Mensheviks and members of the old Duma, along with their families and friends, appeared before the Red Guard at the entrance to the Palace, demanding the right to enter and join their compatriots in defense of the government—and, they shouted, to die if necessary! The ensuing conversation was recorded by Louise Bryant, an American journalist on the scene:

> "'Let us pass! Let us sacrifice ourselves!' they cried like bad children.
>
> Only twenty husky sailors barred the way. And to all arguments, they continued stubborn and unmoved.
>
> 'Go home and take poison,' the Red Guards advised the clamouring statesmen, but don't expect to die here. We have orders not to allow it.
>
> 'What will you do if we suddenly push forward?' asked one of the delegates.
>
> 'We may give you a good spanking.' answered the sailors, 'but we will not kill one of you—not by a damn sight!'
>
> This seemed to settle the business. Prokopovitch, Minister of Supplies, walked to the head of the company and announced in a trembling voice: 'Comrades: Let us return, let us refuse to be killed by switchmen!'"

Towards evening of the same day, writes Bryant, we decided to go to Smolney to be present at the opening of the much-talked-of meeting of the All Russian Soviets. As we crossed under the Red Arch we met a group of Bolshevik soldiers who were discussing the best means of taking the Palace. "The bad part is," said one, "that the Women's Battalion is on guard there and they will say we shot Russian women. . . ." By the pre-dawn hours of the 26th, the soldiers and sailors had simply rushed the Palace without firing a shot, arrested the Ministers and sent them to the Peter and Paul fortress. The Junkers were disarmed and told to go home on the promise of good behavior; the women of the Death Battalion were also disarmed and told to go home and put on female attire.

Soon after it fell into their hands, the Soviet government turned the Winter Palace into a People's Museum. And thus ended the bloodless and compassionate stage of the Russian Revolution.[15]

The Post October Crises

Immediately following the Bolshevik triumph in October came a long series of reversals that spanned the years from 1918 to the end of world war two, to play havoc with the socialist ideals of a free and classless society, and bring great suffering to the Russian people. We shall mention only the major domestic and international dark forces that caused the hardships, from which we must make our overall assessment of the relationship of both the Russian and Chinese experiences to the total survival crisis confronting all mankind today. Listed chronologically they include:

1. The merciless and humiliating Brest-Litovsk peace treaty imposed upon the Russian people by the German military machine during its own last hours, March 1918.

2. The civil war that came in the wake of the treaty, exacerbated by the Allied governments after their victory over the Central Powers, November 11, 1918.

3. The invasion of Russia on all sides by the so-called white armies, financed jointly by the domestic-based industrialists and evolutionary socialists, on the one hand, and the capitalist governments of France, England, Japan, the United States, and now also Germany on the other; carried on *unsuccessfully* by all of them from 1918 to 1922, but *successfully* to the extent of bringing death to millions of Russia's people and a collapse of its economy.

4. The resultant dictatorship of Stalin after Lenin's death, based on Stalin's thesis of socialism in one state threatened by many hostile states bent on its destruction, a position that was greatly strengthened during the emergence of Hitler in the 1930s.

With respect to the Brest-Litovsk treaty, the German government was well informed through its efficient espionage system, that at all stages of the revolution, from February to October, the Bolsheviks wanted peace at any price. They knew that the country was in a state of near economic collapse, and the miserably equipped, often starving Russian soldiers were in massive rebellion as a result of the slaughter of millions of them by the mechanized German military machine. On this matter of violence, popularly associated with revolution rather than war, we shall have more to say at a later point.

Thus, within only days after the October victory, the Bolsheviks sued for peace. On November 10 they sent Ensign Krylenko, Commissar of Army and Navy, to meet with the German High Command at Brest-Litovsk. The Germans pretended to be interested in his proposal for a peace treaty based on no indemnities or annexations, and agreed to a cease fire preliminary to further negotiations. They then stalled the talks while their Generals Ludendorf and Hoffman unleashed a swift offensive along Russia's entire western front. The treachery paid off. With little or no resistance they quickly overran and took possession of one-fourth of Russia's richest and most productive territory, from the Ukraine on the south and northward, through Lithuania, Latvia, and Estonia; by mid February of 1918, they were at the doors of Petrograd, where they stopped to present their humiliating peace terms.

Writes the historian, Alan Moorehead, who cherishes no great love for the Bolsheviks: "As for the peace terms... there was to be no talk of German concessions or withdrawals. The German forces were to remain in occupation of the ground they had already conquered. They were to have full liberty to move their troops wherever they wished, and the Russians were to come forward with substantial indennities. Russia, in short, was to be treated as a defeated enemy. Von Kuhlmann (the German Foreign Minister) summed it all up with the phrase: 'The only choice they (the Bolsheviks) have is as to what sauce they shall be eaten with.'"

On March 2 the Germans issued an ultimatum giving Russia 48 hours to accept their terms or face further loss of vital territory. To put teeth into it, they began bombing Petrograd, making it necessary for the Central Committee of the All Russian Soviet to set up temporary headquarters in Moscow, there to engage in frantic debate on whether or not to accept the atrocious terms. Though the military situation was hopeless, both the enraged population and delegates to the Soviet were for rejecting the treaty and fighting the invaders from house to house. As had happened so often in past crucial moments, Lenin, the lone realist, was able to convince the delegates that acceptance of the odious terms was imperative; the very survival of the revolution was at stake. And so, fortunately, they signed the treaty, for within only eight months came the German's own hour of surrender to the Allies, and the treaty was nullified.[16]

The Russian people had at least been spared the agony of eight more months of devastating warfare, this time within their own cities and food-bearing agricultural areas. What might have happened had they decided to fight on, is conjecture. Certainly, the German military high command would have ordered immediate shipment to Germany of the wheat harvested in the rich fields of the Ukraine, and other resources in the occupied territories, for use by their forces confronting the Allies on all fronts. In this they would have had the cooperation of the big Russian industrialists, the landowning aristocracy and the subservient middle class professionals of both these elites. They had already enjoyed this cooperation in the blitz krieg, to ram through the Brest-Litovsk treaty.

Even so, the respite was only a partial and momentary one, for the most desperate days of the revolution lay just ahead—the terrible civil war, engineered and financed in large part by the Allied governments, as the disruptive strategy within Russia, coupled with their joint invasion of the country. Delayed only due to preoccupation with the war against the Central Powers, the Allies were discussing invasion even before Brest-Litovsk. Military invasion was deemed essential, in order to dislodge the Bolsheviks from political power and put the Bourgeoisie back in. The Allies began a probing action; after the German surrender and civil war gains, they went into high gear. All of them, including the Germans, had enormously lucrative investments in Russia that would be wiped out if the Bolsheviks succeeded in establishing a socialist society.

The historian, Isaac Deutscher, notes that at the time, Russia's economy was dominated by foreign capital:

"Western shareholders owned 90 percent of Russia's mines, 50 percent of her chemical industry, over 42 percent of her banking stock." The journalist, Moissaye J. Olgin, writing in 1917, pointed out that "capital hurried from Germany, Belgium and other countries to share in the high profits. In the metallurgic industry, profits of 100 percent were not unusual. Stock companies oftentimes paid as much as 20 percent in dividends. . . . Oil-wells were being constructed (by British, Dutch, and American companies); a large flotilla of oil-carriers were built on the Caspian Sea; numerous carriers appeared on the Volga. Mechanical and chemical plants supplying the oil-industry were being enlarged or built anew."[17]

To which it should be added that neither the foreign capitalists nor the domestic elites had a continuous interest in ploughing back their high dividends into Russian industry or social improvement.

After Brest-Litovsk, the right wing Social Revolutionaries and Mensheviks, incensed by the signing of the treaty and embittered by their frustrating struggle for socialism *after* capitalism in Russia, joined the upper-class opposition to the Bolsheviks, with a furor that all but surpassed the savagery that so often obsesses the estranged civilians of society, when they resort to civil war to solve their differences! The focus of popular outcry against the treaty was Trotsky, who had the odious task as Commissar of Foreign Affairs, of negotiating it. When the full blast of public scorn hit him, writes his biographer, Jules Archer, he was so unnerved, and his pride so wounded that he wept in private, then resigned as foreign minister. But Lenin, realizing that "We could not have got anything better than the Brest peace," responded by appointing him Commissar of War, to take on the seemingly hopeless task of stopping the International Invasion! And yet—

It was in this role of saving the revolution, that Trotsky's fame as the most important Bolshevik leader, second only to Lenin, rests. But for his personal vanity, his difficulty of working amicably with other leaders, his frequent arrogant and insolent manner with colleagues, especially and disastrously with Stalin, Trotsky would undoubtedly have been Lenin's successor and, perhaps, stand side-by-side in history with Marx, Lenin, and Mao Tse-tung. As to the awesome responsibility before Trotsky, at the onslaught of the multi-nation invasion, Archer gives us a dramatic summary of the desperate state of Russian affairs, from which we use, rather freely, a few striking portions:

> "Was I prepared to do military work?" Trotsky wrote later. "Of course not. I had not even had the benefit of service in the Tzar's army.... The problem was to make a clean sweep of the remains of the old army, and in its place to build, under fire, a new army, whose plan was not to be discovered in any book." The task seemed almost impossible.

The Russians were now hemmed in by German occupation of Poland, Lithuania, Latvia, the Ukraine, the Crimea and the Black Sea coast; a Japanese invasion of Siberia and occupation of Vladivostok; British and French military landings at Murmansk and Archangel; and a rising of Czech Legion war prisoners against the Soviets. White Guard armies were attacking the slim Soviet forces with arms supplied by the Allies.

> "We were between hammer and anvil," Trotsky observed.... "One wondered if a country so despairing, so economically exhausted, so devastated, had enough sap left in it to support a new regime and preserve its independence. There was no food. There was no army. The railways were completely disorganized. The

machinery of state was just beginning to take shape. Conspiracies were being hatched everywhere. . . . To make matters even worse, news came that now the Americans, too, had landed an expeditionary force in Siberia."

In stressing the Bolshevik's untenable situation, Archer asks: "With the military might of England, France, America and Japan supporting the civil war of the White armies against the Bolshevik regime, how could the Soviet Union survive?" But, he adds, Trotsky accomplished the impossible, "expanding a force of seven thousand amateurish Red Guards and guerrillas into a disciplined army of 5 million men. No experienced officers were available to lead and organize them except former Tzarist generals, colonels and technicians of dubious loyalty. He persuaded about twenty-two thousand of them to cooperate, knowing full well that some would secretly divulge his military plans to the White armies and that the Red Guard volunteers, who had brought off the revolution, would resent taking orders from them. He won over his trusted Red Guards with appeals to their Russian patriotism and class solidarity, and the practical plea that "just because a man had been a Tzarist did not mean he could not be converted to socialism."

To counter duplicity among the officers, Archer adds, "he did not hesitate to warn them that their wives and children would be considered hostages to their conduct. He also paired all officers, from captain up, with political commissars, to assure their loyalty as well as troop morale. The system of divided command had its weaknesses, but it gave Trotsky a dependable army. . . ."

"Trotsky had no doubt that some White Officers within the Red Army were betraying key Soviet movements and targets to the enemy, as well as sabotaging battles. When the commander and commissar of a Latvian regiment led a retreat from the battlefield at the height of the fighting, Trotsky placed them under arrest and had them shot. He reported their executions to all Red Army commanders in a flyer turned out by the printing press on the special train that whirled him rapidly from battlefield to battlefield, as need arose. . . . In his long cavalryman's cloak and simple soldier's cap, he exuded a magical air of saving the situation. Rallying the soldiers with ringing eloquence, he inspired them with new hope and confidence that they could fight off the better-equipped, more professional forces of the enemy. And this, indeed, they did."

One final excerpt from Archer's account illustrates Trotsky's remarkable ability of transforming a demoralized army into a determined fighting force taking the offensive and winning it. The occasion was one of the decisive moments of the civil war. "On October, 1919, the British-backed forces of General Yudenich had advanced close enough to Petrograd to see the gilded domes of its cathedrals. Headlines in the European press already proclaimed that Petrograd had fallen. Trotsky arrived to find the city's defenses in total confusion and Zinoviev glumly resigned to its capture. The Red Army units were disintegrating and deserting.

"Trotsky immediately stiffened resistance by a brutal order to shoot every tenth man in those units. He sent a shock force of officers through the city in a whirlwind campaign to take over and reorganize troops and workers. Making fiery speeches everywhere, he vowed that Petrograd would be defended to the last man. His thundering eloquence dispelled the pessimism and defeatism that Zinoviev had allowed to burgeon.

"'We will not give up our beloved Petrograd!'" Trotsky cried out in mills and factories. Seizing spades and rifles, determined men and women marched out to take their place with the troops on the front lines. Where manpower was short, women manned machine guns. Canals, gardens, walls, fences and houses were fortified. Trenches were dug everywhere. . . . Inspired by Trotsky, young workers, peasants and military students fought furiously without regard for their own lives. . . . They attacked the tanks with their bayonets, and although they were mowed down in rows by the devastating fire of the steel monsters, they continued to defend their positions. Awed, White soldiers began to desert."

Nevertheless, the civil war continued in stubborn bitterness, and the military invasion by the European powers, Japan and the United States, dragged on for another two years, bent on crushing the revolution. Faced, however, by an unconquerable army of minimally schooled and militarily untrained workers and peasants, led by a learned scholar who was also an eloquent orator, organizer of consummate talents, and totally untrained military master-mind, it became increasingly clear that both the domestic and foreign counter-revolutions were destined to collapse. By 1921 it was all over, though not without a terrible death toll of 7 to 8 million peasants and workers "mowed down" by the invaders' modern weaponry. Adding to the sorrow and deprivation of the living was the destruction of whole industries. The coal mines had been flooded, railways tracks and bridges blown up, agriculture ruined. It took the new socialist state more than a decade to rebuild its economy by mandatory governmental programs of austere living and equal sharing of what little sustenance there was available.[18]

But in the first flush of victory, great public acclaim heralded the heroic role played by Trotsky in defeating the combined forces of domestic and international counter-revolution. It was undoubtedly his finest hour. Sadly enough, however, it was soon marred by the bitter struggle between himself and Stalin for succession to Lenin's mantle. When an assassin's bullet, though not immediately fatal, brought Lenin to an untimely death four years later, the smoldering hatred between him and Stalin flared into the open. Trotsky's old problems of personal vanity forced even Lenin to question the wisdom of recommending him as the nation's future leader, though he did, indeed, acknowledge him as a man of exceptional abilities, and the most able member of the Soviet's Central Committee. Had Trotsky's petty weaknesses not stood in the way, the subsequent history of the Russian and Chinese revolutions might have been vastly different, and perhaps more successful. Instead, Stalin became Lenin's successor.

The Stalin Dictatorship

If ever there was a man who implored the blessings of both God and the devil, in his quest for power, that man was Stalin. One historian observes that "While it is probably true that Stalin was far abler than some critics have suggested, he was, when compared with certain other of the Bolshevik leaders, a gray mediocrity, hardworking, pedestrian, and uninspired." But long before history made him an enormously controversial figure, Lenin was already aware of the wiley Georgian's ambition to succeed him, and the unscrupulous methods he used to dispose of his rivals. Shortly before his death, Lenin wrote his Testament addressed to the Central Committee (December 25, 1922). It made a frank appraisal of the leading members of the Committee, emphasizing the fact that "Comrade Stalin, having become General Secretary, has concentrated enormous power in his hands; and I am not sure that he always knows how to use that power with sufficient caution." After a particularly trying experience only a few days later, in connection with Stalin's gruff handling of a sensitive political matter, he added a Postscript on January 4, 1923, with the request to Krupskaya, that she make the Testament known to the Party in the event of his death:

> Stalin is too rude, and this fault, entirely supportable in relations among us Communists, becomes insupportable in the office of General Secretary. Therefore, I propose to the comrades to find a way to remove Stalin from that position and appoint to it another man who in all respects differs from Stalin only in superiority—

namely, more patient, more loyal, more polite and more attentive to comrades, less capricous, etc. This circumstance may seem an insignificant trifle, but I think that from the point of view of preventing a split and from the point of view of the relation between Stalin and Trotsky. . . it is not a trifle, or it is such a trifle as may acquire a decisive significance.[19]

Once in power, Stalin began a purge of many of his closest associates in the fledgling socialist state, by way of mock court trials, and murder. It is now part of the all too numerous moments of savagery in human history. The incredible barbarity of this strange man was revealed by his ability to square an apparently sincere belief in the Marxist/Leninist strategy, calling for a dictatorship of the proletariat during the period of revolution, with a ruthless liquidation of his own friends and colleagues—anyone who might conceivably pose a threat to his determination to establish a one-man cult, i.e., the personal dictatorship of Stalin.

To explain this schizophrenic behavior, Deutscher suggests that Stalin, the master of purges, "was Cromwell's and Robespierre's descendant. . . in a country accustomed over the ages to barbarous brutality in its rulers. Stalin, we should remember, was the descendant of Ivan the Terrible, Peter the Great, Nicholas I, and Alexander III. Indeed, Stalinism may be described as the amalgam of Marxism with Russia's primordial and savage backwardness."[20]

Maybe so. Certainly, the ideals of the revolution were immeasurably hurt by the tarnished image he gave them around the world. His myopic view, moreover, of an accomplished socialism in *One* state, Russia, versus many hostile states, fostered a narrow, self-serving nationalism that blinded him to the enormous benefits awaiting optimum cooperation between the Soviet Union and the rising Peoples' Republic of China. Stalin's failure to embrace this golden opportunity with open arms becomes the more appalling in light of the Marxist revolutions that are erupting in many countries, all of them together with Russia and China, comprising half of the world's population.

But we must give the devil his due. Quite a different myth of socialism in one state was also being widely circulated, for which Stalin can surely not be faulted. Concocted by the "enemy-states," says Deutscher—he was himself a prominent member of the Communist Party of Poland during Stalin's time, and expelled from the Party in 1932 as a leader of the opposition to Stalin—Deutscher says, nonetheless, in scathing words, that "an even more deceptive myth—a colossal myth—about the failure of socialism has come to dominate much of Western political thinking. . . . the West, however, has hardly any reason to view this outcome with self-righteousness. For when a Russian looks at the record of the West, in its relationship with Russia, what does he find there? The rapacious Peace of Brest Litovsk, the allied armed intervention against the Soviets, the blockade, the *cordon sanitaire*, the prolonged economic and diplomatic boycotts; and then Hitler's invasion, and the horrors of Nazi occupation, the long and clever delays by which Russia's allies postponed the opening of a second front against Hitler, while the Soviet armies were immolating themselves in battle; and, after 1945, the rapid reversal of the alliances, the nuclear blackmail, and the anti-communist frenzy of the cold war. What a record! What a record!"[21]

We have already touched upon a few critical moments of that record. They make it abundantly clear that if the Stalinist personality cult was a corruption of the Marxist/Leninist definition of the dictatorship fo the proletariat; namely, of the majority or the *propertyless poor*, translated into action for the duration of the revolution by a Central Body of trusted revolutionaries elected by the Party, then Stalin did at least hold a tight rein against the violent efforts of the many hostile states to destroy the One socialist state. The onslaught did, in fact, continue relentlessly from the time of its first failure in 1922 up to and even beyond the second world war.

The subject of violence, during moments of great human distress, opens up a whole pandora's box of myths popularly associated with revolution. We have mentioned it before; we need now to take a closer look at it because these myths, in the light of present-day international developments, are an infinitely greater obstacle to social progress than Stalin's notion of socialism in one state has turned out to be.

18

The Violence Syndrome and Social Revolution

After the first world war and the Soviet Union's survival against counter-revolution, came a period of glorious peace utterances by the great warrior nations of the West, and by Japan in the East. At the same time each of them was feverishly arming for the next military encounter destined to break out between them in 1939. Among the main factors in those war preparations were, again, the German Reich's determination to conquer the Russian Ukraine—bread basket of Europe—and Japan's designs on China's equally rich Manchuria. The rivalry between all the big powers was, of course, for possession of rich and strategic places everywhere.

The author of these pages remembers vividly a prophetic address given at the old Garrick Theater in Chicago, by Frederick Schuman, an astute young professor at the University of Chicago in the early 1930s. He had just returned from an onsite study of the international tensions in Europe. In Germany the industrial elite had just turned over the reins of government to Hitler. Schuman made his overall appraisal in dramatic style. He stood up there on the stage, took out his watch and held it with outstretched arm toward the audience:

> "Now", he said, "I should tell you that, based on human knowledge about falling bodies, this watch will fall to the floor if I open my hand. I cannot say with absolute certainty, but only on the strength of this knowledge that the watch will fall to the floor if I open my hand. But I can say this: To the extent that I know the watch will fall to the floor if I open my hand, to that extent am I certain war will break out in Europe before 1940."[1]

Schuman's prediction, nearly a decade before the violence of the second world war was unleashed, bears a kind of inverse relationship to the popular notion of violence that is supposedly unleashed by people engaged in social revolution against their reigning elites. The notion is created, largely, by the accounts of scholars, journalists, and historians accustomed to the social philosophy and life-style of upper

175

and middle-class society. In fairness, it should, however, also be said that the best of them do stress the fact that people resort to revolution when unrelieved economic hardships and social injustices become unbearable. But the violence syndrome associated with revolution remains.

This prevailing notion demands rectification. It requires, first of all, that we reiterate the biological imperative of the sanctity of life on a total ecological scale, and merge it with the societal imperative of reverence of life among *ourselves*. It is in this sense that the violence syndrome, the killing and maiming of human life, so widely attributed to the leaders of social revolution and their rank-and-file followers, has to be put into proper perspective.

Let us, now, set the conceptual base of the comparative sanctity of one individual human life against another. In order to understand the ultimate meaning of social revolution, and its role in the endangered human animal's struggle to survive, it is necessary to clarify what we have in mind; namely, that the life of one Emperor, one General, or one Minister, blasted out of existence by a bomb or a bullet, is as sacred, no more and no less, as is the life of one Peasant Soldier on the bottom of a mound of corpses, one obscure Civilian Youth strung to a tree, or one Peasant Girl, raped and murdered, when the forces of law and order are let loose in time of social revolution. If we remember this we can, on the one hand, make a true appraisal of the violence committed by people during social revolution and, on the other, of that committed by the ruling governments and their supportive elites during international warfare.

How does the violence syndrome square with the concept of reverence of life, so far as the behavior of peoples in rebellion against their oppressive political and economic rulers is concerned? How does it square with that of their governments, both in time of social revolution and when they are engaged in wars with other governments? Random examples from the records of modern history give us both answers.

In 1850 a rebellion of China's peasants, known as the Taiping (Heavenly Kingdom) Rebellion, erupted in the wake of severe droughts and widespread famine, from 1846 to '48. The spark that set it off came, unexpectedly, from foreign Christian missionaries who had fanned out into the countryside to spread the teachings of Christ. Two things caught the imagination of the peasants: one was Jesus' revolutionary doctrine of humility and love; the other, his lashing of ancient Rome's imperial and landowning aristocracies for their extravagant life-styles and hoarding of great wealth, while the great mass of the Empire's people were starving. Jesus' messages struck home; they applied precisely to the impoverishment of China's peasants at the hands of the corrupt Manchu Dynasty and greedy landlords.

The rebellion was initiated by an amazing, if obscure, village school teacher by the name of Hung Hsiu-chuang. Hung was "converted" by the example of the early Christian revolutionary spirit. It inspired him to sound the call of rebellion from his native city of Canton in south China. The poverty-stricken peasants responded by the tens of thousands, descending upon Canton to join him. They began by destroying the old idols that exemplified the authoritarian teachings of Confucius, then took to the hills to organize their revolution against their oppressive local landlords and despised Manchu Dynasty.

The Manchu stemmed from a coalition of warrior tribes to the northeast of China that had invaded China two hundred years ago. They deposed the native Ming Dynasty, subjugated the peasants, and imposed an arrogant rulership on the nation. They isolated themselves in their heavily armed castle-fortresses, as a contemptuous foreign conqueror, and flaunted the people's cherished ancient Chinese culture. By the time of the Taiping Rebellion, they had earned the deep hatred of the Chinese people.

So rapidly did the rebellion gain strength that by 1853 the ragged peasant army, equipped only with such guns, axes and other weapons as they had captured in their forays upon the great landlord estates, had taken possession of much of South China. Making Nanking their capital, Hung prepared, at once, to launch an expedition to the North, to dislodge the Manchu Dynasty from its stronghold in Peking. Simultaneously, however, he had also to meet the need to create a just and practical system of turning over to the peasants, the land taken from the landlords. He announced to the world that the rebel's plan was to distribute the land among the peasants, who would work it together and share the crop equitably—a forewarning of future revolutions! For the Taiping Rebellion, alas, came catastrophe.

The communal ownership of land challenged the whole system of private property. Faced with this common danger, all upper class contenders for power, foreign and domestic, put aside their differences and united to crush the uprising. The native nobility quickly made peace with the Manchu Dynasty. The Manchu, in turn, subdued their animosity toward the "barbarian" industrial tycoons of the West, whose lucrative operations in China threatened their own existence. Since the foreigners were in danger of being ousted, themselves, they responded eagerly to the frantic call for help.

Hung's army never made it to Peking. Instead, his soldiers were mowed down by the devastating firing power of the advanced military weaponry Europe's armaments manufacturers introduced into the struggle. Yet it took them over *ten years* to blast the determined peasant resistance out of every defendable stronghold across China's far-flung terrain. The perceptive historian, Robert Goldston sums it up:

> By the end of the Taiping revolt in 1864, much of the Celestial Empire had been ravaged and an estimated *ten million people killed*. But the scholar-landlord class had saved its privileges, the Manchu Dynasty had saved its decadent regime, and the western powers had saved their commerical exploitation of China.[2]

What was the body-count of the dead on either side? It is common knowledge that members of the privileged elites in government, industry and agriculture, are never personally on the front firing line. We may safely assume that most of the ten million dead were landless and impoverished peasants. Any doubt as to the extent to which the reigning elites rather than peoples in revolt, spurn the sanctity of life, will be put to rest by the next example.

In 1917 after the Russian revolution had begun, the German army under the command of General Hindenburg, made deep inroads into Russia. The Russian soldiers, ill equipped, ill fed, often starving, and forever out of ammunition, didn't have a chance against the superbly trained German troops who had the most modern machine guns, howitzers and cannon. A laconic note, written by Hindenburg, tells the story of the mechanized slaughter of helpless Russian soldiers: "In the Great War Ledger," he wrote, "the page on which the Russian losses were written has been torn out. No one knows the figures. Five or eight millions? We, too, have no idea. All we know is that sometimes in our battles with the Russians we had to remove the mounds of enemy corpses from before our trenches, in order to get a clear field of fire against fresh assaulting waves."[3]

We have noted the slaughter of 7 to 8 million Russian people by the invading forces of the Allied governments, from 1918 to '21. As to the military confrontations that these and other warrior nations ceaselessly carry on against each other, conservative estimates place the number of dead in the First World War at 10,000,000 and the wounded at 20,000,000! Statisticians and historians of the Second World War find the casualties so much greater and far-flung as to consider them incalculable. Such scientifically planned mass killings by past and contemporary governmental elites make a hollow mockery of their professed reverence of life.

The American invasion of Korea in 1950 to '53 was made under the pseudo name of a United Nations police-action. The world-affairs scholar, Roland Stromberg, wrote the following:

"The greatest sufferers were the Koreans, themselves, whose country, north and south, was reduced to rubble. The civilian death was enormous. Out of a population of 30,000,000 Koreans, perhaps 3,000,000 were killed! (The American losses were 25,000 dead, British 600.) The war was sickening. 'There is no more war,' was Reginald Thompson's final word in "Cry Korea"; he remembered only the slaughter of women and children. To call such carnage 'police action' seemed to verge on the obscene."

Then came the Vietnam war against the rebelling peasants and industrial workers seeking to oust their foreign exploiters, first the French (1949–'54) then the Americans (1954–73); again, more than 1,000,000 dead Vietnamese and millions wounded. (American losses 50,000 dead, many more wounded.) And now the "unthinkable" nuclear arms race!

In contrast to this are the on-location reports on the Russian Revolution by American journalists like John Reed, Albert Rhys Williams, and Louise Bryant, who, though sympathetic to the struggles of oppressed peoples for liberation, were recognized as vigorously independent, truthful, and competent reporters. Their first-hand observations on the respect for life displayed by rank-and-file Russian soldiers, peasants and workers, and the relatively minor violence that occurred before the upper-class counter-revolution struck, are reiterated time and again in their reports.

Trotsky himself had this to say in his *Memoirs*: "When the February victory was fully confirmed, they began to count up the victims. In Petrograd they counted 1443 killed and wounded, 869 of them soldiers, and 60 of these officers." He then cited these figures to show that the initial success of the revolution was *not* bloodless, as many sympathetic though uninformed liberals joyfully declared at the time, but rather that the rank-and-file soldiers of the St. Petersburg garrison mutinied, en-masse, to join their friends and relatives in the insurrection, and were killed and injured in the action. "Yet," he added, "how tiny was this body-count of the dead and maimed, compared to the Great Slaughters perpetrated by elitist governments throughout history."[4]

We have alluded earlier to this self-exterminating behavior of human beings, incited by their governments to engage in periodic forays of mass murder against neighboring and even far removed peoples;

and the people of the "enemy" were incited by their governments to do likewise, and to laud the ugly spectable in poetry and song—a phenomenon that is unmatched by any other earthly creature.

The Russian and later the Chinese revolutions challenged, for the first time in history, this strange killer behavior, successfully for the moment, if only problematically for the future. But in their momentary triumph and subsequent establishment of two firmly rooted communist societies, embracing over a quarter of the world's population, they have made the *myth* of violent social revolution an ineradicable record of history.

19

The Marxist/Leninist Prelude in China

If the writer of these lines had to name the ten greatest benefactors of humankind since the dawn of history, high on the list would be the incomparable Mao Tse-tung: philosopher, post, visionary extraordinary, leader of China's impoverished peasants, in their agonizing but ultimately victorious social revolution of 1949.

Reverberations of the victorious October Revolution in Russia spread quickly to impoverished and oppressed China. the great Chinese patriot, Sun Yat-sen, who led the so-called First Chinese Revolution of 1911 that toppled the Manchu dynasty, discovered the futility of trying to establish a western-style democracy. Although he was elected President of the Provisional Government, the traditional breed of Chinese warlords lost no time in forcing his resignation, each of them eager to restore a new dynasty, with himself as Emperor. This led Sun Yat-sen to ally himself with Lenin in 1921, when the Chinese Communist Party was founded.[1]

During this formative stage of revolt, the CCP was but a loosely organized Marxist group within a much broader nationalist movement, known as the Kuomintang, in a common struggle against the ruling warlords, and Japan's threat of invading Manchuria and China's important industrial areas along the eastern seacoast.

Simultaneously, Karl Marx's socialist philosophy was finding its way to many of the better educated people of China. By 1917 societies had already sprung up in Canton, Nanchang, Shanghai, and Peking, to study ways of achieving social change. Among the young revolutionaries were such now famous ones as Mao Tse-tung, Chou En-lai, Chu-Teh, Lin Piao, Ch'en Tu-hsiu, Ch'en Yi, Liu Shao-ch'i, Teng Ying-ch'ao, (Mm. Chou En-lai), Ts'ai Ho-sen, Li Lisan, Ch'u Ch'iu-pai, Li Ta-chao, and numerous others destined to make history. Some visited Moscow for indoctrination, a duality of contrasting experiences that led to better and costly strife within the CCP. We shall have more to say about this.

China, like pre-revolutionary Russia, was a lucrative colonial possession of the industrialists and bankers of Europe, Japan and the United States, to be divided among them and milked of its coal, mineral and food-bearing resources, on the one hand, and exploited of its farming and industrial human resources, on the other. As in Russia, too, not a few of China's landed gentry connived with the foreign investors, to share in the profitable new commercial and manufacturing techniques, at the awesome price of periodic famine and starvation for the Chinese people.

At the turn of the century the foreign investors, led by the fast growing American multinational corporations, managed to impose upon China the so-called "open door" policy, permitting them to establish International Settlements in China's major industrial centers. One of the legal provisions in these international enclaves gave the foreign personnel the right, should they have violated any civil or criminal statutes, to be tried, not under the laws of China but of their own country.

When a continuous stream of unpunished atrocities committed by these foreigners upon an outraged Chinese people, resulted in what has become known as the Boxer Rebellion, the uprising was mercilessly crushed by the foreign military forces stationed in each International Settlement, followed by mass executions, heavy indemnities, and stricter enforcement of the insufferable open door policy.[2]

More devastating, however, subsequent to the eruption of the Chinese revolution in the later 1920s, was the reality that China had its own Kerensky, in the person of Chiang Kai-shek. Chiang was far more shrewd, ruthless, and powerful than his Russian counter-part. As one of China's wealthiest bankers, a high member of the nation's social and financial elite, and a founder of the prestigious Whampoa Military Academy, Chiang was a shoo-in to become the Supreme Commander of the Kuomintang forces—in behalf of the rich Chinese landowners and of foreign industrialists.[3]

To oversome this Asiatic "military-industrial complex", Mao Tse-tung had to come up with a strategy that was in direct contradiction to the orthodox Marxist/Leninist one. He announced it as early as 1927, in his classic "*Report of an Investigation into the Peasant Movement in Hunan.*" The province of Hunan was his beloved homeland.

Contrary to Marx's thesis of the Dictatorship of the Proletariat, which declared that the role of exclusive revolutionary leadership had to be carried out by the industrial (propertyless) proletariat, Mao's Report called the poor peasants the "main force" of China's revolution. When, in accordance with this assessment, he called for confiscation of the landlords' lands, the party's Communist Central Committee promptly rejected his proposal. Nonetheless, Mao adhered to it with unswerving tenacity throughout the revolution, and against all opposition.[4]

Another of his unprecedented tactics came after the revolution was underway. It demanded indoctrination of the Red Army's soldiers as to proper conduct towards peasants, while engaged in battle in peasant territory. Mao Tse-tung, by then the most trusted and respected leader of the revolution, soon succeeded in instilling into the minds of the top leadership and rank-and-file soldiers of the Red Army, as well as of the peasants themselves and of many CCC members the concept of "service to the people." This became a matter of inviolate daily conduct for commanders and troops alike. It stressed the following Eight Points:

1. Replace all doors when you leave a house.*
2. Return and roll up the straw matting on which you sleep;
3. Be courteous and polite to the people, and help them when you can;
4. Return all borrowed articles;
5. Replace all damaged articles;
6. Be honest in all transactions with peasants;
7. Pay for all articles purchased;
8. Be sanitary, and, especially, establish latrines a safe distance from people's houses.*

It is well to remember that these simple, homey orders, coupled with the overall concept of service to the people, were issued to an army composed almost entirely of young peasants and city workers, who were *totally unaccustomed* to such solicitude for poor people, whether from military, propertied or any other form of authority. After a period of trial and error, to overcome mistrust and encrusted habits on both sides, the instructions were carried out beyond all literal meaning of the words. The soldiers helped plant and harvest crops, mend fences, tools and equipment, repair houses, and aid the older people with their chores.[5]

The peasants responded with great hospitality, and they spread the word that the Red Bandits were not what the landlords and Chiang

---

*Per note by Edgar Snow, in his Red Star Over China, page 173: "This order to replace doors is not so enigmatical as it sounds. The wooden doors of a Chinese house are easily detachable, and are often taken down at night, put across bars, and used for an improvised bed."

Kai-shek's soldiers said they were, but that they were the friends and protectors of poor people! Even isolated warrior tribes, hostile to farming peoples, like the Lolos who had occupied the densely forested and mountainous parts of Szechuan for centuries, and never made peace with the Chinese, were won over by the Red Army during its Long March in 1934, about which more later.

Parenthetically, the writer is of the opinion that without the Maoist dictum, the Chinese Revolution would have been lost; with it, the Red Army proved to be invincible against every combination of superior military armaments, technical or material resources, hurled against it by Chiang Kai-shek and his supporters among the Chinese bankers and industrialists, and those of Japan, Europe and the United States.

The Incredible Causes Of The Revolution

We know of no more unforgettable words, stressing the grim realities that fueled the Chinese Revolution than those used by Edgar Snow. Prior to 1936, when he became the only prominent American journalist able to penetrate the cordon of Japanese and Kuomintang troops, to make contact with the Red Army isolated from the outside world, he had this to say:

> During the great Northwest famine, which lasted roughly for three years and affected four huge provinces, I visited some of the drought-stricken areas in Suiyuan, on the edge of Mongolia, in June, 1929. How many people starved to death I do not accurately know, and probably no one ever will know; it is forgotten now. A conservative semi-official figure of 3,000,000 is often accepted, but I am not inclined to doubt other estimates ranging as high as 6,000,000. . . .
>
> I had come to the East looking for the "glamor of the Orient." . . . (But here in Suiyuan), for the first time in my life I came abruptly upon men who were dying because they had nothing to eat. In those hours of nightmare I spent in Suiyuan I saw thousands of men, women, and children starving to death before my eyes.
>
> Have you ever seen a man—a good honest man who has worked hard, a "law-abiding citizen," doing no serious harm to anyone—when he has had no food for more than a month? It is a most agonizing sight. His dying flesh hangs from him in wrinkled folds; you can clearly see every bone in his body; his eyes stare out unseeing; and even if he is a youth of twenty he moves like an ancient crone, dragging himself from spot to spot. If he has been lucky he has long ago sold his wife and daughters. He has sold everything he owns. . . . Sometimes he has, indeed, even sold the

last rag of decency, and he sways there in the scorching sun, his testicles dangling from him like withered olive seeds—the last grim jest to remind you that this was once a man.

Children are even more pitiable, with their skeletons bent over and misshapen, their crooked bones, their little arms like twigs, and their purpling bellies, filled with bark and sawdust, protruding like tumors. Women lie slumped in corners, waiting for death. . . . But there are, after all, not many women and girls. Most of them had died or been sold. . . . I saw fresh corpses on the streets of Saratsi, and in the village I had seen shallow graves where the victims of famine. . . .

But these are not the most shocking things after all. The most shocking thing was that in many of those towns there were still rich men, rice hoarders, wheat hoarders, money-lenders, and landlords, with armed guards to defend them, while they profiteered enormously—officials (who) danced or played with sing-song girls—there were grain and food, and had been for months; in Peking and Tientsin and elsewhere were thousands of tons of wheat and millet, collected by the Famine Commission (mostly by contributions from abroad), but which could not be shipped to the starving. Why not?

Because in the Northwest there were some militarists who wanted to hold all of their railroad rolling stock and would release none of it to the east, while in the east there were other Kuomintang generals who would send no rolling stock westward—even to starving people—because they feared it would be seized by their rivals.

While famine raged the Commission decided to build a big canal (with American funds) to help flood some of the lands baked by the drought. The officials gave them every cooperation—and promptly began to buy, for a few cents an acre, all the lands to be irrigated. A flock of vultures descended upon this benighted country and purchased from the starving farmers thousands of acres for the tax arrears, or for a few coppers, and held it to await rainy days and tenants.

Yet the great majority of those people who died did so without any act of protest.

"Why don't they revolt?" I asked myself. "Why don't they march in a great army and attack the scoundrels?" . . .

I was profoundly puzzled by their passivity. For a while I thought nothing would make a Chinese fight. . . . I was mistaken. The Chinese peasant was not passive; he was not a coward. He would fight when given a method and organization, leadership, a workable program, hope—*and arms*. The development of "communism" had proved this. . . .[6]

And he did fight, once those conditions became a reality; history has amply recorded it. The fact that he did rise up in a great and victorious peasant army, takes us back to our overview of the ensuing revolutionary developments, a fact that begins with the emergence and coalescence of a young leadership embued with the spirit of revolution and ideas of how to make it triumph.

The Groping Beginnings of Social Revolution in China

After Sun Ya-sen's successful campaign to topple the Manchu Dynasty in 1911, came two and a half decades of searching for viable alternatives to the tyrannical rule of China's warlords in the peasant country, and both foreign and domestic oppression in the cities. It was a time when the revolutionary leadership, so aptly described by Snow as the prerequisite to a poor people's successful rebellion, began to assert itself. The first steps did, indeed, come from exceptional middle and upper class individuals possessing managership, education, keen minds, and a great sensitivity to human suffering caused by social injustice.

Sir Federick Leith-Ross, British Emissary to China at the time, said: "There is no middle class in China, only the incredibly poor and very rich."[7] Nonetheless, things began to happen. Given the setting of a decadent Chinese feudalism, in an era of burgeoning industrial capitalism, the first rebels consisted mostly of bright students, some courageous university and middle school professors, and a few socially conscious and gifted upper class leaders. They came forth with ideas, ranging from minor reforms to anarchism, constitutional monarchy to bourgeoise democracy, anti-militarism to utopian socialism. To unite these dissimilar ideas under a common goal, Sun Yat-sen founded the Kuomintang, calling for a national liberation movement, to liquidate the reactionary landed gentry on the home front, and to prevent Japan from invading China.

Surprisingly enough, this was a program that both Mao Tse-tung and Chiang Kai-shek, the two undisputed heads of the contending forces destined to shape China's future, agreed to support. As a wealthy banker, Chiang had little or no interest in preserving the agrarian aristocracy, and much to lose from Japanese encroachment on the industrial elite's own holdings. Mao, on the other hand, was still an evolutionary socialist, receptive to a system of bourgeoise democracy as a first step to socialism; and thus he, too, became an enthusiastic supporter of the Kuomintang movement. The thinking was also shared by many students, teachers and writers, who were setting the tone of the rebelling societies and study groups in China's cities and towns.

But Mao was an avid reader. In his student days and during a brief career as a normal school teacher in Hunan, he had read the *Communist Manifesto*, Karl Kautsky's, *The Class Struggle*, Charles Darwin's, *Origin of Species*, and the works of such prominent western scholars as Adam Smith and John Stuart Mill. In sharpening his own revolutionary ideas, he was most influenced by his professorial friends, Ch'en Tu-hsiu and Li Ta-chao, who became the leading co-founders of the CCP, May 16, 1921.

The Unfolding of Marxism/Leninism

After the triumph of the Russian October Revolution, members of the societies and study groups flocked to Europe for first-hand observation of events, not only in Moscow, but London, Paris, Berlin, where revolutionary fervor was running high. As already mentioned, there followed the heated debates, reminiscent of the 1903 pre-revolution disputes in Russia, between the evolutionary socialists (Mensheviks) and the advocates of forcible seizure of the state (Bolsheviks). Mao Tse-tung, despite his insistence that the poor peasants are the main force of the Chinese Revolution, sided with the "Bolsheviks", and soon, the pressure of events made the CCP follow him or perish.

Meanwhile, news of the Bolshevik revolution in Russia continued to spread throughout China. The CCP began vigorously to organize railway workers, municipal employees, and other industrial workers, while the Red Army organized the peasants and miners in rural areas. Furthermore, the Party voted at its Third Congress in 1923, to help the Kuomintang, still commanded by Chiang Kai-shek, in its struggle against the ravaging warlords.

The CCP/KMT united front was, however, a shaky arrangement at best, with only moments of reluctant cooperation, and an increasing mutual hostility. Signs of its approaching end soon appeared. On the Communist side came an outpouring of Mao Tse-tung's writings, including the *Analysis of Classes in Chinese Society* calling for more effective organization of the peasants (1926), and the aforementioned report on the peasant movement in Hunan. Both aroused great opposition in the Party and the Kuomintang. Many old friends parted, some became bitter enemies.

Within the CCP, the Fifth Congress of the Party, May 27, 1927, made the infighting official. Mao presented his case to the Central

Committee. It was a moment of personal crisis for Mao, testing his loyalty to the peasants and his judgment as to the options for achieving the socialist goals in China. Even his old teacher, Ch'en Tu-hsiu, voiced strong objection to Mao's thesis. Moscow-trained Li Li-san declared his emphasis on peasant leadership to be in violation of Marxist/Leninist principles; Mao insisted it was but a tactic adapted to the Chinese situation. Nevertheless, the majority of the CCC delegates held to the position that it was the uprisings in the cities, the seizure of factories through armed struggle by the city workers, and the eventual capture of big cities, that proved to be sound tactics in the Russian Revolution.

Mikhail Borodin, Stalin's chief advisor at the meeting, heartily agreed. The CCC not only rejected Mao's thinking, but the Party reprimanded him on subsequent occasions.[8]

Things now moved swiftly and disastrously for the Communist movement. Chiang Kai-shek, whose ear had been keenly attuned all along to the outspoken CCP plans to take political and economic control of China, lost no time in launching his first annihilation campaign of the Communists. Throughout the ensuing struggle he showed himself to be as unscrupulous a political operator as he was a self-seeking Shanghai banker. By the late 1920s his profitable investments in Japan gave him second thoughts about the danger of a Japanese invasion; it actually offered mutually attractive investment opportunities for himself and his banker associates.

But public fear of Japan was mounting. There were strong historical reasons for it, which Chiang could not ignore. In the Sino-Japanese war of 1894–'95, Japan had forced China to cede Formosa and abandon ancient claims to suzerainty over Korea. When she defeated Russia in the war of 1904, for control of important Chinese Pacific ports, she recovered possession of Port Arthur and Dairen, and seized the Russian concessions of South Manchuria. In 1914 Japan made further demands upon China, which had the intent of reducing China to a vassal state; and, when in 1918 the Versailles Treaty awarded Germany's colony in Tsingtao to Japan, this led to the great Chinese student protest movement of May 4.

Chiang had to come up with a plan to allay anti-Japanese patriotic fervor among the people, while, also, striking a crushing blow at the Communists. He thought of a way to accomplish the latter, and to feign making military preparations to thwart the Japanese, who were, in fact, well along in their plans to invade.

As to the Communists, Generalissimo Chiang Kai-shek had, of late, "allowed" Communists to serve on the Central Executive Committee of the Kuomintang, along with his own leaders. When Chou En-lai returned from Europe in 1924, where he had studied socialist theory and practice, Chiang made him Deputy Director of the political department of Whampoa Military Academy while, at the same time, serving as secretary of the Communist Party.

With characteristic duplicity in his dealings with the communists, Chiang began his counter-revolution. He ordered Chou En-lai to prepare an expedition against the warlords of the North, some of whom connived with Japan to serve their own interests. This, lied Chiang to Chou, would be the first step in the anti-Japanese military campaign.

Chou En-lai, though without the experience for such a big undertaking, proceeded to mobilize 600,000 workers from Shanghai and surrounding industrial areas. They eventually took the city, being careful, however, not to touch the International Settlement. Meanwhile Chiang, having lured many Communist leaders to one convenient place, was conferring with Shanghai's bankers and representatives of the big powers in the Settlement, as to the most effective method of striking the first blow at the revolutionaries. We quote Snow again as to their decision:

> They reached agreement to cooperate against the Chinese and their Russian allies—until then also Chiang's allies. Given large sums by Shanghai's bankers, and the blessings of the foreign authorities, including guns and armored cars, Chiang was also helped by powerful Settlement and Concession underworld leaders. Installed in the foreigner's armored cars, and attired in Nationalist uniforms, the gangsters carried out a night operation in coordination with Chiang's troops, moving in from the rear and other flanks.
>
> Taken by complete surprise by troops considered friendly, the militiamen were massacred. . . . Chou estimated the toll of the "Shanghai massacre" at 5,000 lives. He himself was captured by Chiang Kai-shek's Second Division and turned over to Chiang's execution squad. . . . But the brother of the division commander had been Chou's student at Whampoa, and he helped him to escape.[9]

Henceforth, declared the Generalissimo, the Kuomintang is anti-Communist, and any violation of this is punishable by death. With the concurrence of the powerful governments in the International Settlements, he promptly established the *National Government of China* with Nanking as the capital. He announced to the world that his first task would be to annihilate the "Red Bandits" and restore his country to peace and prosperity, a declaration that was directed, of course, to the upper-class elites of the world and their largely supportive middle-class, their professional and technical staffs, and the independent shopkeepers and small property owners; all welcomed the good news and passed it along.

20

The Chinese Civil War That Was a Revolution

After Chiang's massacre of Communists, Mao's supporters and many other CCP leaders fled westward into peasant country. But the catastrophe brought its own reward. By forcing the Maoists into a geographic position from which they were able to lay the ground work for a peasant-led liberation movement, Chiang gave Mao the very setting for which he had been pleading, unsuccessfully, within the Party.

The beginning was made, of necessity, in the provinces to which they had fled: Hunan, Hupeh, Kiangso. There, under Mao's leadership and that of the remarkable General Chu Teh of China's upper classes, the retreating insurrectionists reorganized their forces and began plans to expand. We should add here that Chu was still a high ranking officer of the Kuomintang, but he was shocked by Chiang's breach of trust, severed his connections with him, and joined the Communists.

In July of 1927, only a few months after the Shanghai debacle, many of the CCP's former urban forces had reassembled in Hunan and were being reorganized. When Chu arrived shortly afterwards, Mao had already won the peasants and Hanyang miners of Hunan to the Communist cause. They rallied to his support and organized wide-spread uprisings in Hunan and the neighboring provinces. They joined the fighting force in great numbers, and, as their ranks swelled, they named it the First Division of the First Peasants' and Workers' Army, which was later to become the Red Army.[1]

It was in this crucial start-up period that Chu Teh's military genius and experience began to assert themselves. He was, in fact, to become the most famous and loyal military strategist of the revolution. It was, however, also a time when the Party's military decisions were still being made by the Moscow trained "Twenty-Eight Bolsheviks", headed by Li Li-san and the Soviet Union's international Comintern, whose advice to the CCP Central Committee sometimes carried the weight of an order. There was, also, a deep-felt compulsion at the time, shared even by Mao Tse-tung and Chu Teh, to strike back at the mercenary armies of the Kuomintang for the atrocities committed in Shanghai and other cities.

Given the critical situation, the exponents of the two opposing positions had little choice but to cooperate. Let us, then, touch on a few high spots of the ensuing ten years (1927–'37), at the end of which the validity of Mao's thesis was confirmed and the revolution able to proceed under a united leadership.

On August 1, 1927, Mao's First Army was ordered, in accordance with official CCP policy, to launch the now historic and ill-fated Nanchang uprising. It failed and became one more example of the undesirability of making the capture of heavily fortified cities a prime objective. Nonetheless, a week later the CC, still functioning underground in Shanghai, ordered Mao to prepare an attack on Changsha, the Hunan capital. But this time Mao and Chu held off. They clearly saw their first task as one of consolidating and stabilizing their military control of the Hunan-Kiangsi-Kwangtung provinces, and from there expanding north and west, into other largely peasant territories.

For the next two years the First Army entrenched itself in the mountain recesses and villages of the rugged Chingkangshan chain in Hunan, where nature offers its own well protected mountain strongholds. From this military base they began their attacks on the troops sent there by the Nanking government. Now the emerging Red Army, fighting on its own familiar ground, and with enthusiastic support from the peasants, miners, and other workers, inflicted one defeat after another on the invading forces. Rapidly, it extended its revolutionary control over an ever widening territory. At the same time, Mao Tse-tung and Chu Teh agreed that they must now fulfill their responsibilities to the peasants and the rural industrial workers; namely, to divide the great landlord estates among them and, by democratic election, to establish soviets wherever the communists won control.

The Red Army's military successes made it necessary for Chu Teh to organize his forces into numerous regional, district and local divisions. In response, Chiang demanded and received the most modern weaponry from the European powers and the United States. Though this caused the raw revolutionary forces to suffer heavy losses, the saving result was that for every hundred peasants and workers killed, a thousand replaced them. Many were barely out of their teens; in the course of the struggle, some became shrewd and courageous commanders, others, even famous generals.

Early in 1929, numerous armies, under the over-all command of

Chu Teh, with the loyal support of rising military leaders like Ho Lung, P'eng Teh-huai and Hsu Hsiang-chien, began a series of campaigns that drove Nanking's White Armies out of most of the strategic points of the targeted areas. This ended the Red Army's confinement to its original Chingkangshan mountain base. It was, however, at Chingkangshan that the now famous Maoist guerrilla slogan was first adopted successfully:

1. When the enemy advances, we retreat!
2. When the enemy halts and encamps, we trouble them!
3. When the enemy seeks to avoid battle, we attack!
4 When the enemy retreats, we pursue![2]

Throughout all the long years of the revolution, these tactics proved to be fundamental to victory. But in autumn of 1929, Mao and Chu were ready to heed the CCP-CC demand to attack Changsha, making sure, however, that their forces in the surrounding country were securely positioned and manned against any attempt by the Kuomintang troops to make a breakthrough. One of the Red Army's divisions, the Third Army Corp, led by P'eng Teh-huai, succeeded in occupying the city, but had to withdraw to avoid entrapment by the arrival of heavily armored Chiang Kai-shek forces.

The following year the First and Third Army Corps merged and, commanded by Chu Teh, himself, moved on Changsha again, only to find that the city was more strongly garrisoned than previously, and new enemy troops were continuing to pour into Hunan, to attack all the sovietized areas. Chu wisely withdrew, to engage the new forces on his own grounds where they, and not his own men, would be the sitting ducks. Chu waited for the attack, and it came quickly. First, however, Chiang announced to the world that he would now begin his *First Extermination Campaign* against the communists. Following is a summary of what Mao told the American journalist, Edgar Snow, years later:

Chiang Kai-shek's forces of over 100,000 men began an encirclement of the Red areas. Chu Teh, with only 40,000 troops, managed to overcome their attack by skillful maneuvering and guerrilla warfare. Within four months, Nanking launched its *Second Campaign* with more than 200,000 men; and, again, Chu lured them into wild rugged territory, where the invasion was not only crushed, but the Reds captured 13,000 soldiers and their commanders, along with huge quantities of guns and ammunition. Nonetheless, Chiang kept coming on one month later, this time with an army of 300,000, for a final extermination of the "Red Bandits". He was driven back again, with heavy losses on both sides.

A short period of comparative peace ensued, during which the *Central Soviet Government* was established, with Mao Tse-tung as chairman and Chu Teh as commander-in-chief of the Red Army, December 11, 1931. The other important event earlier that year, as already mentioned, was Japan's invasion of northern China and expansion of its military control of important east-coast seaports.

In April 1933, according to Mao's report, began the fourth and, for Nanking, perhaps the most disastrous of its "extermination campaigns". In short, so badly defeated was its army, that Chiang Kai-shek wrote to Ch'en Ch'eng, his field commander, that he considered this defeat the greatest humiliation in his life.[3]

But now came a crucial moment for the Chinese Revolution, one that was destined to decide its very survival or collapse. The crisis arose, surprisingly enough, out of the chain of striking military successes of the Red Army. It aroused great fear among the big industrialists and international financiers of Europe and the United States. They didn't relish the thought of a communist society in China, joining the one in Russia and making common cause against capitalism. Above all, they did not want to lose their profitable investments in China, as had already happened in Russia. In a common decision to prevent this, they not only rushed shiploads of ammunition, guns, tanks, bombs, planes, and millions of dollars for other supplies and additional troops, but made it a condition that Chiang turn over command of the *Fifth Extermination Campaign* to the experienced and noted General von Falkenshausen of the German army.

Abandoned were Chiang's attempts to engage the enemy in direct battle. Instead, the thorough-going German commander spent a year building hundreds of small blockhouses around an area 200 miles in diameter, to encircle the communists with a ring of steel and bullets. Each blockhouse was fortified with machine gun and artillery fire, and equipped with an instant communications system with the others and with central command. Over all this were 400 aircraft to bomb the Red troops into submission.

Nothing was left to chance. Without resorting to hand-to-hand combat, Falkenhausen began an economic blockade to starve out everybody, soldiers and civilians alike, while bombarding them from the air. Only when the spirit and physical stamina of the Red Army were crushed, only then would his heavily armored troops close in for the slaughter and surrender. Even in this pre-attack period, the enormity of Falkenhausen's success was staggering. According to Chou En-lai, the Red Army suffered 60,000 casualties in the Kiangsi siege alone; the Kuomintang press releases estimated that about 1,000,000 people were killed or starved to death. And this does not include the devastation wreaked upon the people in the sovietized districts in the provinces of Hunan, Hupeh, Honan, Anhui, Fukien. Whole areas, wrote Edgar Snow, were depopulated, sometimes by forced mass migrations, sometimes by the simpler expedient of mass executions.[4]

Everyone close to the struggle—peasants, workers, and soldiers—thought that the revolution had come to a tragic end. Strangely enough, the very flawlessness of Falkenhausen's plans for the Fifth Extermination Campaign, doomed his methods to ultimate failure. His first, and most serious, lowly human error was derived from the thoroughness of his scientific preparations. It took him a long time to build the heavily fortified blockhouses and inter-communications system. This enabled the partisans of Kiangsi and the neighboring provinces to ferret out every step he was planning even before he took it, and to get the information to the Red Army through places where the ring of steel had not yet been fully closed. Most important, they could keep the besieged communist forces abreast of how the meticulous Falkenhausen deployed his troops, where they were weakest and where they stored their guns and ammunition.

In January, 1934, the Central Soviet Government called an All China Congress in the soviet capital of Juichin, to assess the desperate situation. The problem of what to do was assigned to a small committee of trusted leaders. The decision was made, in great secrecy, to try to evacuate the entrapped Red Army, consisting of some 90,000 soldiers and their commanders. The strategy was to move quickly by way of obscure mountain and wilderness routes known only to well informed Kiangsi natives, and from there to reach territory beyond the ring of blockhouses, where the great mass of dedicated partisans will eagerly help the newly established Soviet Government move its headquarters and Red Army to China's vast Northwest. And, thus, began the plans for *The Long March*.

From the standpoint of the far-reaching impact that the Chinese Revolution has been making upon world history, the decision to embark upon the Long March is the First Cause, the *sine qua non*. An enormous amount of fascinating literature about it and the events that followed, has been pouring out of printing presses in every language; and it is available in the public libraries of every country around the world. We shall, therefore, limit our coverage to a summary of five noteworthy developments: the Kiangsi Evacuation, the Long March, the Yenan Period, the Sian Incident, the Communist Triumph.

Parenthetically, we believe it is necessary to make one further prefatory remark, due to the fact that much of this part of our research on the Chinese Revolution was made back in the late 1960s. It is that the bulk of the data comes from the on-location reports by Edgar Snow, the internationally respected American journalist, historian, and visiting college professor in Peking, who, aided by Sun Yat-sen's widow, was the *only foreign reporter* able to penetrate the military blockade isolating the communists from the rest of the world. Why we relied chiefly on Edgar Snow can best be said in his own words when he met with Mao Tse-tung in Yenan, after the Long March: "It seemed to me one of the amazing facts of our age that, during the entire history of the soviets in South China, not a single 'outside' foreign observer had entered Red territory—the only communist-ruled nation in the world besides the USSR. Everything written about the southern soviets by foreigners was therefore secondary material."

The Evacuation

The ceaseless help of the peasants and city workers of South China, to the extent of sacrificing their lives by the hundreds of thousands, was indispensable to the Red Army's escape; with it, Mao and Chu were able to accomplish the massive evacuation of their forces for the targeted date of October 16, 1934. In fact, the first moves were already underway weeks earlier. While some participating peasants in the Kiangsi area "leaked" presumably real but shrewdly misleading information to Falkenhausen's carefully selected men about Mao's plans, small detachments of the Red Army distracted the Kuomintang forces with feigned escape attempts moving north through Kiangsi, when the actual retreat headed south and west.

Most of the estimated 90,000 moved so swiftly and secretly at night that they had been marching for several days before the Falkenhausen headquarters became aware of what was taking place. Having succeeded in withdrawing the regular troops from the northern front and replacing them with peasant and worker partisans, Chu had concentrated practically the whole Red Army in southern Kiangsi. Then, totally unexpectedly, he suddenly mobilized and attacked the Hunan and Kwangtung lines of fortifications. "They took these by assault," records Snow, "put their astonished enemy on the run, and never stopped until they had occupied the ribbon of blockading forts and entrenchments on the southern front. This gave them the roads to the south and to the west, along which their vanguard began its sensational trek (northward)."

Even in these first moments of the Great March, they had, with the help of thousands of peasants—men, women and children—stripped the fortresses of such enormous quantities of bullets, machine guns and rifles, that they had to bury much of the captured loot well along their trail, in the knowledge that the Red peasants would be able to dig them up again in time of need. Until then, thousands of peasant Red Guards continued guerrilla fighting, keeping up an effective rearguard action, which enabled the main forces to get well underway before Chiang Kai-shek and von Falkenhausen could mobilize new troops to pursue them. To lead these courageous partisans, many thousands of whom were captured and executed, the Red Army left behind some of its ablest commanders.[5]

The Long March

Well informed historians and students of the Chinese Revolution see the Long March as one of the most daring and difficult undertakings in all military history. Aside from the fact that the soldiers had to cover a distance of *six thousand miles* on foot and, with the help of some horses and oxen, haul guns and munitions, and such cooking utensils, tools, and medical supplies as the peasants in the sparsely populated surrounding area could make available, there were even more forbidding obstacles to be endured.

By January, 1935, the Red Army had overcome the last Kuomintang defenses, plus those of the local armies of the hostile warlords, and was well on the way to its northern destination. But, again, according to Snow:

> For the next four months the army was almost constantly moving, and the most energetic combat and fighting took place. Through many, many difficulties, across the longest and deepest and most dangerous rivers of China, across some of the highest and most hazardous mountain passes, through the country of fierce aborigines, through the empty grasslands, through cold and through heat, through wind and snow and rainstorm, pursued by half the White armies of China, through all these natural barriers, and fighting its way past the local troops of Kwangtum, Hunan, Kwangsi, Kweichow, Yunnan, Sikang, Szechuan, Kansu, and Shensi, the Red Army at last reached northern Shensi in October, 1935, and enlarged its base in China's great Northwest.

It is estimated that in the year-long trek, the casualties in battle and from starvation and sheer physical exhaustion—during the first winter months alone—were equal to the total number of soldiers who began the march, to which have to be added the losses of the remaining seven months![6]

The Yenan Period

Shifting the retreating Red Army's headquarters to the Northwest, proved to be a master stroke, a long-range blessing that has to be weighed against all the suffering and hardships of the Long March. Among the great advantages gained, in point of time, was the ground work that had been laid in the Northwest, as far back as the early 1920s, by dedicated communist peasant leaders like the beloved Marxist "Robin Hood", Liu Chih-tan. Born of a well-to-do landlord family in Pao An, north Shensi, he, and many other talented young men left home, to be indoctrinated and trained in those years by the founders of the Chinese Communist Party in the central and east-coast provinces. Some attended the Whampoa Military Academy in Canton, capital of Kwangtung and a center of communist activity in south China.

Over a period of ten years, they had established a formidable army, skilled in applying Mao's guerrilla tactics in the wild hills and grasslands of north Shensi. By the time the bedraggled and exhausted soldiers of the Long March had arrived in Pao An, and shortly thereafter set up their capital in Yenan, these partisans had organized soviets and underground military forces in many towns and villages of north China, to spread the communist message. True to the Maoist goals, they had already founded the Shensi Provincial Soviet Government in the village of An Ting, created a soviet training school and military headquarters, and adopted the Kiangsi plan of administering economic affairs.

On the opposite side, all the disadvantages were now on the shoulders of Nanking's generals and mercenary soldiers: great distances from their source of supplies and manpower; unfamiliar, sweeping and mountainous territory; a diversity of native Chinese tribal and peasant inhabitants, all of them harboring a deep hostility against the wealthy east-coast industrialists and their own local big landlords. And all had learned that when the Kuomintang captures a territory, the landlords, high taxes, and oppression come back; and when the Red Army wins, the poor and middle peasants are freed from this.

As to the White Army's mercenary soldiers—the core of Chiang's troops—when faced with guerrilla warfare in wild and desolate country, they were helpless and ran or deserted. Although billions of dollars worth of machine guns, aircraft and bombs, made available to the Generalissimo by the big powers, unleashed a rain of death upon tens of thousands of Red soldiers, it exacted a heavy price from Nanking; namely, that the mercenaries let themselves be lured deep into the hill-country by the Reds, where guerrilla warfare and the loss of great quantities of armaments awaited them. Chu Teh's troops had learned since the very beginning of the revolution, that as much as 80 percent of their weaponry had to come from the Kuomintang's arsenals. Often, garrison towns in the Northwest, occupied by Chiang's forces, were stormed, not to do battle but to strip a machine shop of lathes, hand-tools, dies, and other equipment used in manufacturing weapons. The guerrillas then used them to make their own weapons.

In victory and defeat, from 1936 on, normal life went on in the Yenan cities and hinterland. This was made possible by many hundreds of educators, skilled craftsmen, technical specialists in construction, school and soviet organizers, writers, artists, dramatists, who were attracted to the revolution. Primary schools were built in hundreds of Northwest villages, towns and cities; also, teacher-training, technical and worker's schools. A Red University was established at Pao An, of which Lin Piao, most feared and perhaps most brilliant Red Army commander, was President and gave instruction to the army's young officers.

In this quick summary, the names of but a few key leaders can be mentioned. There was, for example, the remarkable Professor, Hsu Tehli, born in Hunan in 1877, formerly a noted President of a Normal school in Changsha, and oldest man at age 57 to make the Long March. He supervised the entire educational program.

The financing and management of a viable economy were under the direction of Commissioner of Finances, Lin Tsu-han, educated in the classics, and in Sun Yat-sen's time, treasurer and chairman of the General Affairs Department of the Kuomintang. He fled when Chiang began his extermination campaign of communists, and made the Long March at age 55! Then there were, of course, Chu Teh and Chou En-lai, the one the commander-in-chief of the Red Army, from the beginning to the end of the revolution, and often called Mao Tse-tung's third arm, without which Mao could never have succeeded; and Chou, the Political Commissar in the Northwest and, always, the great communist negotiator. In Edgar Snow's words, "no man in China, apart from Mao, held such wide respect among Party and non-Party people alike, as Chou."[7]

While community development was in progress, "veteran" Red officers in their twenties, and "experienced" soldiers in their teens, made up a large part of the front-line fighting forces. When not in battle, they, as well as the military commanders and civilian leaders, observed Mao Tse-tung's Eight Points of Service to the People. Eagerly, they pitched in to help peasants in the field and workers in the shops. If there ever was a period in world history, when the old and the young, the poor and the rich, the educated and the unschooled, were inspired to work together toward a common ideal for a better life, it happened in Yenan.

The Sian Incident

This unusual "incident" occurred in the fall of 1936. It became the turning point, leading to the eventual collapse of the Nanking government. The Reds, with Yenan as their capital, were now in control of two-thirds of China's territory, sparsely populated but mountainous and rugged hill-country where, as Mao had said years ago, "the Red Army fights best." Although they had been forced to retreat to this wild prairie and forest land, to survive, it made them close neighbors of the Japanese invaders who had, since 1931, captured and taken possession of China's enormous, outermost northern provinces: Jehol, Manchuria, Chahar, and parts of Inner and Outer Mongolia, all incorporated into the Japanese puppet state of Manchukuo.

The brutal treatment and massive expulsion of the natives in these provinces convinced Mao that the defeat of Japan had to take precedence over the struggle against the elites of Nanking. The same anti-Japanese fervor obsessed the Kuomintang officers and soldiers, many of whom were from the North, as was their popular commander, Marshal Chang Hsueh-liang, born in Manchuria, ex-bandit ruler of Manchuria before the Japanese occupation, and now given the title by Chiang Kai-shek, of Vice-Commander-in-Chief of the Armed Forces of China. Chang had been sent to the north in 1931, ostensibly to fight the invader—but without the support of the Generalissimo, who demanded a "wait-and-see" policy toward Japan and an all-out campaign to destroy the Red Army, with the result that Kuomintang commanders and troops saw the invader conquer their homeland, while they themselves were immobilized by order from Nanking. In contrast, they saw the Red Army make repeated assaults behind the Japanese lines, at great loss of life. With the help of the peasants, they set up soviets in hidden military posts to observe the enemy's maneuvers and weak spots in advance of further assaults, and to prepare the mass of the Chinese people for the hard struggle that lay ahead, to recapture their homes and farm lands.

This aroused the admiration of Marshal Chang and heightened the

The Chinese Civil War That Was a Revolution

pleas by his officers and troops, to join the Red Army in a mutual campaign to drive out the invaders. Chang already knew that Mao Tse-tung had long been calling for a united front against the Japanese; also, that some of his own officers were secretly negotiating with the Reds for a feasible plan. But most persuasive of all was the fact that thousands of the Kuomintang soldiers, and many officers, were deserting to the Red Army.

The strong emotions for a united front among the soldiers and their commanders in North China, whether they were for or against revolution, and many millions of peasants, brought on the Sian Incident. The project, conceived by Marshal Chang, planned and carried out, in great secrecy, with a few trusted subordinates and, of all people, Chou En-lai, called for a bizarre and truly dangerous plan. Chang knew that the Generalissimo would be unyielding to verbal pleas for any plan to pool forces with the communists to drive out the Japanese, and since he would be visiting Sian in December, some other means had to be found to win him over.

The group then concocted the hoax of having Chiang "captured and arrested" by some Red soldiers who would promptly turn him over to the communists' great negotiator, Chou En-lai! Despite its implausibility, the coup de'tat worked, and Chiang Kai-shek had but one choice, presumably, to face the Red Army's firing-squad or sign the terms of a united front; and sign he did, reluctantly but officially.[8]

A cease-fire between the two armies in the Shensi-Kansu-Ninghsia region was, if not a joint attack on the Japanese for lack of manpower and armament support from Nanking, at least a chance to stop fighting each other and, instead, working together against the common enemy as much as possible. As for the Kuomintang forces under Chiang's direct control on the east coast and in south-central China, disaster awaited them. Suddenly, from 1937 to 1939, the Japanese unleashed a series of lightening strikes along the entire Pacific coast and into the interior, that resulted in a complete route for the armies of the absurdly misnomered "Free China" government of Nanking.

The massive invasion was part of a carefully planned conquest of China's major east-coast and inland industrial centers. Well supplied in previous years with oil, steel, iron and other essential military supplies, made available by the big powers, especially the United States, Japan took possession of Peking, Tientsin, Shanghai, Canton, then moved inland and captured Nanchang, Changsha, Hankow, and other key cities. All the governmental elites, including the Generalissimo and his troops, had to flee to the southwest hills and mountains of Szechuan and set up a new capital in Chungking.

Chiang, having learned nothing from the past, at once organized his forces in Chungking for the next "final annihilation campaign". In contrast, Mao Tse-tung and his political leader, Chou En-lai, were strengthening their position in the Northwest by continuing to set up soviets and winning to their side not only the peasants, but all segments of the population, while the Red commanders who had weathered the hardships of the Long March—Chu Teh, Lin Piao, Ho Lung, and many others—were intensifying their guerrilla warfare behind the Japanese lines.

Mao was the true pragmatist who did first things first. He knew that the survival of the revolution demanded disposing of the invader first. To accomplish this, he realized that he would need the support of the poor peasants, the middle peasants and city workers, but *also* some of the more powerful warlords who had everything to lose if the Japanese succeeded; and, as one historian remarked, at least the *tolerance* of wealthy commercial and landowning people, who had equally convincing self-interests in seeing the Japanese armies defeated. Mao won them over, in large measure, by halting all sovietizing within the Shensi-Kansu provinces, and by calling for elections in the districts controlled by the Reds, in which all people, rich and poor, took part.

The Final Decade—1939–'49
Triumph Of The Revolution

It all began with the overconfidence of Japan's militarists, and the erroneous military intelligence about Japan's long-range plans, that misled the world corporations of Europe and the United States. These plans should have been known by the western powers but were not, as evidenced by their earlier shipments to Japan, of such basic military supplies as oil and metals. The purpose was to keep the Japanese occupied in North China, taking over great tracts of much needed land for settlement by their own 70,000,000 people in Japan, crowded into an area about the size of our state of Montana.

When the second world war broke out in 1940, Japan's real purpose became crystal clear. Mao Tse-tung could have told the West back in 1936 what it was, for his researchers had found it in official Japanese documents. We excerpt a few words from his report to Snow at the time:

> The Japanese continental policy is already clear and is well known. ... The Japanese navy aspires to blockade the China seas and to seize the Philippines, Siam, Indochina, Malaya and the Dutch East Indies. In the event of war, Japan will try to make them her strategic

bases, cutting off Great Britain, France, and America from China, and monopolizing the seas of the southern Pacific.[9]

When World War II broke out, Japan's military leaders were so impressed by the initial victories of Hitler's Luftwaffe and paratroopers behind the French Maginot line, that they joined the Axis powers in 1940 and signed a pact with Germany. And so, Japan bombed the United States' naval base at Pearl Harbor on December 7, 1941. The rest is World War II history and Japan's defeat in 1945. We need but add a few observations on the events within China during this period, that also brought defeat to the Kuomintang and victory to the Communists.

The Revolution Takes Center-Stage

In the early years of the world war, the revolutionaries not only posed the greatest threat to Japan but, according to Snow, provided the leadership in North China for what was much the largest guerrilla organization in the world. Once the Japanese were disposed of, and the Red Army no longer had to bear the brunt of the war against them in China, it was but a matter of time as to how long Nanking could hold on. In 1945 Mao Tse-tung thought the struggle would go on another eight years; it was over in four.

Though fully aware of this danger, the American industrialists and bankers had no choice but to continue backing Chiang in a vain effort to prevent it. And so, they poured more money and military supplies into China, and even sent 56,000 experienced marines and officers, to save their east-Asia investments. They sent over General Joseph W. Stillwell, as Commander-in-chief of the U.S. forces. However, in opposition to this, were the Chinese people generally. Though they had always been skeptical of the foreign powers' intentions in giving so much aid to Chiang Kai-shek, they had gladly accepted American help in the common war against the Japanese invader. But now the entire population was incensed over the enormous amount of military aid the United States was giving Chiang to crush the Red Army, when everyone knew that it was *this* Army, not the Kuomintang, that had fought the war. People had come to revere it as the nation's army of liberation.[10]

Now young men flocked into communist territory to join the Red Army; women and older men, from all walks of life, came to help in every possible way. The number of troops increased rapidly from under a million to three million, and the work of wiping out Chiang's forces began. Suffice it to say that, at last, Chu Teh was able to coordinate the troops of his battle-hardened generals in an offensive to recover the heartland of central and south China. As the troops moved on, they had the support of hundreds of millions of people who helped clothe, feed, equip and transport them, and be their eyes and ears.[11]

As early as 1946 the Americans, fearing the worst, arranged a fifteen day truce between the communists and Kuomintang. They proposed establishment of a democratic coalition. The talks came to naught chiefly because the Generalissimo, in characteristic dictatorial fashion, and no appreciation of his greatly diminished bargaining power, demanded that the communists evacuate their immense and secure North China holdings. The truce ended, and the now highly respected commanders like Lin Piao, Liu Po-chen, Ch'en Yi, and so many others, finally completed the total China encirclement of the Kuomintang, while the equally famed political heads like Chou En-lai, P'eng Chen, Teng Hsiao-p'ng and, again, countless others took charge of sovietizing and managing the civilian affairs behind the Red Army's protecting lines.

The end came in the fall of 1949, when the Red Army dislodged Chiang Kai-shek and his Kuomintang forces from the entire Chinese mainland. With their backs to the Pacific they were rescued by the U.S. Fifth Fleet and ferried to the off-shore island of Taiwan, which has remained their refuge up to the present. In September the communist political and Red Army leaders, and as many excited troops and civilians as could crowd into a big city, entered Peking. The CCP elected Mao Tse-tung Chairman of the new government, and on October 1, before an immense gathering, he formally proclaimed the Peoples' Republic of China. Amidst great rejoicing, he vowed that "never again shall the Chinese people be enslaved."

21

The People's Republic of China

On the day The People's Republic of China was established, the doors to the Chinese people were opened for the first time in over twenty years. Responsible journalists, newspaper editors, scholars and historians—all of them carefully screened, of course, for there was still great danger of sabotage and spy-work by the defeated enemy—traversed the country to see for themselves and talk to people. No longer was Chiang able to dream up atrociously fabricated stories, sent abroad as "official records" about the non-existent chaos, oppression, slave labor, and mass murder in the Chinese soviet and Red Army territories. (The writer recalls vividly some of those weird tales circulated in the United States, via radio and the press, both before and after the founding of the PRC.)

A vast number of on-site reports from foreign professionals were now reaching the outside world. A scant reference to some typical observations will illustrate. The internationally noted French agronomist, Jesué De Castro, visited China in 1957–'58, accompanied by a group of social scientists engaged in a study of the world nutrition situation. At the conclusion of the survey, the sponsoring *World Association for the Struggle Against Hunger* asked De Castro to compile the group's finding's, which were published in Paris in 1961 and, subsequently, in other countries as *The Black Book Of Hunger*. The section of *The Chinese Experiment* began with these words:

> The defeat imposed by the new China on the spectre of hunger that had ravaged her territories and enfeebled her population for centuries, is an event as new and surprising as the conquest of interplanetary space, as satellites, as artificial planets. In certain ways what is going on in China is perhaps still more remarkable. . . . Such is the miracle that has taken place in the past eight years.
>
> I had the opportunity to confirm that it was almost impossible to observe in the population the classic evidence of hunger that I was

accustomed to encounter with alarming frequency in the other underdeveloped regions of the world. . . .[1]

In England, Field Marshall Viscount Montgomery, who had traveled throughout China in 1961, published an article in *The Times* of London. In sum, he stated that everyone whom he saw seemed happy. Referring to the fabricated stories about "devastating famines", being circulated by the China Lobby of the British and American world corporations, he said that he did not see a single case of malnutrition. In certain regions, he noted, the diet was very poor, "but adequate all the same. To speak of famine on a grand scale is nonsense."[2]

Even before the Japanese surrendered, some honest reports got through to Europe and the United States. No less an authority than General Joseph W. Stilwell, Commander-In-Chief of the U.S. forces in the China, Burma, and India area, condemned Chiang for his incompetence and dictatorial methods as a political and military leader. Numerous American journalists—the reputable Albert Payne, Theodore White, Harrison Forman, etc,—wrote about the Chungking regime's corruption, brutalities upon, and exploitation of, the impoverished peasants and workers. "The journalists," writes historian Jean Chesneaux, "were extremely critical of the Kuomintang, especially, once they had witnessed the simple, brotherly society of Yenan. . . . On May 1, 1944, the American magazine *Life* described 'Free China' as a strange combination of the Spanish Inquisition and Tammany Hall."[3]

In light of the flood of reliable reports like the above, and the encomiums in behalf of the revolutionaries, only three influential nations gave immediate recognition to the Peoples' Republic of China: the USSR, Britain, and India. Others soon followed, but it took a quarter of a century before most of the world's nations finally recognized it; and even then not the United States!

The unceasing hostility that our country, as the leading world power, displayed toward the PRC for a long time after the revolution, made a deep and lasting impact upon the Chinese people. During those crucial formative years of the newly established communist state, bitter experience had taught Mao Tse-tung, Chu Teh, and their military and political associates, and the people, that the continued presence of the U.S. Seventh Fleet in the waters between the Chinese mainland and its offshore island of Taiwan, was primarily to probe for internal dissent and weaknesses in the PRC. The purpose, everyone assumed, was to exacerbate these and, if opportune, to strike with all military might. This would be done, of course, by the "legitimate Chinese democratic government of Taiwan", with the friendly aid of the American people and concerned nations of Europe!

That opportunity did not materialize; but the presumption of intent was amply confirmed by subsequent history. We need allude only to a few examples, because they determined the immediate domestic and foreign policies of the PRC.

Mao's proclamation of the People's Republic of China had no more than re-echoed around the globe when the China Lobby of the predominantly American owned multinationals "persuaded" our government to resume its anti-communist offensive against the PRC. This called for the same ingeniously deceptive propaganda of seemingly pursuing peace while engaging in war, adopted throughout the revolution. Now it meant heeding the calls for help from the industrial and landed aristocracies of Korea, Vietnam, and Cambodia—all bordering China—to stop the PRC's efforts to infiltrate communism among their people. Their pleas were promptly met.[4]

While engaged in these maneuvers the United States was able, by sheer economic and military power, to coerce the United Nations into retaining Taiwan as the legitimate representative of the Chinese people. Eventually, however, the folly of barring one-fourth of the world's population from a bona fide world agency became too much for 150 U.N. member-nations to stomach. On October 25, 1971 the General Assembly ousted Taiwan and replaced it with the PRC. Nevertheless, it took eight more years before the United States could bring itself to face up to the necessity of recognizing the People's Republic of China. The pressure came from our deteriorating conditions at home, the grim reality that the Chinese and Russian revolutions had taken on global dimensions and were giving birth to social revolutions among poor people around the world.

The international tensions and continuing external threat of annihilation, instead of causing fear and discord during the first ten years of PRC, served only to strengthen the already strong bonds of loyalty and common purpose between 800 million Chinese people and their trusted political and military leaders. That trust had grown into an almost worshipful reverence of Mao Tse-tung, in gratitude for his unswerving and successful struggle in their behalf during the long years of the revolution.

Immediately after the revolution, on February 15, 1950, the People's Republic of China and Soviet Union signed a thirty year treaty of "friendship, alliance, and mutual assistance" that lasted only ten years. The reason for the unexpected termination reveals fundamentals of such great importance that it needs to be examined carefully, both for its direct impact on the two nations and its long-range bearing on the NSHS thesis. Before our study is terminated, this may give us that long awaited "real" answer to human salvation.

Under the treaty, the Soviet Union extended invaluable financial and technical aid, the only aid given by any foreign government at the time. This enabled the new China to move swiftly in strengthening its domestic economic base and international military posture. The effective use that the PRC was able to make of the Russian help, came to light in the summer of 1950—only months after the end of the Chinese revolution—when the United States invaded Korea, under the guise of a U.N. "police action"; and was forced to accept a cease-fire three years later; and again in the early 1960s when our government greatly expanded its "undeclared" war against the North Vietnam Communist regime. The USSR and PRC jointly helped the Vietnamese—the Chinese, out of fear of an invasion as the American troops began to take positions close to their border.

Shortly thereafter, the underlying Russian help to China astonished foreign military experts: on October 16, 1964, the PRC exploded its first atomic bomb; in 1967 it fired off the universally feared hydrogen bomb. With respect to domestic civilian affairs, foreign visitors revealed an unprecedented development of China's most important natural resources: coal, iron ore, tin, antinomy, tungsten, petroleum. To this must be added rapid progress in the construction of manufacturing plants, machinery and equipments; research laboratories, as well as advancement in the medical, nutritional, and technological sciences; and, in response to the ever-present external danger posed by the United States and its western allies, the development of air and land military weaponry.[5]

We can summarize all this by taking a quick look ahead to an incident that occurred in the summer of 1975, when a delegation of the American Society of Newspaper Editors visited China for nearly a month. Clayton Kirkpatrick, Editor of the Chicago Tribune, one of the largest papers in the United States, had much to say. We excerpt a few paragraphs from his frank and honest report that ran in the paper for a week:

> In a scant quarter century, the Communist government of the People's Republic has sought to remold one of the world's oldest civilizations into a new role as the leader of the third world—the poor, the weak, the economically undeveloped nations.

> By all the evidence available to a visiting journalist, it (PRC) is delivering a relatively comfortable standard of living to 800 million

Chinese. It has achieved a degree of popular support that promises long term stability. In a nation where political oppression, revolution, and hunger have been endemic for centuries, these are extraordinary achievements.

. . . China is a rigidly moral country. Theft is virtually unknown. Streets are safe at any time of the day or night. . . . Corruption in a public official is a capital crime equal to treason. . . . Affluence is avoided.

China, as befits a Communist country, has no recognized religion, but if it had one Maoism probably would be the choice. Reverence for Mao is almost universal among citizens of the People's Republic. His writings are studied and quoted in much the same way that the Bible is studied and quoted in Christian countries. . . .

Kirkpatrick concluded with the following:

China is a major power now, and its strength will continue to increase. Under careful management it would seem that the United States could achieve a guardedly friendly relationship. . . . This would require coordination by the U.S., China, Japan, and Russia.

If it cannot be achieved, it appears clear that China will pursue her policy of trying to unite the developing nations of the Third World, under Chinese leadership, to create a power structure that could eclipse the United States and Russia combined.[6]

Small wonder that our government finally decided in 1979, to recognize the People's Republic and exchange Ambassadors.

There was, however, another side to this Chinese domestic scene, that seemed to emerge suddenly, to perplex the visiting foreign scholars and journalists as much as the country's progress amazed them. It came into view in the late 1950s as a movement expressing great dissatisfaction with the way the People's Republic of China was running things. What mystified the spectators from the rest of the world most, was the fact that the government's venerable Chairman, Mao Tse-tung, started the movement—in the name of the People's Republic!—and that the former impoverished masses, who had benefitted the most from the new communist social and economic programs, were the main force behind the uprising. It became known as the *Great Proletarian Cultural Revolution*. We shall continue to refer to it as— *The Cultural Revolution*.

There is a twofold significance to this "strange" revolution: its importance to all of us, as an attempt to find that missing link to human salvation; and, its unfortunate mistakes that brought failure to the search, even though Mao Tse-tung almost had the link within his grasp. The revolution stirred up great social turmoil and, since it bears closely on the Ultimate Imperative with which we conclude our study, it needs careful scrutiny.

Why would Mao Tse-tung have wanted to start a Cultural Revolution at a moment when he was held in the highest esteem by the Chinese people and his many loyal comrades of the revolution just won? The fact is that he had a strong and valid reason. Put simply, it was to make sure that the long struggle, in which so many had died and those who survived had endured great suffering, would now give birth to a just and *classless* People's Republic. Mao and his closest associates had good cause for their concern. The reason can be stated in a few words.

We have noted the unstinting cooperation between the Red Army generals and troops, and the civilian leaders, shop workers and peasants, during the Yenan period. Irrespective of rank, all worked together for nearly fifteen years in a beautiful classless society, to help each other until Chiang Kai-shek's mercenary soldiers, the Generalissimo himself, and the members of his corrupt government had been defeated and driven out of China.

Now the victorious communist partisans—generals, educators, soviet (political) heads, engineers, shop managers, technicians, writers, rank-and-file workers—flocked back into the cities. Things started out the Yenan way, but after a few years, gradually but visibly, small shops became big factories; simple machines and hand tools were being replaced by complicated machinery. Scientific and intricate technical methods were being introduced into production. Business administrators and specialists in the new techniques had to receive advanced education in order to perform their complex duties. These rapid changes also made the work of government officials more complicated. In short, contrary to the Mao Tse-tung thought and the Yenan spirit, an upper and lower class was reappearing!

All this worried Mao and thousands of his colleagues, the Yenan veterans. The great mass of the people wondered too, for they were beginning to be adversely affected by it. The Maoist desciples were not only carefully watching the development but doing everything possible to find ways of putting an end to it. Schools, libraries, and workplaces throughout China were supplied with millions of pamphlets and books stressing the Mao Thought, and these were avidly read and discussed wherever people gathered.

From the very day the People's Republic was founded, efforts were made to preserve the Yenan way of life. Functionaries in the so-called higher positions in government, education, industry and the professions, were required to keep in active touch with everyday repetitive physical work. Some success was achieved in having them do occasional work as members of an assembly line, as drill press operators, as workers in the rice fields, etc. Even school children were assigned to simple and non-hazardous farm or factory work as part of their classroom "book learning." It was a praiseworthy effort, but not enough to stem the rising tide of an unanticipated socialist *class* society.[7]

Mao's fears were aggravated when he headed a delegation to Moscow in 1957, to celebrate the fortieth anniversary of the October revolution. What he saw and studied while in Moscow made the Cultural Revolution all but certain. A number of things remained fixed in his mind, and they determined his course of action.

Readily discernible was the fact that, granting the progress made by the USSR toward industrial and military goals and the improvement of the material living conditions of all the people, the people themselves seemed to play no part in the decision-making process, or in influencing the direction, priority, or specific objectives to be pursued. That, said Mao, was left to the presumed expertise of the Party leaders and specialists in the diversified areas of local and national affairs. (We defer, for the moment, any assessment of Mao's deductions about either the USSR or PRC socioeconomic developments.)

Mao took particular note of the Soviet Union's popular and well publicized system of giving generous incentive rewards in the form of wage increases or bonuses to industrial workers for meeting or excelling production quotas; of bestowing honorary citations to any individual whether at the lowest occupational level or the highest leadership position, for distinguished service to the nation. Such citations might include monetary rewards and, if the person's accomplishment was considered to be of great importance, also some type of personal status reward like the use of a private automobile with chauffeur, commodious residential quarters—whatever seemed appropriate as a token of society's appreciation.

For Mao this fostered the very materialistic culture values from which sprang the world's most recent class society, capitalism—the age-old class distinctions between self-serving rulers and the masses. Mao had no doubt that the practice, already showing its ugly head in his own country, would proliferate if not stopped at the outset. His dim view of these "unsocialistic" practices in the Soviet Union became even more frightening to him, when coupled with the startling decision by Stalin's successor in 1953, Nikita Khrushchev, to improve relationships with the West.

Having received the approval of the ruling Social Democratic Party,

Khrushchev changed Stalin's motto of one socialist state against a host of enemy capitalist states to "peaceful coexistence"; he then visited the United States in 1959. The purpose: to exchange thoughts with its leaders in government, industry and agriculture, on possible ways of cooperating in the mutual interest of both countries.

This was truly frightening not only to Mao Tse-tung and other key leaders of the People's Republic of China, but also to the great mass of the people. All of them had fresh in mind the enormous financial and military aid given by the United States to Chiang Kai-shek; and even now its Seventh Fleet was still menacingly cruising along China's east coast. By the early 1960s when the aforementioned fears of American designs upon the People's Republic were intensified by the Vietnam war, a wave of anti-Soviet feeling swept over China. The Soviet Union was accused of deserting the socialist cause at a time of great danger from the West under the leadership of the new world power, the United States. USSR government officials, particularly Khrushchev, were branded as "capitalist roaders," and their "betrayal" of the revolution was seen by Mao Tse-tung and many comrades of the Yenan days as the work of the rising class of privileged Russian elites eager to imitate the American affluent life-style.

Mao's relentless castigation of the Soviet Union's leadership after his return home, so angered Khrushchev, that he secured the approval of the all powerful Central Committee, to cancel all further aid to China. In light of the great importance of that aid, as already noted, many of Mao's most respected old freinds now holding high office in the PRC, began to differ with him. Though they feared the consequences of Khrushchev's rapprochement with the United States, they saw nothing so objectional in Russia's domestic practices of rewarding its working people and dedicated leaders in government, the sciences, business and education, for work well done. Others were in favor of appeasing instead of alienating the USSR because they felt that the People's Republic was not ready to go it alone.

But Mao was concerned with fundamentals, and there he was right; but in his tactics among friends—in both China and Russia—he was dead wrong. Liu Shao-chi, President of the People's Republic, a great admirer of Mao Tse-tung, and a scholar whose writings carried authority second only to those of Mao, made this opening comment about the report: "In China the question of which wins out, socialism or capitalism is already solved." Mao replied, bluntly, with the warning that the revolution was far from won and could well be lost if the new *upper classes*, already solidly entrenched in Russia and gaining power rapidly in China—a provocative statement itself—are allowed to grow and thus transform the People's Republic into a class society ruled by the new governmental and industrial elites in their own interest, as is happening in the USSR.[8]

And so began the preliminary battle for and against the Cultural Revolution. Bitter and divisive though it became, it was not fought with guns and bullets, but with slogans, words, accusations and especially, Daziboa; i.e., "everyman's newspaper" of China—great strips of paper filled with contending ideas and pasted on walls, posts, doors, and kiosks all over the country. Anybody could post one, and everyone else was free to respond, to scribble remarks on a poster already up, or to write and post his or her own daziboa beside the others. At the height of the verbal revolution, Mao posted his own daziboa, and it was taken up by every "real" newspaper throughout China.[9]

As the controversy spread nation-wide, the masses sided with Mao Tse-tung, the government, professional and industrial leadership with Liu Shao-chi; and when the latter were called capitalist roaders and unsocialistic "revisionists," the Cultural Revolution was on. Though much has been written about it, we shall touch only briefly on the specific issues, because they really did not come to grips with the causative problem, and thus by-passed the very goal of a classless society sought in common by the leaders on both sides of the conflict. The most unfortunate part of it was the failure of the clear-thinking Mao Tse-tung of old, to identify the problem to be resolved by his otherwise sound idea of a Cultural Revolution. Let us make a quick survey of Mao's laudable purpose in launching the revolution, point out his inappropriate and often unjust condemnation of his former comrades in arms, then move on to the more judicious objectives of the concluding NSHS Ultimate Imperative.

Mao's First Demand

This was for the right of the "masses" to share in the decision making process in government and industry. To 800 million Chinese people, 80 percent of whom made their livelihood from the soil, Mao's demand was on target; and so it was to the city workers. He had only to say the word, and they would be at his side to wage the new revolution.

There was no gainsaying the fact that living conditions in the cities were outstripping those in the countryside, and rank-and-file workers were having less and less voice in determining the management and operating policies in their workplaces, on the ground that they did not have the knowledge necessary to cope with the complicated new industrial equipments and techniques. The peasants on their part were discovering that while development and installation of modern machinery and manufacturing processes in the large industrial centers were receiving prompt attention, the equally urgent need to increase agricultural production was seriously neglected, a decision-making fallacy emanating exclusively from leadership expertise that hurt peasants and city workers alike. All felt deeply that it was perpetuating the age-old upper class exploitation of the masses who, by their daily closeness to elemental productive work, alone possess the wisdom that the mainstay of life is mother nature's supply of food and raw materials to feed and clothe and shelter us. And the Chinese people remembered well the terrible famines that decimated countless millions of them through the centuries, under the rulership of upper class elites and their learned professionals.

Although this was becoming a familiar reality by the 1960s, Mao Tse-tung knew that the practical power of lining up the political and Party hierarchy for or against him was in the hands of PRC President Liu Shao-chi, Defense Minister, Pen Teh-huai, Peking's Mayor, Peng Chen and his Deputy, Wu Han, a prominent historian and professor at Peking University—all one-time trusted comrades in the Yenan days—and some two million minor Party functionaries, the cadres, who together with growing numbers of other top Party leaders, constituted the "capitalist roaders."

It is only fair to say that, for the most part, they sincerely believed, and were correct, that in modern society the complex management and technical responsibilities must of necessity be entrusted to specially trained and educated practitioners capable of carrying out their leadership roles *for* the masses if not jointly with the masses. In disapproval, the daziboa revealed the anger of students and workers with party cadres, eager to join the new elite of upper class communist leaders. Millions of daziboa called for re-educating "this elite of lazy party workers that indulged in idleness and hated work, ate too much and owned too much, strove for status, acted like officials, put on bureaucratic airs, paid no heed to the plight of the people and cared nothing about the interests of the state." The pro Liu daziboa countered by blaming the masses for lack of understanding of the difficult leadership responsibilities, and insisting that improper conduct by cadres can only be corrected by and within the party structure; to which the Maoist posters responded with a call to the masses to reform their own cadres in every school, factory and farm enterprise.

In these verbal battles on the eve of the Cultural Revolution Mao was, nonetheless, continuously being outmaneuvered by the upper echelon of the governmental and increasingly powerful industrial hierarchy. His campaign to instill into the thinking and attitude of millions of minor cadre functionaries the idea that they were the servants of the masses, and to persuade the higher officials to bring the masses back into the decision making process in the political and economic affairs of state, fell on deaf ears. And despite his awareness of the great esteem that the common people had for him during the long and bitter struggle against the Kuomintang and Japanese armies, he did not know or perhaps fully realize the extent to which their loyalty to him carried over into the peace-time concerns of the People's Republic. This he discovered in 1966.

In August of that year, Mao put his prestige on the line, by pasting up his own famous daziboa in Peking, calling on the students, workers, and peasants to *"Bombard the Headquarters."* It was broadcast at once via radio to every city, town, and village across the nation. Now the masses had their order direct from Chairman Mao, and they lost no time in making their first assaults on the citadels of the anti-socialist bureauocracy: the seats of government, the universities and factories in the big cities. To Mao's amazement the revolution erupted like a pandemic tidal wave inundating the educational and industrial centers, then engulfing the strongholds of the "renegades" in the countryside.

Now the powerful and revered Chairman of the Chinese Communist Party took over. All the radio networks and major newspapers were immediately at his disposal. Every hamlet, town and city received his message. He called for a nation-wide campaign of education directed to helping the nation's peasants and workers regain their lost rights and responsibilities. On August 8, three days after Mao had posted his daziboa, the party's Central Committee held its Eleventh Plenary session with Mao Tse-tung presiding. In a fiery speech he berated the members for their failure to lead the masses, then demanded that they remove the Cultural Revolution's "arch-enemy," Liu Shao-chi, from his position as the party's Vice Chairman. Mao knew full well that at this moment all the government and party bureacrats, the majority of whom were still in Liu's camp, realized that the eyes of the entire nation were upon them. They voted by a slim margin to replace Liu with Mao's still loyal comrade, Lin Piao, who was himself the most famous general of the Chinese revolution.

In the following months millions of students and leaders of China's proletariat poured into Peking for Mao's instructions on how to achieve his first demand to restore Yenan rights to the masses, and, indeed, just to see their venerated leader. One estimate put the number at 130 million! Now a wealth of fascinating theories and studies began to pour forth from printing presses around the world. To reiterate, for our own broader NSHS purpose, we shall but touch on the major issues, leaving it to the interested reader to consult the specialized treatises listed in our closing Notes.

During the high point, from 1966 to '69, the Cultural Revolution focused on the following goals:

Worker participation in the decision-making process in the socially owned shops and factories.

Development of agricultural Communes (cooperatives) to accomplish the same purpose, and to improve farm equipment, machinery and techniques.

Compulsory re-education of the so-called upper class professionals, as well as countless numbers of cadres, in government, education, and industry. This required them to spend some time doing labor work, to teach them the fundamentals of service to the masses.

Reform of education, from the elementary schools up to the universities.

The necessary leadership to put these programs into action came as much from the bottom—peasants, city workers and students—as from the top: Mao Tse-tung, Lin Piao, Chou En-lai. The most important grass-roots organized groups that promoted and monitored demands of the Cultural Revolution were the *Red Guards*, *Revolutionary Committees*, and the universally respected *People's Liberation Army*, which had its beginnings in Yenan. but the first and most vigorous individuals who called for the revolution, were university students in the big cities like Peking and Shanghai. When the faculties refused to change the centuries-old careerist education, students not only boycotted classes en masse, but made common cause with workers in factories and shops, who were equally unhappy with the return of the old upper-class system of limiting decision-making and management responsibilities at the workplace to "educated" experts.

To help start the rebellion, the newly formed Red Guards, also composed mostly of students and young people generally, swept into the big cities to serve as the "Shock Troops." They arrived in Shanghai by the thousands. To balance their impetuousity and inexperience, came the competent members of the People's Liberation Army. If all of them failed to accomplish Mao's fundamental objective; namely, of *revolutionizing formal education*, they did have some temporary success in making re-education of the highest governmental and party leaders, as well as millions of the cadre functionaries, mandatory. This meant being transferred to farms and factories for specific periods of time, to do the physical work performed daily, from year to year, by the masses.

The Cultural Revolution achieved more permanent and meaningful results in behalf of the rights of both peasants and city workers. In industrial centers this pertained to the ability, in large measure, of the *Revolutionary Committees* to secure worker participation in the decision-making and management functions at their workplaces. The question frequently asked at the time by foreign visitors to the PRC was "how can workers run a factory when they really don't know how?" A part of the answer was given by seeing worker education and decision-making in operation in shops and factories, and by sitting in on a regular session of a plant's Revolutionary Committee discussing, jointly with top management, everyday production and management problems. The agenda might relate to improving an old-fashioned work tool, reducing or increasing a production quota, correcting defects in the flow of an assembly line, purchasing a much needed piece of modern equipment from a foreign country or designing and making it themselves.( )

Greatly expanded by the new Revolutionary Committees, the experience led to the wide-spread practice by shops and factories, in the peasant country as well as the cities, to set up "university" sections giving advanced technical courses *inside* the plant, to which the combined party and revolutionary committees elected gifted workers for instruction during working hours while being paid their regular wage. Upon completion of the course the workers were assigned to the more complicated duties for which the course prepared them. The significant result was that, as of this writing (Spring 1981), such formal on-the-job technical and scientific education has become a basic part of China's system of worker education at their places of employment.

To this positive side of the Cultural Revolution we should add a word on the mandatory re-education program for all the upper-echelon elites, whether they were known as capitalist roaders or not. That it was not quite so positive will illustrate why it did not last. In short, they were immediately relieved of their office responsibilities and sent to re-education centers. As already noted, if assigned to factories, they had to work as floor sweepers, stock clerks, assembly line workers, or whatever; and, if to farms, they had to learn how to do the physical labor of planting crops, cultivating and harvesting them. Often they had to be sent considerable distances, especially if the re-education center was in the peasant country.

The captive students soon learned that the duration of the re-education period would be several months or longer and, therefore, often sent for their families. Most of them had returned to their former positions by the end of the Cultural Revolution, some never did return. But for all of them the revolutionary education was official, initiated under Chairman Mao's own order to Bombard the Headquarters, and carried out by the more or less coordinated but certainly enthusiastic forces of the student and worker Red Guards, the now Mao-controlled central and local party committees, and the steadying hand of the long experienced People's Liberation Army.

Mao's greatest contribution to China's well-being, before and during the Cultural Revolution, was, no doubt, his ceaseless emphasis on helping some 80 percent of its people, the impoverished peasants. Significant, perhaps beyond all else, was his contribution to the development of the Communes. The peasants, inspired by Mao's teaching of self-reliance, organized a system of small cooperatives in 1958 known as Communes. They were completely developed by 1964, and have since become an enormous fountain of nourishment for all China. A word of explanation is in order because they not only anticipated the spirit of the revolution but had to endure one of China's most disastrous droughts during their formative days. Coupled with the unfortunate timing of an overly enthusiastic Maoist social program for a Great Leap Forward in agriculture and industry, the two ventures ran into trouble due to nature's own great eruption.

The start-up problems of the Communes were thus cited erroneously, and in no small part willfully, by the western powers, including the alienated Soviet Union, as the causes of China's troubles during the hard years of the drought. In contrast, and to set the record straight, the sympathetic yet highly respected student of the Chinese Communes, Anna Louise Strong, who lived periodically in China for many years, declared the unique structure and organization of the Communes as the sound base of their subsequent remarkable success. She summarized the multiple features of that base as follows:

> People's Communes in China arose, not as an experiment in equalitarianism, but as a merger of agricultural cooperatives to create a larger unit for better control of the rural environment, and especially, but not exclusively, for water control and irrigation. In early 1958 most of China's more than half billion peasants were in 740,000 agricultural cooperatives with an average membership of 160 families. When the year ended, they had merged into 26,000 communes, usually on the scale of a township, with an average of several thousand families. . . . Still later it increased three-fold by subdivision in some provinces to fit local conditions; but the commune throughout remains the form which merges all the cooperative

farming in the country, and to which practically all peasants belong. . . .

It (the commune) assumed not only the handling of agriculture but of local industry, commerce, education, home defense on a township scale. . . . The third aspect of the Chinese People's Commune, in which it differs most sharply from all other forms of farm collectivization anywhere, is that it combines government power with production. The commune is both the upper level of the combined farming cooperatives and also the lowest level of state power at the township level. The peasants survey the total resources of their township and have the state power to use them.

What first recommended this locally was that improvements like local roads, reservoirs and irrigation canals could be done with authority at once by local initiative. One husky commune chairman from Manchuria told me in 1958, when I asked who paid for local roads: 'Nobody pays for roads. We just make them.'

Finally, Anna Louise Strong said in retrospect in 1964:

In the three hard years of unusual natural disasters, the communes saved the country. . . . Many experts believe that without the communes, the disasters of those hard years would have cost millions and possibly tens of millions of lives.[10]

This overview of the main events of the Cultural Revolution takes us to Mao Tse-tung's regrettable mistakes that prevented him from reaching his goal: the establishment of a classless socialist society. The mistakes were:

1. Failure to differentiate a capitalist class society from other class societies that have existed throughout history, and still exist today.
2. Misjudgement of upper-class leaders in the Soviet Union as "capitalist roaders".
3. Erroneous presumption that the "communist" society during the Yenan days offered a sound base for a classless society.
4. Devastating results of the mistakes.

An assessment of these shortcomings of the Cultural Revolution will conclude our chapter on the People's Republic of China.

Class Societies

It has been a basic socialist tenet since the time of Karl Marx, that the class struggle in a capitalist society is between an upper class of wealthy owners of *socially created* wealth, and a poor—in Marx's day, propertyless—working class that created this wealth; that the capitalist upper class must be overthrown and divested of its unjust title to such property, in order to establish a classless society within the above definition.

The simple fact is that there have been, since the dawn of history, and still are many other kinds of upper and lower class societies in which poverty and oppression are and always have been the lot of the lower classes. Beginning with antiquity, there were the warrior classes with their conquered peoples; the ancient *upper-caste* pagan priesthoods, in conjunction with the powerful landowning nobilities, jointly using their privately owned tax collectors and military forces, to fleece the impoverished peasants and/or slaves of their produce; the same agricultural class-system persisted into the middle ages and early modern era of feudalism, in western Europe, pre-revolutionary Russia and China, and in much of the rest of the world. Then came the capitalist class societies in contemporary industrial nations, followed by an entirely new hierarchy of *non-property* owning political, educational, industrial, and professional upper class elites in the communist countries, versus the masses.

This diversity of class societies throughout history not only made it incorrect but most unwise to call the Soviet Union's leaders "capitalist roaders"; and it was no less serious a mistake for Mao Tse-tung to brand the PRC leaders with this derogatory name. To be justifiably labelled as capitalist roaders, they would avowedly have had to be advocating the re-establishment of some kind of capitalist system of private ownership of their country's socially necessary means of production. Since they were all devout Marxist/Leninists, the erroneous designation was absurd on the face of it. What, then, might Mao have done to make his call for Cultural Revolution valid? We shall come to that later.

The Yenan days, extending over nearly fifteen years, were an unforgettable experience for the millions of people who lived in the great Northwest or went there, to help the civilian leaders and Red Army win the communist revolution. But the beautiful cooperation between the leaders and rank-and-file workers did not make the communist controlled communities of North China, with Yenan as their capital, a classless society. On the contrary, it was the daily life-and-death struggle during the military encounters with the invading Japanese and Chiang Kai-shek's armies, that made the fullest kind of cooperation a survival necessity for everybody, regardless of one's normal class status.

When peace returned, people resumed their accustomed class roles, circumscribed, however, in both the Soviet Union and People's Republic, by the abolishment of the right of *any* individual or *class* of individuals to own socially created property or other forms of socially necessary wealth. Liu and many other leaders during the Yenan period tried to explain this to Mao, but to no avail. In point of time, Mao's failure to heed their advice was his first mistake.

Unnecessary, too, was Mao's call for the *mandatory* "re-education" of the PRC's governmental and professional upper classes, requiring them to do physical labor, so that they would learn to understand the importance of worker participation in the decision-making and management functions at their places of work. This coercive method only served to create ill-feeling and divisive forces within the People's Republic.

Had Mao Tse-tung been better informed about developments on the world scene, he would have known that this same learning process was already taking place quite naturally, not only in the USSR, where it was thought to be a sensible collective way of improving production methods and equipments, and worker happiness, but also in other countries. The Japanese, after losing the war, adopted the policy out of sheer urgency to solve their old problems of over-population, lack of all but small deposits of oil, coal, metals, minerals, plus fast-growing economic problems. Europe's capitalist countries, where the Marxist socialist movement was politically strong, had long been practicing worker decision-making participation in industry; and by the late 1970s even the large privately owned corporations in the United States, motivated by their own rapidly deteriorating competitive and profit-making situation, domestically and internationally, began to negotiate similar plans with the labor unions.

This takes us to what was, beyond question, Mao's most serious mistake: alienation of the Soviet Union by his inappropriate and, to the Russians, insulting name calling. In anger and, again, with full support of the Communist Party, Khrushchev canceled the Friendship and Mutual Assistance pact. Mutual animosity replaced the mutual friendship so desperately needed by both countries. Feelings of suspicion and hatred became increasingly intense in the coming years. Instead of collaborating to the utmost in every field of common interest, the only two strong and potentially secure communist nations became bitter enemies! Soon they were rehashing old disputes that should have become obsolete, along with the Russian Tsars and Chinese Dynasties, over conflicting "rights" to independent territories having common borders with the two countries.

The continued drifting apart has, amazingly enough, turned the PRC toward the United States, a move for which it condemned the USSR some twenty-five years earlier for deserting the socialist cause. The USSR, on the other hand, has become a nuclear-armed world power, which the American giant multinational corporations are determined to destroy in order to regain their lucrative investments around the world, even if it takes a nuclear war to do it. Given that grim reality, as of this writing (March 1983), exacerbated by the new war-obsessed Reagan administration's tenacity to win a nuclear war against the Soviet Union, Mao Tse-tung's mistake will have been far more disastrous for mankind than anyone could have imagined at the time.

As we conclude this chapter, we can only hope that an aroused American public will prevent the "unthinkable" cataclysm from happening, at the ballot box and in every other peaceful way possible. We should also focus our thoughts on what the state of human affairs might be today, had Mao never made the mistake of antagonizing the Russians, and the two countries had continued their cooperation, and had greatly expanded it up to the present. Consider, for a moment, the fact that the USSR has, alone, and despite its confrontations with the PRC, become a world power on a par with the USA, and that the PRC is now a powerful nation itself, despite its estrangement from the USSR. It is reasonable to suppose from this that the combined strength of the two nations would be so overwhelming, it would deter any nation, including ours, from planning a nuclear attack against them. Such a two-nation power bloc, having a population of more than a billion, plus the help of numerous friendly nations in all parts of the world, would have an enormous influence today, hopefully, for peace and the well-being of all members of the human family.[11]

Having made this observation from the point of view of the Chinese and Russian people themselves, we believe that a meaningful suggestion from an outsider would have to be that their two governments had better put to an end their hostilities toward each other *quickly*, in their common survival interest.

22

Proposal: A Peaceful Revolution In The USA

We have finally arrived back home, to our own country, the United States of America. We have said some harsh things about our homeland, but really not about the great mass of everyday people. You will recall that the harsh words were against our own self-centered industrial aristocracy, whose enormous hunger for material wealth and power over others, calls for much more effective counter-action by everyday people than harsh words, alone, can produce.

In this and the following chapter on the proposed American Revolution, we envisage, first, a peaceful method of restructuring our domestic economy; second, a continuance of our search for a way by which the governments of the world can abandon the international jungle, and create a peaceful world community. Once we have documented the evidence in behalf of this twofold societal objective, both we and the reader come face to face, for the last time, with the NSHS Ultimate Imperative.

We have noted that the "four revolutions, though based on just cause and motivated by lofty ideals", did not come up with the answer to that Imperative. We did, however, make the bold prophesy that a careful examination of the accomplishments and shortcomings of those revolutions and, indeed, of our ideas for a peaceful one in the USA, will enable us to detect more readily the elusive cause of, and answer to, so much misery among the peoples of our planet's badly misnomered civilized nations." It is, therefore, proper to introduce the missing link in our search, when the evidence is in, which means at the end. But now to these two chapters, in the hope that they, too, will bring us a bit closer to our destination.

The Comparative USA Heritage

Wise and creative people through the ages, have pondered the vision of a better world, and sometimes they have acted upon it. The founding fathers of our own nation waged a war of liberation against the British, to establish a democratic government; and they laid down the principle of democracy as the cornerstone of our Constitution. The dream of a democracy, over two hundred years ago, must again inspire us. We have to face up honestly to the fact that the democratic process has been so thoroughly corrupted in our country, by the new industrial aristocracy, that the vast majority of our people have lost faith in it; and they are overwhelmed by the thought of being powerless to do anything about it. Nearly half of our population does not bother to vote, and of those of us who go to the polls, many feel that their vote really doesn't count.

This is common knowledge. But people can and *must* do something to rekindle the democratic spirit. We must not confuse the *corrupters* of the democratic process with the *principles* of democracy itself. We have stated earlier that, if history teaches us anything, it is that no self-seeking ruling class—exemplified by the ancient warrior and ecclesiastical tyrannies, the later agricultural aristocracies, and today's industrial elites—can rule for long, if the collective Will of the people demands its termination.

To implement that Will we need to begin by recognizing the great differences in past and present socioeconomic realities in the United States, compared to those in pre-revolutionary Sweden, Mexico, Russia, and China. We could no more engage in successful social revolution, today, the way the people of those countries had to do it, than they could have done it our way in their time. This can be illustrated strikingly, by listing the dissimilarities in two contrasting columns:

The Eve Of Revolution In

Sweden, Mexico, Russia, China (60 to 170 years ago)	**The United States** (Today)
For centuries the people had been oppressed by their ruling monarchs and land-owning nobilities.	We in the USA are accustomed to a life of material abundance, and political freedom.
On the eve of revolution, 85 to 90 percent of the people lived in dire poverty; periodic famines decimated millions of them.	Less than 20 percent of our people live in poverty; the great majority enjoy a comfortable to luxurious standard of life.
Except for Sweden, the people were mercilessly exploited by foreign industrialists, on the one	Our people, blessed with rich food-bearing lands, a heritage of freedom and democracy, left to

hand, and the landed gentry, on the other.

The people had little or no voice in government. All political power was vested in monarchs who ruled "by the divine right of kings", and in their subordinate aristocracies. This power was, however, being challenged by the rising class of foreign, as well as by the native industrialists.

The revolutions succeeded because the ruling castes possessed no decisive superiority over that of the rebelling populations, in the knowledge, control, and use of prevailing military armaments. Travel by air was in its infancy; the same can be said about radio and TV communication. The nuclear bomb and other devastating nuclear inventions were non-existent.

us by our forbears, have never feared oppression by foreign conquerers.

The Constitution under which our government was founded over 200 years ago, makes the heads of state, and legislative personnel, the servants of the people who, except for some appointive offices, elect them for a term of years. Our people cherish this right and realize that it is now being endangered by the industrial elite.

Travel is faster than sound, communications instantaneous. Sophisticated weapons of war, in any form, and computerized techniques of covert surveillance of private and collective activities are possessed solely by our industrial tycoons. This makes the old military strategy for social change obsolete *within* an advanced industrial society like the United States.

These realities make armed insurrection for basic change in the United States, an act of collective suicide. But the weakness is more than offset by the two hundred year-old democratic heritage, giving strength to our people that remains undiminished. This is, of course, the power of the ballot box, which provides us with weapons that put the odds of winning a peaceful social revolution greatly in our favor. We can fire a thousand of them to every one the wealthy elites can. If pointed in the right direction, they hurt no one and benefit all people, rich and poor.

With the superior power of the ballot box in our hands, people should be ready and eager to fire away. Simple logic dictates that we *begin* the firing on the home front, then join other nations in a common effort to build a just and peaceful world society. We shall start by listing three major domestic targets:

Transferring big private-profit corporations to privately-owned, non-profit Rochdale Cooperatives.

Transferring the earth's non-replaceable resources to Social Ownership.

Preserving and expanding Small Enterprises operated for Private Profit.

It will be helpful to note that two of these programs retain private enterprise; only one eliminates it.

There is, fortunately, very good precedent for the first proposal on private enterprise. It is supplied by the successful operations of many large *Rochdale Cooperatives* around the world and, to a small extent, in the U.S.A. These non-profit, private enterprises cover a wide range of large-scale business undertakings in wholesale and retail merchandising, manufacturing, banking, insurance, housing, healthcare, farming, and transportation, to mention just a few. We shall describe them in more detail after stating briefly the purpose of all three programs.

Significantly different preparatory legal and statutory steps are necessary to transfer to social ownership the immense holdings of giant multinational corporations engaged in the mining of oil, coal, minerals, metals, precious stones, and other limited deposits in the earth's crust and seabed, as well as such slow maturing products of the soil as timber stands. This includes not only extraction of these non-replaceable resources, but also the manufacture of closely related products. The time has come when they can no longer be wantonly depleted for private profit, but must be collectively owned and managed in the common interest by each nation. The well-being, perhaps the very survival, of the human family depends upon their long-term availability.

The program to preserve and expand small businesses operated for private profit is based on the *wisdom* of restoring small personally managed profit enterprises. We have in mind such venerable pursuits as decentralized family-owned farms, serving small food stores in their immediate neighborhoods with tree-ripened fruits and fresh, organically nourished vegetables; also, small manufacturing ventures turning out high quality articles like chairs, tables, cabinets, art objects, etc., all having the distinctive features of the skilled craftsman who designed them for their beauty and durability. From an equally important standpoint, the latter are needed to counter the shoddy quality and sameness of much of today's mass-produced merchandise coming off the assembly line.

Rochdale Cooperatives

What is a Rochdale Cooperative?

The name goes back to 1844, to the little town of Rochdale, England, where a group of poor weavers, inspired by the great humanist, Robert Owen, got the bright idea of pooling their pennies in order to buy the necessities of life wholesale. They began by organizing "The Rochdale Society of Pioneers" which sold to the members at cost, the food, clothings, shoes, and other things it had purchased for them at the reduced wholesale prices.

The project was so successful that they next founded a Cooperative Wholesale Society. Soon they began talking about establishing a wheat and corn mill, a printing plant, and a sickness and death benefit society. Their idea spread quickly among working people throughout Europe and other parts of the world; it expanded into every kind of cooperative merchandising, buying and marketing farm produce, manufacturing and service. By the early 1900s the simple but shrewd operational rules created by the Rochdale pioneers became popularly known as the Rochdale principles.

Described broadly, these principles call for democratic control, open membership, no religious, racial or political discrimination; service at cost; finally, and not to be underestimated, financing of membership education. In practical organizational terms, the Rochdale principles translate themselves into the following operating policies:

1. Ownership of the Cooperative by the members who buy one or more nominally priced shares, to supply the investment capital and the operating and expansion funds.
2. Executive responsibility by a Board of Directors, including representatives of the employees' labor unions, elected by the members.
3. Board of Directors' authority to seek limited interest-bearing loan capital from members, governmental or private lending agencies.
4. One vote per member in all decision-making processes, regardless of the number of shares he or she may own, or the official position the member may hold.
5. No dividends to members on the shares they own. Instead, the Cooperative makes refunds to every member out of surplus over costs, in proportion to the dollar amount of purchases the member has made by the end of a given accounting year.[1]

The provisions of points #4 and #5 distinguish the Rochdale principles from those of commercial corporations operated for private profit. To illustrate: in a profit corporation, the number of votes a stockholder casts is in proportion to the number of shares he or she owns. This means that a few big stockholders can and usually do control the corporation's policies. Since the profits are paid to the corporation's members in proportion to the number of shares they hold, the few wealthy owners take the lion's share.

This is not possible under the Rochdale principles upon which consumer and producer cooperatives throughout the world are largely modelled. Assume, for example, that a cooperative has a surplus of 3% over operating costs, to be refunded to the members. A large family owning just one share but having purchased, say, $2,000 worth of goods, will receive $60; a single member who invested in 10 shares because of his desire to see the cooperative succeed, but has made only $500 worth of purchases, receives a $15 refund. He can, however, buy interest-bearing Co-op bonds.

No one makes a profit or grows rich on the Co-op. All the "profit" goes back into the community as a refund to the member patrons, and since Rochdale cooperatives stress high quality and honest weight, and sell at competitive prices, even non-members do well by trading at the local Co-op.

You will be interested to know that these Co-ops have grown enormously since 1844 and become a part of the life of working people in most countries other than the United States. A few highlights are worth mentioning:

Great Britain: Number of members belonging to consumer, producer and service cooperatives, more than 13,000,000 or 24% of the population; annual business in U.S. dollars, over $6,000,000,000.

Sweden: Over 1,200,000 or 14% of population;

Finland: 1,250,000 or 24% of population;

Iceland: 40,000 or 21% of population;

Norway and *Denmark*: together about 1,000,000 or 10% of population.

France: 3,000,000 members in urban cooperatives; 1,000,000 in agricultural cooperatives; 600 Rochdale societies operate producer cooperatives mostly in building, metallurgy, electricity, paper mills, printing and books.[2]

The Soviet Union and People's Republic of China

Cooperatives play a large role in their economies. Contrary to their origin in the West, they grew out of centuries of oppression by autocratic governments. This makes their background and present operations quite different from those of western Co-ops.

Communist Bloc Countries

Yugoslavia: holds particular interest for us in its development of worker self-management enterprises, combining the principles and collective goals of western cooperatives with those of communist societies. They merit careful study.

Hungary: producer cooperatives provide 11% of the nation's total production; consumer cooperatives, 64% of all retail trade; state-owned stores 34%.

Rumania: cooperatives account for 30% of all clothing and 34% of furniture production, and similar high proportion in the metal trades.[3]

It is important to inform our people that in these and other industrially advanced countries, a strong political alliance has been built up over the years, between members of Rochdale societies and socially conscious labor unions, as well as thoughtful people generally. Together, they exert their combined pressure upon government through political parties controlled by the coalition. Their candidates are committed to introducing legislation and supporting existing laws necessary to their common well-being or being ousted from office at the next election.

This political power of organized people can also be achieved in our country. Its absence explains why the daily press, TV and radio have been able, without effective public counter-action, to withhold information about the steady growth of cooperatives in other countries.

Even scholarly books are all but silent on the subject, for the bulk of them are financed by Foundations whose donors are the Rockefeller, Ford, IBM, Exxon, and other giant corporations. They have no intention of publicizing the success of Rochdale cooperatives.

It should be pointed out, too, that the big chain-store corporations like Safeway, Winn-Dixie, Jewel, K-Mart, etc., have through the years vigorously fought the development of cooperatives in the United States, especially in urban centers where most of our population is concentrated. Although there are some large farmer-owned cooperatives, they are forced by the overwhelming power of the giant private-profit corporations to model their operations more on those of commercial companies than on Rochdale principles.

The same problem confronts a scattering of small Rochdale food cooperatives that are struggling to survive. Even the very few successful ones have to sell at the exorbitant prices set by the big food chains that not only own and control the supply from the farm to the outlets, but also the granaries, railroads, banks. There are, in fact, documented cases of refusal by banks to make loans to financially successful co-ops having more than one store and planning to open additional ones, solely to prevent them from acquiring a serious competitive stature vis-a-vis the private-profit corporations.[4]

In contrast to this, large Rochdales around the world are able, because of their dominant position in all fields, not just in food, to force competing profit corporations to keep their prices down and their quality up, on the threat that if they don't, they, the Co-ops, will do it for them.

Now there are, no doubt, uninformed people among us who will object, at once, to the Rochdale system on the ground that, if Europeans are supposedly doing so well with their Co-ops, how come that we in the United States have achieved much greater prosperity over the years without the Co-ops? The question deserves an answer, but it first raises another question.

Do they know that most European nations have much less food-bearing acreage per capita than we have, and though they have a long history of impoverishment, have largely wiped out poverty? Norway, Sweden, Belgium, Holland, East and West Germany, to list just a few, give us some surprising answers. Only 5 percent of Norway's land is arable and 10 percent of Sweden's, compared with 47 percent in the United States. Population density in the two Germanies is 580 per square mile and nearly 1000 in Belgium and Holland, compared with 57 per square mile in our own country.

Just stop to think for a moment what our economic and environmental situation would be if our population were 10 times greater per square mile, as it is in East and West Germany, or over 2 billion; or 19 times greater per square mile, if compared with Belgium/Holland, for an astounding 3½ billion! Add the startling conjecture of what our living conditions would be if our food-bearing lands, compared to those of Sweden and Norway, were 5 to nearly 10 times *less* than the 47 percent with which nature has endowed us.

Social Ownership Of Unreplaceable Resources

The transfer of large-scale private-profit corporations to social ownership demands invoking the state's power of Eminent Domain, a legal question that has to be resolved because the food and energy crisis has created a national emergency. This means that we have to start implementing our programs where the going will be the most difficult; i.e., with the big conglomerates and miltinationals. Their control of the American way of life, penetrates, literally, every social and economic facet, from manufacturing warships to baking bread, from running railroads to financing baseball teams, from raising grain and hogs to running banks, from endowing universities and the opera to manufacturing toothpaste.

On the face of it, this and the formidable opposition that the tycoons at the head of these corporations will mount against any attempt to confiscate their lucrative properties, account for the notion that the task to change things is hopeless. In countering this state of mind, one must persist in reiterating that it is a grave error to let surface appearances deceive us. Underneath lies the historical reality that all elites are inherently weak, despite their dazzling display of wealth and power; they are, and always have been, easy to topple by a well organized people who know where they are going when the time for fundamental change has come. Every student of history knows this; too many people do not yet know it.

The undisputable fact is that power for good and for bad is achieved by a knowledgeable and unified leadership, and if that leadership has behind it the weight of numbers and the wisdom of substantial segments of the people, no group of aristocrats is a match for it. This should be especially true for us Americans because the democratic spirit runs deep with us; and that also holds among the best of our industrial elites. They are not the heads of an oppressive foreign state, and they believe in the power of the ballot. So, if we stop saying things are hopeless and begin, instead, to pull our numbers together around attainable goals, we can bring about the needed changes in our economy *peacefully* within the democratic process.

There are some distinct advantages in starting where the problems are the most serious and the power and management knowledge the greatest. Among the heads of many multinationals and conglomerates are some resourceful and imaginative leaders who are cognizant of the needs of the times. More than a few of them can be counted upon to help bring about an equitable transfer of ownership; their executive and top management staffs have nothing to fear from the change. Except for cases of serious abuse of subordinates, they will be left essentially intact, because most of them probably rose to their key positions through tested competence in the fiercely competitive struggle that characterizes large-scale profit enterprises.

Rank-and-file employees—factory workers locked into automated production lines, mechanics, clerks, salesmen, all have much to gain and nothing to lose. They will be less subject to the speed-up pressures that are ever present in the mad race for profits among rival corporations. There is, in fact, good evidence that production per man-hour will increase, as has already happened in industrial nations where progress in private and collective non-profit enterprise is much farther along than in our country. When that occurs, employees know that their productive efforts are not primarily directed to enrich a few wealthy owners at the top.

To be sure, there are no shortcuts toward accomplishing these far-reaching changes. It is also well to be forewarned against the illusion that success will come from isolated or sensational victories at the polls by momentarily prominent individuals; hard experience leaves no "ifs" about this futility. Only an organized, determined people striving year in and year out to achieve sound political and economic change along the lines suggested by this activist appeal, will assure progress.

But how long can people wait while conditions become unbearable? And what are the implementing methods by which the goals can be attained? Beyond any doubt, these are pertinent questions. Before answering them we have to remove two great obstacles barring the way to our goals. The one pertains to the legal matter of *Eminent Domain* involved in confiscating the misnomered private properties of giant multinationals and conglomerates; the other, to the current pace of history.

The power of Eminent Domain gives the state the legal right to condemn and take possession of private property, with specification of the owner's right to just compensation. This power may be exercised in order to meet one or another form of national emergency: a natural catastrophe like an earthquake, flood or hurricane; an invasion of our country by a foreign country, or some other serious threat to our nation's safety and well-being.

All three of our socioeconomic programs are relevant to the state's power of Eminent Domain. It is especially true of the program calling for conversion to social ownership of the properties of huge conglomerates operated for private profit, in areas of non-replaceable resources. This does not mean that the state or government will operate these enterprises; it can, and should, give an operating license to a properly organized and financed Rochdale cooperative, or to a number of them.

Implementing the power of Eminent Domain does, however, present an enormous, but not impossible, problem. Reputable attorneys and law school professors advise us that, historically, the state has applied this power only to specific property located in a particular place and with respect to a particular emergency. There is no precedent of our government ever having used the power against largely privately-owned agri-industrial corporations, engaged in a wide range of businesses in all parts of the country and around the world, primarily to make money. The connection between the alleged threat that these corporations pose to our nation's well-being and, in a more final sense, to all nations, should they decide to make the first strike in nuclear warfare, has never been established either in a court of law or by federal legislation. In fact, contemporary law in the United States thrives on a contrary pseudo-individualistic concept.

Fortunately, our Constitution, one of the world's great Charters of human freedom, leaves the door open for proper action to protect and preserve that freedom. The *Original Amendment V* of the *Bill of Rights*, adopted December 15, 1791, says that no person "shall be deprived of life, liberty, or property, without due process of law; nor shall private property be taken for public use without just compensation." We should remember, too, that it is a creation of courageous, though fallible human beings, who could not envisage all the social problems apt to arise over the centuries after their time. This is why they wrote a prior *Article V* setting forth the process for *amending the Constitution*. To date *twenty-six* Amendments have been added.

The framers of our Constitution were also the leaders of a great revolution that had just freed the settlers in the New World from the oppressive rule of the British landowning aristocracy and its rising class of wealthy merchants. Their minds were surely not on these two foreign elites when writing the Bill of Rights, but on preserving the newly won liberty of the early settlers. Benjamin Franklin, Thomas Jefferson, James Madison, Thomas Paine, among the wisest and most influential leaders of the founders of American Union, saw the need for the Original Amendment V as a protection of the properties of the great mass of the people: their dwellings, farms, cattle, timber stands; their personally owned small businesses as well as the belongings of professionals and craftsmen like doctors, carpenters, teachers, lawyers, printers, blacksmiths. They were not thinking of the immense property holdings accumulated by the wealthy.

Was not the anti-social nature of this very difference what the American Revolution was all about? The "rebels" were, indeed, confronted by virtually the same difficult problems and their causes that we in the 1980s have to resolve, only their oppressors were foreign and ours are domestic elites. There was, however, yet another side to this difference. It was in the fundamental, *non-human* created nature of land and title to it, and its elemental life-sustaining produce, that still constituted the major source of wealth and power separating the upper classes from the everyday working people in the 1700s.

Little did anyone dream that in the course of two centuries an industrial era, complex and unprecedented, would emerge; and that an upper class would again succeed in acquiring title to huge aggregates of a new kind of *socially* created property, the collective ownership of which is indivisible from human well-being.

We have made this brief background statement to counter the deeply inculcated notion, in the thinking of the general public, that the intent of *Amendment V* of the Constitution's Bill of Rights applies to all property regardless of its origin, size or purpose—and for all time. It is hardly a sign of paranoia, if one assumes that the most vigorous advocates of this misconstruction are people who own lots of property. More serious, however, is the length to which the wealthy corporate elites will go to brand as subversive any effort to reveal their erroneous and self-seeking purpose. This takes us back to the question: how do we begin implementing the necessary socioeconomic changes?

Our friends of the Bar stress the importance of beginning with the basic legal step provided by the Constitution: invoke the power of Eminent Domain, by means of a *twenty-seventh* Constitutional Amendment. Following are the proposed title and a summation of the contents:

THE SOCIAL JUSTICE AMENDMENT TO THE CONSTITUTION OF THE UNITED STATES

Section 1. The natural and social resources of the United States are the property of the nation, and shall be taken and used for the best interests of the people of the entire nation and not of private owners, except that control of these resources shall be taken from private owners only by due process of law, and with compensation based on a fair computation of the present owners' percentage of title in relation to that of the present and past *non-owner* participants, whose physical and mental labors created the far greater portion of the corporation's total worth.

Section 2. The major means and media of communications, of transportation, of energy, of public utilities, of credit and the media of exchange, of social welfare and security, as well as the major service and production enterprises functioning within both the earth's biosphere and in outer space, are and shall hereafter be the property and province of the people of the United States. They may be licensed to the shareholding members of privately owned nonprofit Richdale Cooperatives, except that the control and governance of these matters and of the materials, equipments and manifestations, shall be taken from the owners of corporate and/or partnership enterprises, operated for private profit, only by due process of law, and with compensation as set forth herein in Section 1; and the Congress shall make the laws governing these things.

Section 3. Corporations and other types of groups of persons or organizations, for profit or not for profit, shall possess only those rights and powers that are specifically granted to them by the law; and the formation, amendment, consolidation, or dissolution of such organizations shall be subject to laws duly adopted by the Congress.

Section 4. Local voter control of communications, utilities, public welfare and the other types of resources named in Sections 1 and 2 above, may be continued where such local control patently is effective and beneficial to the people of the area and of the nation, but this value judgment shall be made by the Supreme Court of the United States through a Special Masters Chamber consisting of nine persons, one each to be named by each Justice of the Supreme Court, except that neither the local control nor Supreme Court value judgment shall in any manner replace or jeopardize the ownership of such locally controlled and managed social property-resources by the people of this nation, as specified in the above Sections 1 and 2.

Section 5. Small farms, small industrial enterprises, and other small businesses, owned and operated for profit by private persons or organizations, shall be exempt from the foregoing provisions of Sections 1 through 4; but the cutoff criteria as to size, capital assets, and range of such small enterprises, shall be determined each three years by the Congress of the United States; and the decision of the Congress that a private-profit establishment has become a subject for private non-profit Rochdale Cooperative or societal ownership and operation, shall not be effective until it has been reviewed as to due process by the Supreme Court of the United States, Special Masters Chamber; this procedure shall, however, be subject to the further mandate that the Supreme Court forward its findings, as to constitutionality, to the Congress within one year after the Congressional decision was made, in the absence of which the decision of the Congress shall become effective.

This Constitutional Amendment, if adopted, and allowing for such refinements as may be deemed necessary to meet the nature of the opposition and public mood, at the time it is under consideration by Congress and the American people, will open the door to equitable government legislation. However, in re-examining the present wording of the proposed Amendment, we think one phrase in Section 1 needs clarification. It pertains to the provision that compensation be "based on a fair computation of the present owners' percentage of title, in relation to that of *present and past non-owner participants*, whose physical and mental labors created the far greater portion of the corporation's total worth."

This requirement rests on the social philosophy underlying the three major planks for restructuring our economy. It was stated beautifully many years ago by a famous French philosopher who put it this way:

> You are undone,
> If once you forget that
> The fruits of the Earth
> Belong to all of us;
> And the Earth itself,
>
> To no one.
> Jean Jacques Rousseau
> 1753

Now, if the fruits of the earth belong to all of us, then the yield of hand and brain belongs to every participant helping to bear the fruit. Irrespective of the nature of one's specific role in a productive or service enterprise, be it as a rank-and-file worker, a technical, professional or management specialist, a tiller of the soil, a musician, a sculptor, *they all own it* in a very inclusive sense. This holds equally for the top executive and the day laborer on the lowest ownership rung, but, for all of them, only in a passing sense, for eventually it all goes back to *Mother Nature* owned by no one.

Where does this leave the biggest working stockowner? As one of the multitude of transitory owners, he, too, is included. And the outside investor? It just leaves him on the outside if he has never done a day's work.

We move on to—

The Pace of History

Today's incredibly swift pace of history exerts an inevitable impact on the conditions to be encountered by all of us Americans, irrespective of the role each of us will play, let us say, during the rest of the decade of the 1980s. We have in mind the international power struggle that is coming to a head, and in which we, in the United States, may be affected more dramatically than the people of other countries. The setting goes back to World War II, at the end of which Great Britain had to relinquish its status as the leading world power to the United States. In light of this, consider the following:

With travel faster than sound, and audio-visual communications over great distances instantaneous, a year today is like a hundred years in the past—a past that moved at a snail's pace compared to history's present dizzy pace. The full impact of the political meaning of this has yet to be felt.

If, for example, we compute the accelerated speed of current history against the lumbering pace in the past, say, at a ratio of ten to one (a conservative if not a precise and surely not a conjectural figure), then, based on the observable movement of contemporary events and those of recorded history, we come to this remarkable finding: the 34 year old United States World Empire, measured from its high point in 1947 to its discernable decline in 1981, has a remaining time continuum of perhaps another ten to fifteen years at the most, when compared to the equivalent time-span of the world's two longest surviving past Empires, the Roman and the British.

To put it more specifically: the Roman Empire lasted about 360 years (equal to 36 years today by our historical slide-rule), from the time of its generally accepted zenith in the reign of Hadrian (98–117 A.D.), to its fall in 476 when the last of the Roman Emperors, Romulus Augustulus, was deposed by the Goth, Odoacer. The British Empire lasted 184 years, from its moment of greatest glory in 1763, when England defeated its archrivals, France and Spain, to emerge as mistress of the sea—a period of less than twenty years in today's technological age.

This tremendous speed-up in the flow of human events is the premise from which we Americans must face up to the fact that the United States World Empire has about run its course, and that fundamental societal change is upon us.

If this projection makes sense, then the reason becomes doubly clear why people who have not yet reached advanced age, have a strong personal stake in joining with others to plan against the rough days ahead; they will have to live through those days.

Some of you may have watched the TV program in 1976 when the popular commentator, Alistair Cooke, addressed Congress to celebrate the Bicentennial Year of the American Revolution. He recalled that only about a third of the people were for the Revolution; two-thirds were either against it or couldn't care less. To this we should add that, according to the record, only a handful *worked* for the Revolution. Benjamin Franklin is credited as having told his fellow revolutionaries, "we have to hang together because if we don't, we will surely hang separately."

Benjamin Franklin is telling us revolutionaries of today's highly organized American industrial society that, like the founding fathers of American Union, we too "must hang together", by organizing around a sound and workable program, to restructure our economy. Only our collective strength can win a peaceful revolution at the ballot box; and the industrial elite, with all its wealth, will be powerless to defeat us.

23

Proposal:
A Peaceful Revolution
in the USA
(Continued)

We have set forth the political action that should enable us Americans to restore our cherished democratic heritage. Yet, even with the swift pace of current history, it will take some time to accomplish this—thirty or forty years? According to our historical slide-rule, it may not take that long. But in the interim, millions of our people will be enduring great hardships. We can help minimize them, by organizing politically, and electing candidates sincerely committed, not only to the three major programs, but to the need for *immediate legislative action* to deal with these hardships.

Let us list some of the most pressing needs—without reference to the global imperative of a nuclear freeze, for which everyone must work, lest no one be alive to deal with anything—and specify in a few words what ought to be done quickly about:

Pockets of Extreme Poverty

Occupational Employment and Training

The Tragic Social Injustice

The Plight of Small Business

Rights and Responsibilities of the Elderly and Handicapped

Regional Integration of Industrial Centers

Worker Self-Management Enterprises

Solar Energy

We shall discuss these problems as domestic issues, then show their interrelationship with the mounting world crisis. Their global dimension thus merits your careful examination, and collective political action with other concerned people.

The seriousness of pockets of extreme poverty can be stated in a few sentences. Upwards of 15 percent of our population lives below the poverty line. This translates into more than thirty million people in the

239

United States, the richest nation on earth, who are hungry, undernourished, ill-housed, and highly vulnerable to disease. Most unforgiveably hurt are children, the aged and infirm. Medical science tells us that prolonged malnutrition of children under the age of six can damage them physically and mentally for life. If the industrial nations of Europe, possessing less abundant food-bearing resources per capita than we do, and many more people per square mile, can wipe out extreme poverty, then we, from even the simplest humanitarian standpoint, ought not to tolerate it one minute longer than is necessary to eradicate it with all speed.

The other immediate action proposals offer some answers to ending this social blight upon our nation.

Occupational Training and Employment

Our nation is entering the decade of the 1980s with multimillions of normally employed people out of work, plus many who are underemployed. We have to strive for enactment of comprehensive federal and state laws for occupational training of unskilled workers, who constitute the great majority of the unemployed, and for absorption of all others in a balanced system of badly needed public works and cooperation by private enterprises.

We must, of course, recognize that this will be one of the most difficult initial programs to implement, because training and reemployment, in both private industry and public works, have to be planned and financed by the big private-profit corporations, matched by government subsidies. It's an undertaking that neither wants. First, the corporations like nothing better than a substantial supply of unemployed workers, to strengthen their labor contracts and, if failure to agree on terms results in a strike, to have a good supply of unemployed workers available to help break the strike. Second, the whole idea of underwriting truly meaningful training, cuts too heavily into their profits, while the mere mention of public works is equivalent to high treason.

This is why it is so important to move rapidly with a growing body of organized citizens, unified under the basically sound long-range programs outlined earlier. The need takes us to the key part of the "immediate demand" for full employment and occupational training: *a new kind of public works*. The time has come when public works employment in our country—long established elsewhere—must be accorded the dignity of providing essential year-round services to the state and community in many seriously neglected fields. This cannot be brought about by haphazard crash programs. In fact, it calls for a permanent system of federal/state funded public works designed to—

1. Redevelop the inner cities of large industrial centers;
2. Develop scientific land-use programs, from the findings of which can be established new industry-agriculture related cities of moderate size;
3. Help poor rural urban communities improve their public facilities and services;
4. Provide inexpensive transportation for people going to and from work;
5. Restructure the federal and state highway system to make possible speedy development of an interurban mass-transit passenger service;
6. Accelerate low-cost housing programs;
7. Conserve forest lands, plant and animal wildlife.

In order to operate efficiently, these public works programs must be supplemented with paid occupational training. They need also to be part of a system of quick and easy shifts of interested workers and their families from high unemployment areas to places where there is a labor shortage.

As previously noted, such just plans are well advanced in societies that have made considerable progress in both nonprofit privately owned large Rochdale Co-ops and socially owned agri-industrial enterprises. We Americans can and must take the same first hard steps that other peoples, too, had to take to reach the more distant goals; and along with a good beginning goes adoption of an annual wage for all registered working people, payable 12 months of the year and sufficient for a decent standard of living.

The Tragic Social Injustice

This tragic injustice had its beginning in the year 1619, when a gang of seafaring merchants of the lowest order of depraved human beings docked their ocean-going schooner in Chesapeake Bay. They brought a "cargo" of fellow human beings, captured in western and central tropical Africa, to be sold as cheap work animals to the early European settlers in the New World. The first people they contacted were Britishers living just off a small inlet of the Bay, in a territory known as Virginia, named after the unmarried Virgin Queen Elizabeth.

These despicable merchants in African slavery had been doing a profitable business for many years with wealthy families in England, some of whose adventuresome members had taken off for the New

World, to settle in Virginia. The traders knew, therefore, that they had willing buyers for their cargo of Negro slaves.[1]

Developments after the white settlers had won the American Revolution and founded the United States of America, need no repetition here. A few words, taken from an authentic report about what happened, will do. They touch on the experience of one remarkable slave who, as a young man, managed to escape to the far North some years after he had recovered from a not unusual, almost fatal, beating by his master, because it was discovered that he had learned to read! He would have died had he not been able to drag himself into the bushes of a nearby woods, where an aged slave couple got him to their log hut, washed his wounds, secretly nursed and fed him until he was reasonably well.

This dark American never knew the exact date of his birth; sometime in 1817 or 1818 or 1819? He didn't know. The researcher writes:

> His first years were spent in a kind of breeding pen, where, with dogs and pigs and other young of the plantation, black children were raised for the fields and turpentine forests. The only bright memories of his childhood clung round his grandmother's log hut. He remembered touching his mother once. After he was four or five years old he never saw or heard of her again.

Barely out of childhood, he was put to work in the field:

> They told him that he was a slave, that he must bend his back, walk low, with eyes cast down, think not at all and sleep without a dream. But every beat of the hoe against a twisted root, each narrow furrow reaching toward the hill, flight of a bird across the open field, creak of the ox-cart in the road—all spoke to him of freedom.

While he dreamed of freedom, he was also experiencing the grim reality that he and all slaves were auctioned off to the highest bidder. Buyers felt at their bones and muscles, to gauge their strength. Children were taken from their mothers, fathers were separated from mothers, all precisely as was the custom in selling horses, oxen, cattle, hogs, to meet the requirements of the buyers.

This is what the researcher wrote about one slave; she could have written much the same about any slave. She did, however, drive home her point of the tragic injustice of it all, by selecting this particular slave. His name was Frederick Douglass. In 1838 he finally succeeded in escaping via the underground railroad. In the course of his adult life he became a famous Abolitionist, newspaper editor, and statesman. In 1889 President Harrison appointed him Minister to Haiti.[2]

Much has been accomplished to rectify the terrible suffering endured by these Negroid people since President Lincoln announced the Emancipation Proclamation declaring the slaves free. So much more still has to be done! In this decade of the 1980s far too many "white" people are plagued by deep-seated notions, nourished by our forebears over the years, denigrating the human traits of Negroes. To help them overcome their phobia, we would urge them to read a good book on the biological sciences. We quote one prominent geneticist:

> Do race differences in *coloring* have any practical significance? It was formerly doubted that they did, but there is growing evidence that many if not most of the surface racial traits do have what is called "adaptive" value—that is, in a given environment a particular trait confers some special benefit on individuals having it and may lessen the chances of survival for individuals without it. For instance, the heavier skin pigmentation of Negroes serves as a natural protection from the damaging ultra-violet rays of the hot sun and adapts them better to living in the tropics, whereas Whites are at a disadvantage (being, for one thing, more likely to develop skin cancer). On the other hand, in colder and cloudier areas heavily pigmented skins tend to block out the sun rays which are essential for vitamin-D production (important in bone growth); and thus, in the temperate and northern regions, light-complected persons are favored and darker-skinned persons are at a disadvantage (with their children more prone to develop rickets). So, too, heavily-pigmented eyes can be a shield against intense sun or against the glare of snow and ice in the Arctic; and heavily pigmented, thicker and more naturally oily hair might be more advantageous both in tropical environments and in Arctic regions.[3]

One further bit of information, available in any standard Encyclopedia, may be helpful to those among our white population who are troubled about the seemingly inferior life-style among the so-called blacks of today. We cite the following comparative historical data from the Columbia Encyclopedia:

> Many African Negroes have lived in a far more advanced stage of material culture from ancient times. Negroes were one of the many peoples who invaded Egypt, and they influenced and were influenced by the civilization which developed there. In the period c. 1700–1580 B.C., Egyptians and Nubians (Negroes) mingled freely, and black men came to hold important positions in Egyptian government.
>
> Much later, beginning c. 741 B.C., the Nubians initiated a campaign of conquest which held Egypt in subjugation for about a century. In

the northern and western sections of Africa an indigenous Negro culture flourished for centuries before the Arab invasions in the 7th century A.D.[4]

Looking at this ancient "achievement" of black culture, that made Negroes invade the lands of other nations and kill people in wars of conquest, we might ask, in the spirit of Natural Survival Through Human Selection, were the Blacks, then, a better race of human beings *because they looked and acted as we Whites do today*?

Returning to the present, we think that the most effective and just way to give black people every opportunity to build a *better* life, and to give white people every chance to *atone* for the indescribable misery our ancestors inflicted upon Negroes for over 300 years, is to do the following: make the immediate political action programs advocated in this and the preceding chapter heartily available to them, and to other disadvantaged minority groups as well.

The Plight Of Small Business

So far we have charted the course necessary to divest our industrial aristocracy from the ownership of socially created properties. The part leading to a healthy system of Small Business has still to be traversed. This can be done rather quickly because the road has been well travelled and has adequately supplied the needs of the people for many years, until the elites closed it for their own purpose. Of course, it is true that small, personally managed businesses, as well as small Rochdale Cooperatives, cannot thrive and make their distinctive contribution to our economic well-being, so long as the big private-profit corporations control the economy.

They not only control the supply and kinds of merchandise available to the public, but to the wholesalers and retailers as well, whether these are small independent companies or subsidiaries of the big corporations—or Co-ops. The trick is accomplished through "vertical" absorption of traditionally independent firms, extending from the source of the raw materials to the consumer; and by a similar "horizontal" takeover of companies across the board, in virtually every major field of production and service.

The net result is that small businesses, no less than chain outlets of the giants themselves, not only have to sell at the high corporate prices, but supply the public with essentially the same low quality merchandise. Alas, only a few octogenarians (like the writer) know, from personal experience, that you could once buy luscious tree-ripened peaches, plums, apples, at the little grocery store down the street. If you needed only one or two tomatoes, onions, or ears of corn, you didn't have to buy them pre-packaged in quantities you didn't need, and pay for the packaging into the bargain; and the corn and tomatoes, like the fruit, were luscious because the storekeeper bought them himself the day before from the farmer on the outskirts of town. If you went to the corner hardware store to buy a couple of screws or picture hangers, you didn't have to buy them prepackaged in ten times the number you needed and at least ten times the price two would cost.

But this isn't the worst of it. There is the pseudo-scientific speed-up of the yield of the earth's food-bearing lands, by injecting strange chemicals into the soil and then getting a quick output of an atrociously adulterated food unfit to eat. This mad rush to plunder Mother Nature's generous but limited storehouse of life-sustaining resources, and to replace it with more lavishly yielding "scientific" production, makes us mere human animals look as though we're trying to play God to Mother Nature.

We must get back to the work of immediate counter action as regards the crucial role that Small Business must again play in the production and distribution of food. There is an inherent uniqueness in the necessity for us human cultivators and caretakers of nature's life-sustaining soil, to get its precious foods to the dinner-table promptly and in all their nourishing and delectable state at *harvest-time*; and *no sooner*, and with no artificial gimmickry to improve on nature's God-given wonders.

Except for such popular and nourishing foods as pineapples, oranges, bananas, that are enjoyed the world over but can best be grown only in warm and tropical climates; or apples, grapes and peaches, best grown in temperate zones and sometimes requiring shipment over great distances, this inviolate domain of sustenance for every living creature, now demands vigorous governmental action to bring the land's produce and us human consumers close together again.

Unfortunately, this elemental answer for the restoration of Small Business in all food categories does not present itself in connection with the countless millions of customer rip-offs perpetuated by the big conglomerates whenever we make purchases of non-food articles like kitchen utensils; electrical appliances, a wash-machine, a TV set, an automobile. In today's scientific age the complications in the production and distribution of such commodities offer no easy ways by which to transfer parts of the process to Small Business. Obviously, they have to become a part of large-scale non-profit enterprises. There is also emerging, belatedly in the United States, a hybrid form of *capitalist/*

worker self-managed large-scale corporate business, about which more shortly.

In whatever socially healthy direction specific efforts have to go, in order to restore and expand much needed Small Businesses, the responsibility for *immediate* action rests with politically organized everyday people, hopefully, along the lines advocated in this treatise for a Peaceful American Revolution.

Rights and Responsibilties Of The Elderly And The Handicapped

There are approximately 22 million people in the United States over 60 years of age. An estimated 5 million are able-bodied, experienced, in need, and eager to be gainfully employed. There are an additional 2 to 3 million physically disabled, but mentally alert, younger adults equally in need and desirous of suitable training to fit them for full or part-time employment.

So far as the elderly are concerned, most people recognize their right to retirement-benefits, assuring them the necessities and comforts of life and needed health care. Beyond this minimal right there is, however, the importance of restoring a full life-span of productive service for all adults regardless of age, who want to be gainfully employed. This does not gainsay the fact that along with advancing age goes a decline of physical strength, endurance, and ability to maintain the productive pace of younger years. But in our over-emphasis of these physical abilities for productive service, we tend to forget that with age frequently also goes an unimpaired skill, a steadier application, and sometimes a wisdom that comes only with the experience of years.

A grave injustice sometimes becomes an open door to a great opportunity. We have in mind, once again, the giant multinationals and conglomerates, some of whose leaders are civic-minded and creative entrepreneurs. The opposite kinds of problems posed by them and the unemployed elderly—and also the handicapped—can actually be joined. Strange as it may seem, they can become the open door to an unprecedented creative program that is in the common interest of the elderly, the handicapped, and the big corporations. Supported by governmental financial aid, it would call for:

1. Attractive incentive awards to multinationals and other large corporations that have set up accredited *Senior Citizen Corporate* Divisions employing mainly persons over 60.

2. Exemption from federal-state corporation taxes for these Divisions.
3. Supplementary tax credits on a graduated basis above a specified minimum number of workers over 60 years of age in the new Divisions.
4. Hourly wage rates for the elderly in the new Divisions that are somewhat lower than prevailing ones in competitive industry.
5. Preferential governmental procurement policy for the products of a corporation's Senior Citizen Division. This shall apply to anything from paper clips, office furniture, tools, and to every governmental level, from the local to the national.

Such a program would, furthermore, call for similar incentive awards to corporations willing to set up and operate Sheltered Workshops for the handicapped able to work at their plants full or part-time, and for the severely disabled who cannot travel but are able and eager to do productive work at home. There is a long history of noble attempts by social agencies to meet this need. The record is painfully clear, however, as any practitioner can testify, that social agencies, divorced from the regular manufacturing and merchandising operations of industrial corporations, cannot cope with this task alone. We stress the importance of making the change with this closing observation:

> Sheltered workshops for the handicapped both at the plant and for those who are Homebound, must be made part of established industry. Only in this way can they benefit from the combined input of the professional services of social workers, medical and occupational therapists, and the expertise of business corporations engaged in manufacturing, merchandising, and sales promotion.[5]

Regional Integration Of Industrial Centers

The urgent need for this has to be put bluntly. This is because there is prevalent among suburbanites a grand illusion that the quiet, tree-shaded lanes of their suburbs, and widely spread and nicely appointed homes, neatly tucked away from the noise and hubub of the big city—that all this is exclusively the result of their own thrift and wise community building and planning. The fact of the matter is that suburbs would be non-existent were it not for the sustaining nourishment given them daily by their physically dirty, overcrowded, overburdened, bedraggled, impoverished, and altogether unbeauteous mother-city.

All of us frequently hear the righteous pleas made over TV and radio by the mayors and leading citizens of these suburbs, to be let alone and run their own affairs, to get their nagging mother-city off their backs, with her constant begging for help to feed and house her too many laggardly children.

We call attention of suburbanites to these facts:

1. Their employed adults are completely dependent, for their handsomely paying positions, on the public service, transportation, and communications system radiating from the mother-city out across the nation; on the skilled and unskilled labor of millions of workers living in the mother-city; on the network of executive offices still located largely in the mother-city and occupied by company executives and their staffs, many of whom do not live in the city but in the suburbs.

2. Millions of suburbanites work in the mother-city and draw their salaries from firms having installations there; they make daily use of the city's public services, streets and public buildings, but they pay little or nothing for using them. If they drive to and from work, they purchase no city licenses though they use the streets and other public services for their cars. They are not residents of the mother-city! If they own their own homes in the suburb, they pay no property tax to the mother-city, though she is starving for funds to meet the expenses they, the suburbanites, help her incur. They pay little or no city sales tax, for they do most or all of their family shopping in the suburb, though they have the benefits of the city's police, fire, power, light, water, sanitation.

Any thoughtful child knows that this draining off of the mother-city's revenue by suburbanites who use, but don't pay their fair share of the expenses incurred in providing the public services they use, *is wrong*. The Mayors and leading citizens of suburbs should understand this even better, because they know *there would be no suburbs without the broad lap of the mother-city*.

Worker Self-Managed Enterprises

Having just referred to this, let us begin by reiterating that Worker Self-Managed large-scale enterprises, to be politically and economically meaningful, have to be based on the intent of the two major programs outlined in this study: social ownership of the earth's non-replaceable resources, and non-profit, privately managed other large businesses, functioning as Rochdale Cooperatives.

We must not confuse this fundamental with hundreds of examples of invitations now being offered by our industrial elites to their employees, to participate in *Employee Stock Ownership Plans* (ESOPs). Such plans are far from allowing a transfer of ownership-control from a corporation's wealthy owners to the employees. In rare cases, generally when a comparatively small firm of a thousand or fewer employees is about to collapse or has to shut down its plant, do the employees have a chance to buy it and run it as a worker-managed enterprise, and to hire and fire its trained and experienced technical, specialist, research, and management personnel.[6]

ESOPs really reflect a long overdue awareness in our country, that the old system of adversary relationships between employees and owners is done for in much of the rest of the world, and is undermining the competitive ability of U.S. based conglomerates in international trade. It would, therefore, be a mistake to equate what our elites are offering to employees with what is happening around the world. We must keep in mind the fact that our country is still the military and economic arsenal of the misnomered "free enterprise" system of pure capitalism. Most other industrially advanced nations, regardless of the merits of their socio-economic ideologies, have gone communist, socialist, or into a mixture of the two with a lingering capitalism. Within these evolving lifestyles, the anti-capitalist political parties often take control, or seriously challenge the pro-capitalist parties for control, of the state—and business!

Viewed from this frame of reference, Worker-Managed Enterprises take on a very important domestic and international set of functions. A quick global overview shows that, in addition to large cooperative ownership, recent developments of worker-managed production and service enterprises have become increasingly prevalent in communist Russia, China, and the nations of Southeast Europe, particularly in Yugoslavia.

In Yugoslavia, government and party leaders have discovered, as have the leaders of other communist states, that outright *state* ownership of all large-scale socially created agri-industrial properties is not a cure-all of the evils of capitalism. It, also, suffers from an absence of the fullest possible play of individual initiative and creativity, so ardently and improperly lauded by the industrial elites of the United States as being their distinctive contribution to human progress. The simple truth is that the contribution is much more effective if not allowed to be misused or corrupted in order to benefit a few rather than all of the contributors.[7]

On March 2, 1982 the Ford Company and the United Automobile Workers Union announced an agreement to set up an ESOP plan.

Ford, one of the four largest American world corporations, offered to guarantee life-time employment to some 80 percent of its employees, and to work out a system with the union for worker participation in the company's decision-making processes and responsibilities; also, an equitable plan of profit-sharing by the workers. The union agreed to make corresponding concessions, with respect to wages, paid time for holidays, and other kinds of fringe benefits, still to be worked out.

The whole idea has aroused a great deal of pro-and-con discussion among working people and the public generally. It bears watching.

Solar Energy

From an ultimate survival standpoint, the world energy crisis is one of the fundamental problems facing mankind. To date, the earth's major energy resources are oil, coal and nuclear power, used and misused by the industrial elites of a few nations to make money rather than to serve society. It is, thus, not surprising that the Research and Development (R&D) specialists of the big conglomerates have been instructed to give solar energy an image to look like something for science-fiction; this, notwithstanding the fact that nuclear/fossil power is polluting the earth's biosphere to a dangerous extent, and despite the fact that many of the world's noted scientists in the energy field urge vigorous R&D work in solar energy.

The reasons for opposing this are obvious: there are huge profits to be made at every stage in the present energy business. The opportunities extend in every direction, from extracting the oil, coal, metals and uranium, to refining, processing and converting them into the end products. Those products may include anything from building a house, a bridge, a municipal heating or lighting system, to a nuclear bomb, a missile, battleship, chemical defoliant. The most alluring part is that the R&D costs are chargeable to operations before computing the profits!

Few, if any, of these immediate profit lures have presented themselves in Solar Energy. The Sun's rays are free and no way has yet been found to package and sell them at a profit. Not so long ago the disillusioned Senator Abourezk, of South Dakota, had this to say after his bill for a solar energy appropriation was defeated:

> While the Atomic Energy Commission is trying to deceive the public into thinking that solar energy is 'way down the road and decades away', Exxon, Gulf, and Shell have bought up solar power companies (and are) doing whatever they can to make that prophecy come true.

But as the great poet, Robert Burns, said a long time ago: "The best laid plans of mice and men gang aft aglay." Something has happened that has upset the best laid plans of the oil experts, and they are suddenly investing heavily in solar energy. One of the reasons is that in 1968 Dr. Peter Glaser, an engineer at Cambridge, invented and later patented, an apparatus that can convert solar energy to electricity, beam it to earth via microwaves from a *Satellite Solar Power Station* (SSPS) some 22,000 miles above the earth, and then reconvert the microwaves back to high voltage electric power by means of receiving antenna on the ground.

Nonetheless, as Senator Abourezk warned us, the oil and coal barons are still down-playing solar energy while busy at work on it, to assure their control of what they now see as an emerging market. They have been orchestrating public opinion so successfully for so many years that solar power is not only far down the road, but that it will not, for a long time in the future, meet more than a mere five to ten percent of our country's power needs. It, therefore, comes as no surprise to find the deliberately fabricated notion accepted as fact by most people.

As of this writing, some of the multinationals and other large corporations, reported as investing heavily in SSPS and similar projects, include Martin Marietta, McDonnell Douglas, Honeywell, Raytheon, IBM, General Electric, Gruman, Boeing, Rockwell. The journalist, Adam Hochschild, who has interviewed the SSPS inventor, reports that "if (these) backers have their way, a prototype Satellite Solar Power Station will be aloft within a decade." And the initial cost to develop the technology alone is mind-boggling. Estimated on the low side by one of the participating corporations, it will be anywhere from $40 to $80 billion; mass-production after that, says Glaser, himself, will cost $7.6 to $15 billion for *each station*—to be paid out of your and all of our tax and purchasing dollars, say we.

The dangers of SSPS are variously described by energy scientists as potential environmental catastrophes and lethal weapons. Science writer, Paul Brodeur, declares the microwaves to be a particularly insidious form of pollution because you can't see or hear them as they beam down on a five-mile wide antenna. People in airplanes and birds flying through the heated column of air the microwave creates, will be heavily radiated. Rain, clouds, and hail all tend to disperse microwaves. Even if the SSPS beam is 99.9 percent on target, five million stray watts of electricity will still be bombarding people nearby. Dr. Aden Meinel, Professor of Optical Sciences at the University of Arizona, compares an SSPS to "a giant microwave oven cooking all people, plants and animals caught by the wandering beam."[8]

This is the dark side of the picture, not of solar energy itself, but of the dangers of its misuse by private-profit conglomerates motivated primarily to make money for their stockholders. There is, fortunately also an attractive side, revealing the countryside and urban residential areas dotted with small, decentralized solar energy units generating their own yet coordinated solar power, owned and operated by Rochdale Cooperatives. Bear in mind that this is the main point of our very brief survey of the solar energy pros and cons.

The sun's rays are present everywhere in one form or another. They can be converted on-the-spot into a system of diversified solar power capable of generating energy *continuously*, in all weather and all seasons. Solar engineers know that this can be done by integrating the sun's rays with their indirect power in prevailing winds, ocean-depth and surface heat-exchange, and compressed gases below the earth's crust. These don't have to be piped, shipped, flown or carted from places of supply to places of need!

We Americans are only now becoming aware of this, and of the fact that during the past few decades, hundreds of thousands of small heating units have become standard equipment in many parts of the world—in homes, public buildings like schools, libraries, churches, museums, and in a rapidly growing number of commercial buildings. In Australia, solar water-heating is required by law. Government subsidized solar energy R&D work in Japan, France, Scandinavia, and Israel, much of it done by Co-ops, has left us far behind in the wide use of solar power.

There is another truly beautiful part of the picture, aside from its natural aesthetic qualities. This is the built-in Rochdale principle of private, non-profit ownership. It enables the operators of small, self-sufficient units to systemize and share their knowledge and experience through regional R&D bodies, the entire local and area complex being owned and controlled by the Cooperative's small shareowners drawn from the great mass of the people.

Finally, we do not want to say that outer-space solar power stations are inherently bad. However, given the great unsolved outer-space problems, and the costs and dangers, mankind had better move slowly and cautiously. Stressing the fact once again, this amounts to a political imperative calling for the dislodgment of our industrial aristocracy from the controls.

On The World Front

The World Affairs part of this study can be stated more briefly than the thoughts that we shared with you on Domestic Affairs. This is obviously not because the subject is less important, but rather because no one government, including ours, can or should do more than contribute its own thinking and resources to global efforts embodying the pooled input of all peoples around the world.

Few knowledgeable people question the need for a globally dimensioned system of just world order. How such a system can be established is a subject as thorny as it is pressing. Basic, however, to any plan for practical work organization is its ability to help the member-states defeat their two most deadly enemies: the spectre of hunger wherever it raises its ugly head and the despoliation of Mother Nature's limited food-bearing resources by wanton military and technological destruction.

The longing for a just world order has eluded humankind through countless centuries. In our own time the United Nations is but the third futile attempt to reach the goal. There are many reasons, on which it is wise to cogitate as we strive with other nations, regardless of their cultures or economic systems, to build a better world.

The aspiration has to surmount a huge wall of international difficulties that are deeply rooted in a host of outmoded ideas. They rest on the notion that self-preservation demands a bitter struggle for survival because nature does not provide enough food for all. Although the assumption goes back long before Charles Darwin gave it his scientific blessing as a dubiously universal law of nature, the important thing is that it still dominates human behavior. People in the big warrior nations rely primarily on their military might for success in the "struggle of existence."

Countering this ancient belief in the inevitability of international warfare is a whole new world of realities that has suddenly emerged and obliterated the very foundation of the prevailing warrior cults. Many people do not know that the explosive discoveries in science and technology now make starvation anywhere in this planet unnecessary and immoral. It happened so suddenly, we can't quite accept it as being real. People still think in the obsolete thought patterns of nature's scarcity and the struggle to survive. Our industrial aristocracy, in its greed for money and power, *sees to it* that we Americans continue to hold the notion.

The Conundrum of the United Nations (UN)

The UN is a step in the right direction. But why has it made little, if any, progress to-date? We must remember that it was organized, not by representatives of the world's common people, but by spokesmen for the elites of the five victorious nations of World War II. The UN

Charter gives any one of them the power to veto (nullify) action that the majority or perhaps the total membership of some 150 nations wants to take on major issues of war and peace; one lone nation of the big five can still the voice of 146 or more other members. This makes it necessary to alert ourselves to the UN's underlying plight.

We are aware that the UN is not a pioneering institution, but the third in a line of similar "world peace" organizations. They go back 165 years, each spawned in the wake of a devastating war: the Holy Alliance in 1815, after the Napoleonic Wars, which called upon the Princes of the victorious nations to end the scourge of war; the League of Nations in 1920, after World War I, to make the world safe for democracy; now the UN. All of them were set up by the victors of the latest war to give international sanction to the spoils of war. None of them was given the authority to confront the *causes* of war, or to call upon the member-states to get rid of them!

Fortunately, a ray of hope has begun to shine for the UN. Since the early 1960s a growing number of the impoverished member-nations, frustrated by the western powers' adamant refusal to shift the UN's basic tenets from so-called peace-keeping to protect their lucrative international holdings, to globally dimensioned economic improvement, have organized their own mutual assistance organization, while retaining UN membership. It began as "the 77"; and after the rich oil producing nations (OPEC) joined them, their number increased to 103, or more than two-thirds of the total UN membership.[9]

Ridiculed at first by the big western powers, they soon astounded them by making rapid progress in helping each other develop their agricultural and industrial resources; and even more strikingly, by protecting each other against the former colonial powers of the West, through a unified foreign relations policy, and collective action in their common interest. They are now known as the *Organization of Non-Aligned Nations*—meaning non-aligned with both the big communist and capitalist nations. As a result, it is no longer a simple matter for the rich warrior nations, in collusion with the landed aristocracies of the now organized and vigorous "103" nations, to exploit their peoples to the hilt and dominate their internal affairs.[10]

It is wise not to put much credence in the TV and radio news broadcasts, or in those of the daily newspapers, about the revolutionary happenings in the Third World. Remember, these news media are owned lock-stock-and-barrel by the multinationals, whose lucrative world-wide possessions are being jeopardized by the collective policies of the Non-Aligned Nations. This is why the trigger-happy politicians in the White House, and in both Houses of Congress, at this writing (Spring 1983), are doing a lot of sword rattling.

It may seem strange that, if the one-time profitable investments of our industrial aristocracy are mainly in the countries now dominated by the "103," the present incumbent of the White House is not preparing a nuclear strike at these nations, but at the Soviet Union. The answer is not hard to find. So long as that powerful nation stands in the way, a major military campaign against the leading nations of the Non-Aligned, would be strongly opposed by the Russians. Once they were destroyed as a contender, the road would be clear to our giant corporation's possessions in the Third World. What can we do to prevent the present political office holders in Washington from carrying out this plan of the Reagan Administration? We can throw the rascals out at the next Presidential and Congressional election.

We return to a more pleasant ray of light for the United Nations. Now that this world agency is no longer owned outright by five big powers, and the Non-Aligned can match their strength, in and out of the UN, the possibility of restructuring it into a democratic and effective world body, brightens. The National Missions to the UN, and all concerned people, can henceforth focus their thinking on ways to create a *United Nations System*, capable not only of ameliorating international tensions, but of becoming a positive force in transforming an international jungle into a peaceful world community. Let us call it –

A United Nations System Of World Service Federation

We propose that the UN/WSF, like the present UN, be a free association, a non-political world agency of nation-states. Unlike the UN, it will engage in socio-economic undertakings in a collective manner never before attempted on a global scale. A few things that it will *not* be, warrant mention. It will have neither armaments, military manpower, nor other coercive powers over the member-states. It will not be a military or "governmental" supra-state.[11]

Now, let us go in for some unorthodox thinking. First, the UN/WSF System will, in concurrence with the member-states, shift its priorities in international collaboration from the sterile war/peace efforts to organized action in the areas of common national and world needs; i.e., to eliminate poverty and disease, environmental pollution, food and energy shortages. Second, in order to accomplish this, it will have to set up two autonomous World Organizations within the system. The one will mediate conflicts arising out of *clashing* national interests, that might otherwise result in war. The other will help the member-states meet their *common* needs, in the solution of which all of them want desperately to cooperate out of self-interest.

The structure and functions of such a UN/WSF cooperative system may be described as follows:

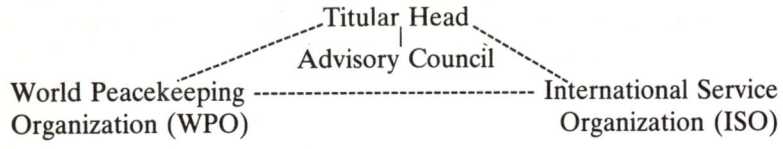

THE UN/WSF SYSTEM*

```
                    Titular Head
                         |
                   Advisory Council
World Peacekeeping  ----------------------  International Service
Organization (WPO)                          Organization (ISO)
```

*The dotted line indicates the voluntary cooperative relationship between the System's world bodies.

The World Peacekeeping Organization (WPO)

WPO will provide a mediating service to the member-states, to help them resolve their clashing interests short of war. It wisely leaves jurisdiction in common interest services to the cooperating but independent sister organization, for it takes no great vision to see the futility of trying to mix the sordid business of war versus peace and the mutual desire of all nations to meet their common needs. That mixture has plagued the United Nations since its very inception, especially as it relates to the violent international conflcts engaged in covertly by the giant multinational corporations of the big powers. To keep the lid on these conflcts, the member-states will naturally send delegates to the WPO who are qualified in the art of collective persuasion to prevent war.

The International Services Organization (ISO)

In this independent global body lies the hope of a troubled world. The International Services Organization will help the WSF members coordinate and pool their knowledge and resources in an all-out attack on the now overriding world needs they know they must solve together. To this end ISO will not only provide assistance for their collective action programs in the civilian areas previously mentioned, but also in the research and development of oceanic resources, solar energy, and other vital outer-space undertakings whose time has come.

As in the radically different experience and world outlook requirements of WPO, we may assume that governments will send delegates to ISO who have outstanding qualifications in the common interest fields coming under ISO jurisdiction. Specialized staffs will, actually, perform the planning, research, and internal ISO coordinating and administrative tasks, under the direction of appropriate delegate committees.

With respect to the ISO member-nations themselves, it should be emphasized that both the authority and responsibility for carrying out particular projects in health, conservation, agriculture, industry, etc., for which the delegates have voted to give matching grants and/or loans to requesting nations, *that authority will remain with the recipient nations*. ISO will, however, retain the right to make regular field checks in order to report to the delegates that the terms of assistance are being met or, if not, to take suitable action including, if necessary, suspension or termination of the agreement.

The Cohesive Structure Of A UN System of World Service Federation

The autonomous operations of WPO and ISO are not as free-wheeling as this quick summary might imply. The fact that they will have to deal with problem-solving in two essentially incompatible world phenomena—clashing versus common national interests—makes it imperative for the two bodies to maintain the closest kind of work relationships. To assure this, may well be the most important task of the system's Titular Head as the presiding officer of the UN/WSF Advisory Committee, composed of the major chairmen of both ISO and WPO. The present UN's Secretary-General would be the logical person to fill that office.

In the beginning, and until such time as the member-nations feel a greater sense of security under effective world organization than they do now, the role of the Titular Head will be symbolical rather than powerful. But the importance of the role is not to be under-estimated. Significant unifying functions will quite logically attach themselves to the dignity of the Titular Head's office. As the Advisory Council's chairperson, elected by majority vote in each of the two world organizations, he or she will lend prestige to the Council's recommendations for common action. The Head would be vested with the authority to call WPO and ISO into joint session on problems of great concern to the peoples of the world, and to address the meeting in a plea for unity and understanding. He might meet with individual Heads-of-State on problems of particular interest to them and, thus, facilitate fruitful dialogue between governments and their key representatives in the UN/WSF system.

Annual Levy Payment By The Member-States

The UN/WSF system will require a mandatory annual levy from each member-state equal to ½ of 1 percent of its gross national product (GNP), with the provision that the bulk of it, perhaps 90 percent, be allocated to ISO and only 10 percent or less to WPO and the office of the Titular Head. The reason for this seemingly lop-sided formula lies in the fact that in the time-span of a few historical seconds, the balance of basic, long-term human concern has shifted dramatically from war/peace issues to the hunger-energy-ecology crisis confronting all mankind. Herein lies the fate of modern man. Herein lies the work of the ISO world body.

The UN/WSF Finance And Population Weighted Voting Formula

The weighted voting plan to be explained *here applies only to ISO*. It need not be used by WPO, unless the members choose to do so, because that world body limits its functions to mediating-services which do not entail pooling enormously large monetary, material and human resources, to enable the member-nations to meet their common civilian needs. Its persuasive role to help them resolve their clashing national interests short of war, calls for collective moral force not material investments.

The ISO Finance/population formula, on the other hand, is designed to provide an equitable voting strength to the delegate or delegates of every ISO member-nation. It accords a numerical voting weight to the representation of each nation, computed on a 50/50 basis (a) for the nation's population-count and (b) for its levy payment. For purposes of explanation, let us assume hypothetically, that ISO adopts a total of 500 votes as a conveniently divisible number representing all its members; that 20 billion dollars is the year's total ISO revenue; and that all the delegates represent the world population of 4 billion people.

Based on these totals, one half of the 500 ISO votes are cast for total population and the other half for total levy payment. Each member-nation's numerical vote is then determined on this 50/50 basis; i.e., its share of the 500 votes is equal to the ratio of its population to the total 4 billion population *plus* the ratio of its levy payment to the total 20 billion dollars paid in by all the ISO members.

You will be interested to know that an actual compilation of the relative voting strength of all present United Nations member-states (152), based on the 50/50 weight of population and levy payment, reveals a surprisingly attractive voting balance. It gives no single bloc of nations, based on political ideology, wealth, or population-count, a majority vote without substantial help from nations outside their particular bloc. And since the only business coming before ISO is of a common interest nature, which poses no unsolvable problems, this plan of voting rights is eminently fair for rich and poor nations alike.

The Top ISO Priority

It bears repetition. The task of wiping out hunger and starvation, and of preserving man's habitat on Earth, is top priority. A number of scientists engaged in exploring outer space are, amazingly enough, proposing a practical first step that can bring speedy results. Their "down-to-earth" idea is—

> to short-circuit the absence of adequate communications and transportation facilities among the world's impoverished nations, by beaming action-oriented information via internationally planned and financed space satellites to countries in need of constructive help in developing their basic resources.

Such broadcasts, if made integral to the pooled assistance of ISO, including the use of trained personnel, regular air-freight shipment of materials, supplies, tools, and equipments, can accomplish miracles. In this unexpected way do astrophysicists propose methods to solve one of mankind's oldest and most stubborn problems. Their long-range plans for researching and developing solar energy and other promising cosmic resources may well prove to be equally on target.

One query that may still be in your mind regarding the need to separate the WPO and ISO functions and carry them out in two independent world bodies, merits answer. Aside from the UN's present structural inequities, to which we have already alluded, there is a compelling psychological reason. It is that the same delegates can't mediate a clashing issue between two nations or blocs of nations on Monday, and come up with findings that favor one side, to the hurt of the other—the latter, in all probability, being one or more of the UN's poor nations; then, on Tuesday, decide on the pros and cons of a common interest matter, all in a perfectly happy mood! This is precisely why two-thirds of the UN's member-nations—the Third World—established their own world organization of the Non-Aligned.

In concluding this study and advocacy of a UN/WSF global system, it is necessary to refer briefly to a false concept, prevalent in the West, as to what the nature and purpose of such an agency should be. It pertains (a) to the idea of *World Government*, and (b), *World Law*.

With respect to the first, we shall be wise to bear in mind that in past as well as present-day primitive society, the term "government" has meaning only when applied to limited territorial political units like tribes, city-states, nations. The people of such in-groups, if drawn together by strong ethnic, religious, and/or language ties, can live with government legislation and laws that are expressive of their common cultural heritage; they can and do give enthusiastic support to their government's exploits against real or imagined foreign enemies.

At the world level there are no strong cultural ties. And by definition, "world government" would have no foreign enemies—unless we manufactured one from another planet. Even more fantastic is the idea that government, at any territorial level, is essential to peace and justice. There has never been a war in all history that was not planned and carried out by government. *Correction*: except one kind of war—revolution AGAINST government. The American Revolution is a beautiful example.

So far as international affairs are concerned, government, which history reveals as being oppressive more often than not, and the *only institution* that has declared and fought all wars, World Government would not only be highly suspect but dangerous. Should it happen in the next few years or decades at the most, the strongest warrior nations or bloc of such nations would very likely take it over in toto.

During the formative years, World Law would be equally inadvisable, but only in the sense of unwanted nation-centered legalistic derivation and wrong timing. Laws are but a codification of long established social practices among culturally and otherwise broadly unified nations, tribes or other territorial in-groups. A UN/WSF will be wise to avoid getting itself entangled in a web of such laws, for they are as diversified and conflcting in international affairs as are the governments that enact them.

One may say in good logic that, genetically, every existing body of laws and statutes has come out of the distinctive lifestyle of a particular people. And since warfare between governments throughout history encompasses many more years than do periods of peace, government laws are hardly good building material for a soundly structured world organization.

It follows from this that a UN/WSF can function very well without trying to adapt itself to these and a host of other in-groups legalistic complications. It is reasonable to suppose that once the wisest leaders and substantial segments of people in a large number of nations are strong enough to launch a UN/WSF successfully, they will bring to the undertaking sensible ideas about World Law. They will proceed pragmatically by developing international policies based on day-to-day experience over a number of years, and retain those that bring clear victories over hunger and old tensions between nations. In time the most successful of the policies will surely become known around the world. Eventually, they will merit codification into law. And so will *evolve* World Law.

Space and, indeed, wisdom prevent entering into a multitude of specifics in this initial study. More comprehensive treatises are already being written, and others may be expected to follow. They will have to include the role of such non-governmental organizations (NGOs) as the *Specialized Agencies* that are privately funded and external to the present UN, though cooperative with it. Suffice it to say that the major service functions of these Agencies will probably be absorbed by UN/WSF because the Agencies have only miniscule funds compared to the mandatory levy payments from all the UN/WSF member-nations. These will consist not only of monetary, but also of in-kind payments.

We may assume that the relative value of each of these kinds of payment, in terms of percentage of GNP, will require intensive study, as will the GNP concept itself. This is because many impoverished and largely agricultural nations do not rely nearly so much on *monetary* as on *in-kind* "media of exchange". This does not mean that the important services of the Specialized Agencies should be discontinued. Some of the most important research and experimental work is accomplished by small, independent organizations like these and other privately endowed groups. It is a case of small being beautiful. But large is beautiful too, like the blue sky of a summer day.

We are nearing the end of our thesis on the larger subject of the endangered human animal. We have stressed the urgency for us humans to heed two life-preserving imperatives: enlightened frugality and reverence of life. Short of fulfilling them, we humans may not survive, or ever attain a genuinely humane culture.

24

The Ultimate Imperative

We have come to the end of our search for the missing link to human wellbeing. You will recall that at various stages of the search we emphasized the importance of two, yet unfulfilled, prerequisites to reaching this goal: *Enlightened Frugality* and *Reverence of Life*.

In Part I we discussed mankind's gross violation of the second requisite, by the brutal mistreatment and misuse of our sentient kin in unlike form, as well as by social injustice and warfare among our own kind.

The Prefatory Comment to Part II credits the social revolutions, to be reviewed, for the limited accomplishments they achieved. But it also points out that they have found neither the cause nor cure of the social inequities that continue to plague us humans, adding that "the real and attainable answer still awaits fulfillment." The comment concludes with a sort of promise; namely, that if we study the pros and cons of the revolutions, we may be able to discover the real answer.

To date, in the fall of 1983, the great majority of us, especially, those among our political, economic and military leaders, not only continue to resist the pleas of creative thinkers, calling for the biological changes set forth in the early portions of our study, but, also, to persist in perpetuating social injustices and devastating military ventures that endanger the survival of the human species.

Throughout our inquiry we have, thus, observed the many ways in which mankind *spurns* both reverence of life and enlightened frugality. However, while pondering the failure of the Biological Imperative to square the colossal debt we humans still owe our kin in unlike form, and the similarly futile struggle of the Marxist revolutionaries to lead the poor and oppressed toward a more just and peaceful society, we think we have found the missing link! Presumptuous though this statement may seem, we shall now document the supportive evidence.

We must begin with the two prerequisites; they are really opposite but inseparable parts of a single fundamental. Reverence of life pertains to our spiritual life-experience; enlightened frugality, to the materialistic side. How to give them the strength that will, literally, *force* us humans to put them into practice, is the question we need to answer now.

Since the conceptual base upon which mankind has to build a radically new kind of spiritual and materialistic way of life, we may well classify the dual transformation as revolutionary. A spiritual, more precisely, a Religious Revolution, will have to lay the corner-stone for the materialistic one. Let us call the latter an Occupational Revolution.

The Religious Revolution

A societal mandate for this revolution implies the urgency for basic change in the existing theological tenets that motivate human beings deeply and *erroneously*. Contrary to this indictment is the age-old assumption that theology—or formal religion—has played an important role in meeting moral problems in the past, and continues to do so in the present. The fact of the matter is that theology, especially the western variety, has done nothing of the kind, as disclosed in the painful findings of this and numerous other studies. The reason lies in theology's *unGodly* false concepts.

A shocking thought? Not at all. There is, moreover, a brighter side to it, which, we trust, will become clear as we explain why theology can and must learn how to play its intended role. Mankind needs to envisage this challenge of the religious imperative as being the foundation of human wellbeing and happiness. The evidence is overwhelming that, in a materialistic sense, no other institution has been able to lay this spiritual corner-stone. Theology can do it, because the religious experience is the most profound endowment bequeathed to us frail and miniscule beings in God's beautiful and wondrous garden of life.

We come to the heart of the problem. What is false in theology the world over? If false, what can be done about it? The answer to both questions has to be *very brief*, because the unknowable "truth" permits of little more than thoughtful human conjecture. We may, thus, say the following:

There is but one all-embracing theological fallacy: the introvertive notion that we atrociously violent and greedy human animals have been created in God's image! Given the awesome totality of countless trillions of plant and animal life forms, all of them God's children, it behooves theologians to cease uttering the nonsense that we humans, particularly, are created in God's image. This irrational demeaning of

God—or of the divine Being by any other name—*is* the extraordinary theological fallacy, and it plays havoc with the spiritual love and compassion needed by and for all of us.

If every transitory life-form, ours, those of all flora and fauna, as well as of equally momentary inorganic ones—a little stone on a hill, the sound of music, the beauty of a sunset—are a part of God, our theologians had better rethink, drastically, their concepts of the identity of God.

On the face of it, the absurdity of a finite organism trying to attribute a specific form to God is indisputable. But this does not gainsay imagining that all creation—ourselves, every other kind of existence on our planet—is what we human animals may reasonably perceive as being God; and to this we must add our faith in God's infinite dimensions and characteristics, revealed in the boundless space of the Cosmos, its uncountable Galaxies, Solar Systems and Planets, trillions of which, probably, support a great diversity of living creatures. This universal, awesome, beautiful and loving Being is God.

Some people, in and out of churches, will say that they see nothing new in this, even though they agree that there is little reverence of life among us humans. We are, however, not talking about people generally, but about theologians. It is important to bear in mind that so deep and obsessive a feeling as the religious experience, gives them an immense power in shaping that experience for their congregations, be they Jews, Christians, Buddhists, Moslems, or whatever.

There are, to be sure, a scant few and, unfortunately, not too well known innovative-minded members among the world's theologians, who do take cognizance of the Godliness of all living and inorganic beings. These creative thinkers merit our attention, for they are the hope of successful theological change.

Going back more than two thousand years, there was Buddha (the Gautama) who, at age 29, renounced his "evil and sensuous life" as the son of a rich family in ancient India. This led him to rebel against established theology, and found the Buddhist religion, in the 6th century B.C. Its tenets demand that we humans "harm no living creature, and keep the mind free from evil and devoted to good."[1]

We have already mentioned the English anthropologist, Sir Edward Tylor, who first used the term *animism* in his work *Primitive Culture* (1872), setting forth the theory that primordial man attributed a soul to all living creatures and inanimate objects; also, George Perkins Marsh, one of the founders of the conservationist movement, who wrote, "the bubbling brook, the trees, the flowers, the wild animals were persons to me, not things." The great Indian statesman, Mahatma Gandhi, himself a believer in Hinduism, and a true activist for reverence of life, called protection of the cow "one of the most wonderful phenomena of human evolution. The cow means to me the entire subhuman world. Man through the cow is enjoined to realize his identity with all that lives."

At the outset of our discussion we noted that reverence of life is practiced more widely among people in the far East and South than in the meat-eating West. Opposition to a Religious Revolution may, therefore, be much stronger from western theologians and the champions of a spurious materialistic abundance. It is the old story that crucial moments of change are met with unyielding resistance from the beneficiaries of the status-quo.

In fairness to the theologians of the West, we must say that the outlook is not all that dismal. We have the determined, if still lonesome, pioneers of much needed theological progress. One of these creative thinkers among today's small minority of open-minded theologians, recently put the problem to me in reverse fashion. He said that theology, at any given moment in human history, including the present, is not the cause of its own static, often outmoded concepts. The real cause is the prevailing *social philosophy*, set forth by the leading theorists and practitioners, in universities, politics, business, dissident religious groups and, indeed, in all walks of life. In large measure, that philosophy is the moral foundation of momentarily right and proper human conduct.

The theologian then concluded his observation by pointing out that theologians, unlike social philosophers, see themselves as the conservators of the best in religion since its presumed beginning. *Consequently*, theology is a strong conservative force in human affairs.[2]

This is truly a thoughtful, life-sustaining commentary, not only for us humans but for all of God's children. On the one hand, it takes cognizance of the role played by momentarily dominant, down-to-earth philosophical intuition, in shaping the concepts and practices of theology and, on the other, recognizes the great power of an intrinsically conservative theology that resists change of its "divinely endowed" dogmas, unless forced to change them by the pressure of a new social philosophy.

This takes us right back to the creative minded biologists, ecologists, conservationists, as well as social revolutionaries, in their common struggle for a just and peaceful society. Let us assume that, in the course of time, the new philosophy will enable them to make substantial progress, and that theologians throughout the world, will be moved by an overwhelming desire to preach the new gospel of the universality of God. It seems reasonable to suppose that their parishioners, everlastingly plagued by the unanswerable question as to whence we came prior to birth and whither we go after death, will take to heart the admonition not to harm or mistreat our land-based plant and animal kin, or to pollute planet Earth's streams, lakes and oceans. If they will not do this out of gratitude for sharing with all God's children, the beautiful garden of life, they will, surely, do it out of fear of eternal damnation in the fires of Hell.

Though all this may be a very difficult goal to reach, the threat of human extermination compels us to make it an actuality. Once attained, it becomes the corner-stone of the equally important—

Occupational Revolution.

It would be a move of great wisdom for any nation to start an occupational revolution. Since its purpose is to minimize human violation of reverence of life, the move must, certainly, be made by the people of the United States. The evidence of our horrendous failure to do this has, of course, been the major subject of Part I of this study. We have, also, as you will recall, discussed specific ways of abandoning our predatory inter-species behavior; and, in these necessarily few first pages of the Ultimate Imperative, have proposed a similar abandonment of false theological concepts, prerequisite to achieving human reverence of life.

We in the United States, now have to confront the prevailing individual-centered philosophy of "me first" with a new social philosophy, advancing the other half of the dual NSHS fundamental: Enlightened Frugality. And this, you will ask, calls for another revolution? Yes, in our occupational practices. But this one may be much easier to win. Unlike the old revolutions, it might, surprisingly enough, be rather enjoyable to all parties concerned.

To make an appraisal of the nature and objectives of so unusual and, allegedly attractive a revolution, suggests the forethought that this might be done most effectively, and clearly, on the presumption that we in the United States have already reached the goal, and have learned a great deal from the experience.

This achievement will, however, require us to project it well beyond thirty years into the future, on the further presumption that we have prevented a nuclear holocaust by the adoption of a sufficient number of the socioeconomic measures, set forth in the previous chapter, to assure the survival of the human family; i.e., social ownership of unreplaceable natural resources, establishment of privately owned non-profit Rochdale Cooperatives, and preservation of small, personally managed profit enterprises. Let us, then, present the futuristic picture in the following manner:

A National Committee of educators, business leaders, vocational specialists, researchers, and other social scientists is visiting us from another country that, like other countries, has not yet adopted our unorthodox education-occupation system. They are eager to learn something about how it works. Our own Reception Committee includes knowledgeable social engineers who planned the system, and practitioners who operate it. We shall designate the visiting participants by the initials VP, and our own committee members, by OCM.

The Chair of our committee has graciously welcomed the visitors, and the VPs have responded with equal cordiality in expressing their thanks for the opportunity to learn about our interesting occupational programs. The interplay of sensible questions and answers has begun, and the VP Chair has made the first remark:

> I should tell you at this opening session why we have asked permission to visit with your committee. Our people have been eager for some time, to become better informed about your remarkable occupational undertaking.
>
> Although we are a very small country, both in size and population, and our national economy is still mainly agricultural, industry has been developing rapidly this past decade. It has brought some benefits and, as you well know, some problems.
>
> We are aware of the problems that afflict the big industrial nations of the west, not just in their domestic affairs but, especially, in the danger of a nuclear war. We have, however, been impressed by your nation's remedial industrial programs, made into law over a period of some years, that have helped reduce such serious problems as pollution of the earth's biosphere, domestic unemployment, crime, immense wealth for the few and impoverishment for the many. Now you have accomplished a nation-wide occupational transformation, that seems to be creating new blessings for your people!
>
> Since yours is the only nation that has done this, we are eager to learn from you, what we need to do to bring some of these benefits to our own people, before the industrial problems hit us harder.[3]

This concluded the VP's initial statement, and the OCM Chair responded again:

> We feel honored, and are happy to have you with us. You are right in your assessment of the old industrial problems, but I have to correct you about the extent of the new occupational system's operation. Its provisions are embodied in our federal, state, and local law, but it is not yet operative on a nation-wide scale. I am sure our committee members will be glad to explain how things are functioning at this stage.

For a moment the OCMs looked questioningly at each other, then gave a kind of collective nod to one of the operating heads, apparently, because of his expertise on the subject. He acknowledged the nod and, with a pleasant smile to the VPs, proceeded.

> It would be wonderful if we could say that our system of dual psycho/physical education-occupation—more about that shortly—were already in effect throughout the nation. No doubt, you realize that we could not restructure our long-existing and complex system of basic education, vocational training and agri-industrial operations, overnight.
>
> It took over a decade just to start the plan. But, once the decision was made by government, business and the sciences, to go ahead, we practitioners, struggling with a malfunctioning, actually, an irresponsibly overdeveloped computerized productive machinery, were ready and eager to replace it with the dual education-occupation human machinery.
>
> In order to avoid costly start-up mistakes that would seriously endanger the sound principles of the system itself, we set up a number of demonstration centers in 2003. We did this, in cooperation with a few states having large industrial cities and interdependent agricultural areas, and whose economic situation was still very bad, due to continued factory closings, high unemployment, and the inevitable suffering by the people.
>
> As we made mistakes in these limited centers, and learned from them, we gradually broadened the scope of operations, until now, twenty years later, the majority of working

people are within the system, and the rest are clamoring for us to move faster, so that they, too, will be in it. I would urge you, our welcome guests, to remember this when you return to your homeland. In fact, I would. . . .

Even before the OCM had finished his last sentence, one of the VPs raised his voice, to shout laughingly, "We'll remember while we're still here, and we'll prod you with a lot of questions about it, as we visit your workplaces."

"Please do," said the OCM in the same good spirit, and resumed his comments:

I started to say that you will be pleased to discover that any country, industrial or rural, will be a much happier place in which to live, when its people have carried out an occupational revolution. Should your people decide to embark on such an exciting undertaking, we will help you in every way we can.

At this point, one of the OCMs interposed, to suggest that it might be a good idea to explain, now, just what our occupational principles and administrative methods are. The Chair agreed and, turning to the VPs, said that, for this task we are fortunate to have with us our famous and beloved social philosopher. For valid reasons, she wishes to remain anonymous at present. I *may*, however, tell you that twenty two years ago she was the inspired theorist and leader of the Occupational Revolution. Today, over two decades into the Twenty First Century, she is perhaps our best informed historian of the revolution. Making a bow in her direction, he said, "It gives me great pleasure to present to you the National Chairman of the United States Occupational Confederation (USOC).

The prominent lady arose, and stood silent for a moment. To the surprise of the VPs, they were not only looking at the top officer of USOC, but at a very attractive young woman—young, because she was, along with an unquestionably laborious public affairs career, still in her middle forties. And so, it was natural for the VPs to respond with hearty applause to the introduction of this remarkable woman. When the hand-clapping subsided, she thanked them and went directly into her assigned dissertation. She began in a light vein:

Our Chair has asked me to take on the rather large task of reviewing some of the major events, before and since the Occupational Revolution, and of explaining the resultant theoretical education/occupation basics of our American society, as they have developed over the years, and continue to support us in 2023.

I promise to make my comments as brief as I possibly can, though they will be a bit more lengthy than those of the previous speakers had to be. I would, therefore, appreciate it, if you will ask me questions or make observations, as we move along, lest I become too wordy and put you to sleep!

My memory tells me that the historical setting in the late 1990s, which made possible our contemporary occupational life-style, needs only a quick review, because all of you are somewhat familiar with it. You will recall that our country's economic conditions became increasingly worse during the first half of the previous decade and, subsequently, unbearable for the great majority of our people.

In 1989 a common feeling of desperation drove them, by the hundreds of thousands, to heed an earlier futile appeal, to launch a genuine grass-roots political organization, which quickly became the American Common-wealth Party (ACP).

You will also remember the socio-economic programs that enabled the amazingly fast-growing ACP to elect a large enough number of federal, state and local candidates, to implement those programs throughout the nation, gradually but surely. There was, of course, bitter opposition from many of the wealthy industrial tycoons, who hated to relinquish their great power and privileged social status.

I think it is important to mention here, that we and they learned an ancient lesson from the struggle; namely, that when the time comes for fundamental social change, no small group of elites, with all its wealth and military weaponry, can stop an informed and well organized people from making the change.

There was, moreover, another, more interesting lesson for *us*. We learned that improved living conditions and social relationships, give birth to new ideas about human well-being. We discovered this, both from a deeper insight into our own aspirations for lasting well-being, and from what we had learned about the peoples who had successfully waged the older, so-called Marxist revolutions. In our way, we had disposed, in large measure, of both the outmoded agricultural and the still vigorous industrial aristocracies.

This brings me to the heart of the subject I want to share with you. In only a few years, some of us began to notice that, despite substantial gains made, much the same upper and lower class inequities that plague the other post-revolutionary nations, were still with us!

Our lofty ideals of creating a truely classless and democratic society in the United States, had not eliminated the two oldest social classes of all. Suddenly, we found ourselves face to face with the common yet crucial knowledge that those classes had existed many centuries before the modern industrial age. . . .

The OCM speaker hesitated and put the fingers of one hand to her lips, presumably, in a thoughtful posture of how to link this knowledge to what she had just called the heart of the matter. She smiled, and continued:

I am simply referring to educators, physicians, lawyers, chemists, business executives, successful writers, artists, musicians, politicians, etc., on the one hand and, on the other, factory workers, unskilled laborers, farm workers, office clerks, blue collar workers, truck drivers, plumbers, etc.

We know that, for the most part, the members of each group perform useful and necessary productive services. But we also know that, throughout history, the inequities of income and social status between the bottom and top group, have driven ambitious individuals, and others dissatisfied with their lot, to outdo their rivals in the mad chase for monetary rewards and social prestige.

We became obsessed with the fear that these self-seeking, individual against individual, struggles for sheer personal advancement, would nullify our short-term ACP programs for a democratic way of life. Ah, yes, it has always been so since time immemorial.

Our own mad search for a solution drove us to scour every public and university library, with no luck, for an idea that might throw some light on our seemingly unsolvable problem.

One night, when our hopes were at their lowest, a group of us met to commiserate with each other. After a while, our senior colleague in his seventies, and a psychologist by profession, thought he should brighten things up a bit. So he related a story that his grandfather told him many years ago, about a multi-talented friend whom they called the renaissance man.

Though this man never made a living by his numerous talents, he greatly enjoyed them. Without any formal training, he could play the violin, cello, and other musical instruments, with considerable skill. He loved to do strenuous physical work outdoors, and every fall he would help his farmer friends do the hard work of harvesting their wheat and oats crops. He was a poet, and often, on a Sunday evening, read his beautiful word-creations to family and friends alike. He enjoyed doing just about any kind of . . .

We wouldn't let the psychologist finish, because four or five of us jumped up like so many Jacks-in-the-box, to holler "Stop! Don't say any more." I shouted, "You got something—the idea we've been looking for!"

That put us to work into the wee hours of the morning. Wittingly or not, our story-teller had given us the key to our search. The task before us now was to put the education/occupation plan into clear and convincing language. Since I was something of a renaissance woman, myself, they shoved the job on to me. As a result, you dear VPs are visiting us a quarter of a century later, to learn and to profit by our experience.

You will be interested to know that, to attain our dual occupational goal, it was necessary, first, to restructure our entire educational system, from the kindergarten to the youth, the university and, perhaps most gratifying, the adult stages. Let me give you the theoretical base for all this.

We started from the premise that human beings are neither all mind nor all matter, but that they are a composite of both. We called this the psycho/physical base of the new learning and achievement objectives. To meet the need for totally different educational concepts, we coined the motto 'as the handle must fit the tool, so must education fit the individual to the twofold role he or she is destined to play, in youth and in adult life.' For the full-life cycle, it meant that we have to prepare the young for their adult role as efficient and happy physically productive and mentally productive co-workers.

After some twenty years since the demonstration projects were begun, our social engineers have acquired sufficient operating knowledge, to help me present a good picture of today's education/occupation process. With respect to the three age-stages, I have often urged that a child's psycho/physical education must start in kindergarten—in fact, even before.

It may surprise you, when I tell you that the ground on which we build is the play world, that all-absorbing preoccupation of child-life, through the enchanted medium of which every child endows its activities with an elixir of pure pleasure.

In play we find genetically all the interests of youth and of adult life. It is at once imitative and suggestive of the adult pursuits. It differs from them only in that it is not burdened by the element of responsibility—though it is none the less absorbing and exciting for want of it! With a sense of pure romance, the child pursues its play objectives, sailing the high seas in a tub, building great houses of paper, harvesting the ripened grain, riding wild horses on a log; in short, conducting without inhibition, all the productive ventures of adult endeavor.

The ever widening experience of these vicarious adventures becomes the first subject of exploitation for the pedagogue. Upon its fertile soil he builds the educational structure of the child. He fashions it to the exclusion, however, of all ethical and impersonal considerations. He proceeds only gradually to a synthesis of the purely personal with the larger social environment.

Proceeding within this framework, we have, therefore, focused the education of young children on the perspectives and consequent interests of childhood. Our primary concern is, of course, the elementary psycho/physical wellbeing of the child.

As a teacher, when not performing my physical work, permit me to say that this is attained, on the physical side, through the development of motor coordination, formal gymnastics, walking, swimming, games of physical exertion, travelling, and extended association with people and things. In the mental and kindred behavioral areas, the creative and aesthetic urge, there are some basic, self-assertive desires in every child, that demand expression very early. They offer the first glimpse of a child's aptitude for color, sound, design, rhythm, proportion, etc. To facilitate their release, children are taught to indulge freely in simple creative arts: drawing, music, handicrafts, dancing.

All of you well know that such first efforts are of a purely groping nature, but not for long. Soon the child begins to display proficiencies in one or more of these natural endowments. To open the way to mental growth, and the sharing of these experiences, we do introduce the child, at an early stage, to the art of reading, writing, and to the elements of mathematics.

As part of the childhood learning process, we also include a simple, descriptive study of some of the natural and biological sciences. Sessions on these are held out of doors, and are directly related to observation. The old classroom book-learning of broad cultural subjects is hardly a part of this.

I think that at this juncture I should mention a very important decision we made shortly after we had adopted the educational values and techniques I have just outlined. It was that the development of the physical and mental—including the aesthetic—aspects, must proceed hand-in-hand with an on-site knowledge of the ever-expanding environment of the child-world. From the synthesis of the two, opened a path of absorbing adventure.

Children now embark on exploratory journeys, first on small, then on larger ones. They go alone and in groups. The circle of the observable world is gradually enlarged until it has encompassed the entire globe, giving to the child both visual and mental perspective.

"A complete circuit of first childhood impressions and responses having been made, the initial stage of educational training comes to a close. The threshold of youth has been reached. The child is ready and eager for new things. It has been made conscious of its own psycho-physical potentialities; acquired a love for the great out-of-doors, and for its kin in both human and unlike forms. It has experienced the first inclinations towards certain aesthetic, physical and creative values. But the habitat is still a personal and particularistic one.

The child has felt the thrill of first contacts, the stimulation of first acquaintanceships; it has sensed the breadth and magnitude of its human existence. Over a period of some ten years it has traversed the far corners of the planet, and has enjoyed the pleasures of expanding motor activity. It has surveyed the Earth, but has not pondered it. The wonders of the natural and of the social world are still made of simple childish stuff; they are still one-dimensional—the present. There has been no attempt to integrate or to evaluate. The inner unity of things past and present is yet a closed secret. The child-world is but one of seeing and doing in the present.

Up to this point, the task of education has been one of building strong the bodies of the young, and of opening wide the portals of the spirit. On this note, I should like to move on to the second stage,—the education of youth . . .

Our speaker was stopped short by a young VP, who began waving her hands vigorously. "Please, may I ask a question?" The answer was a cheerful "yes." She then declared, "I am fascinated. Never have I heard anything so beautiful, and *sensible*, a way of educating young children! Surely, educators gave the idea their hearty support. Am I right?" The answer came with an appreciative smile, and the speaker continued:

Let me say first, that your question, itself, is fascinating; but as to support for us, you are both right and wrong. In the beginning, public reaction to the whole psycho/physical theory was pro and con. The most prominent and authoritative educators called it everything, from ridiculous, impractical, stupid, impossible. The old individualistic scholars joined the majority of business leaders, to condemn it as wasteful day-dreaming and incalculable extravagance. In contrast, was the unexpected enthusiastic support of large numbers of people, in all walks of life and economic levels.

Another eager VP jumped up to ask, "Was this not due to the terrible increase of unemployment, ever since the 1980s, caused by the replacement of productive human beings with so-called computerized technological robots, not only in your country but in all the industrialized nations?" The question brought an instant turn of heads and affirmative nods from all the OCMs. From the speaker came these words:[4]

> Ah, you have hit the nail on the head! Beyond any doubt, the principle of mandatory psycho/physical productive service, required of every able bodied adult, and beginning with the education of our young, was a God-send. It is what brought us the decisive support of seriously concerned leaders in education, agri-industry and, especially, of both leaders and a hundred million rank-and-file working people, whether unemployed or still on the job. Things were so critical, we worked day and night, to win people over to our proposal.
>
> There was, fortunately, also a really cheerful side to all this, that greatly encouraged us. You have to understand that we Americans cherish our democratic heritage. Most of us have a kindred inner feeling of the wholesomeness of doing daily productive work of a simple and physically exhaustive nature, *balanced* with an equally exhaustive daily occupational service of a more intensive kind: technical, artistic, administrative, executive, creative.
>
> It takes no great imagination to deduce from this, that many adults welcomed the dual occupational lifestyle. The beautiful part of the idea was that it did not, necessarily, pit adult members of society against each other in bitter conflict, irrespective of their status as wealthy property owners or poor wage earners; nor did it expect the adults of either community to alter their present occupational careers, for which our ancient single-vocation education and training institutions prepared them in childhood and youth.
>
> Although we soon found that it was too late for adults along in years, to benefit, personally, from the new psycho/physical educational system, this did not deter a substantial number of our elders from the satisfaction of participating in the building of one—for their children, their children's children, and, in truth, for posterity. In doing this, many of the rich felt that they had nothing to lose during their life-time; and the poor saw a better life for their own children.
>
> The OCM speaker was about to move on to the youth period, when an older, somewhat dignified looking member of the VPs, who had

been listening intently, asked permission to make a short comment and ask a question about it. This was gladly given.

"I am much pleased," he said, "by your practice of matching young children's domestic education with gradually broadened global visits to other nations. I realize that, for purposes of optimum communications, many nations—including yours and ours—have adopted Finnish as their official world language, supplementary to their native tongue. Consequently, conversation is no problem for your children when visiting those countries."

He looked around, thoughtfully, then continued. "You may be interested to know that Finnish was chosen, because it is a philological mixture of old Finno-Ugric and Indo-European linguistic stems, thus making it relatively easy for both Western and Asiatic peoples to learn from childhood on.

"This brings me to my question: why do you eliminate so-called book knowledge from childhood education, as you stated earlier? It seems to me that, aside from the ability to converse, the youngsters have an equally important need, and *desire*, to understand the beauties of the countries they visit, as well as those they see while going to and from their destinations. It seems to me that they need some book-learning in geography, perhaps, history and, oh . . . other cultural subjects. I shall appreciate your comment on this." His words were welcome to the OCM speaker:

> I am glad you have brought up the whole matter, because it deals with fundamentals. Yes, the children do need information on the geography of the places and countryside they are visiting; but, the learning process is not of a general nature, nor is it dependent much on books, during the childhood period. The teaching focuses on the specfic area of a given visit, and takes place en-route, in sessions that are planned and supervised by a geologist who gives the youngsters an on-site description of the landscape, and a bit of its geodesic history. They loved it from the very beginning.
>
> Unlike your question about geography, your reference to other cultural subjects takes us back to a stormy period, extending from about 1992 to 2003. We were locked in bitter controversy with our opponents, over the proposed system of psycho/physical education for children.
>
> I should remind you here that, in order to relate your pertinent question on the role of culture in childhood education, to the total subject that prompted your National Committee to visit our country, we are by-passing, for the mo-

ment, the basic information about the youth and adult stages. They embrace education, dual productive services and, in a progressive way, culture. Any reference to them now will become clear when I give you an over-all picture of the two stages in my closing statement.

With respect to the heated dispute, it seemed to us that, since the educational and vocational training, during the youth stage, is to prepare our young people for their dual productive services in the adult world, childhood education must be re-oriented in a manner pertinent to those long-range objectives. Although our logic proved to be sound, after some years, we would never have attained our goal, but for a more powerful force than discussion, by itself.

I have in mind the continuing problem of wiping out massive unemployment, caused by the aforementioned displacement of human labor with computerized, technological robots. Many of you are undoubtedly familiar with the enormity of that problem in the late 1980s, before the American Commonwealth Party took over. By the year 2000, robotry had reduced our normal labor force of a hundred million to little more than one fourth of that number!

We shall forever be indebted to the ACP founders. Their programs had put nearly half of the jobless people back to work, when our disputes began. However, the grim fact that upwards of thirty million were still unemployed, plus the bewildering nature of the cause, was too much to bear. As our verbal battles went on, a mounting wave of desperate voices inundated the opposition to our proposed remedy. Our rescuers included many reputable industrial engineers, researchers, courageous educators, industrial leaders, and distressed people everywhere.

In 2004 Congress established the Demonstration projects. Today, the psycho/physical concept flourishes in education, agri-industry, the arts, the sciences. The improved employment situation, alone, has surpassed our highest expectations.

The OCM speaker paused, to look smilingly at her questioner:

From this quick overview, my dear VP scholar, I hope I can explain, in similarly brief fashion, why the standard cultural subjects are absent in our childhood educational curricula, before I move on to the final topic. I shall simply list the main arguments we used against the opposition in those tense days, state them in the same words we used then, against the very study-courses that your elementary schools, and those of other countries still use. I shall even mention geography as we no longer teach it.

"*Geography*: The study of all the configurations of the planet, and of geological phenomena—this, at a stage when the child had not yet even had the opportunity of observing them with its own eyes, still less of comprehending them!

"*History*: A review of the entire story of the complex adult world from the beginning of recorded time to the present—this, when the child was still deeply engrossed in the external phenomena of its own limited child-world.

"*Economics*: The study of the laws affecting the production and distribution of social wealth, though the child knew not yet how to manipulate effectively even the basic tools, and had never produced an ounce of anything.

"*Civics*: The study of formal communal organization, the subtlest of all the social sciences!

"*Literature*: The fictional interpretation and portrayal of every imaginable experience in the whole gamut of life!

Considering the short time-span since we abandoned these subjects and others of like sophistication, we are amazed at ourselves, that we should ever have made them the first objectives of childhood education. Why the child should be expected to evidence either interest in or appreciation of them, makes no more sense to us now, than to expect the infant to drink before it could suck, to sing before it could talk, or to dance before it can walk. We thank God that first and last things in education have found their proper place in the United States.

During the coming week you will be making your own appraisal of our ongoing educational programs. I shall, therefore, conclude these few retrospective words with but one more comment. It pertains to a rather startling and, indeed, very important disclosure that has already come out of our comparative studies of the old and new educational systems. We have learned that to try to impose upon young children, the ideology of the adult world, in addition to that of the child world, stultifies future development. Our past experience has shown that it does great damage to the equilibrium of the child's personality, because the mental burden of a world unexperienced is too heavy to bear.

Now comes the sad consequence. I'm sure that you thoughtful VPs are also familiar with it, from your traditional educational practices. The ensuing fatigue and ennui have but one effect. The child-mind, repelled instinctively by an artificial body of knowledge, develops a growing aversion to it; and, upon the attainment of maturity, this aversion becomes a fixed idea. The resultant stunting of mental growth thus alienates the adult from a genuine and an abiding thirst for knowledge.

Both your and our records give ample proof of this. Freed in adult life from the cultural impositions that came too early in childhood, they shied away from them for the play-world that came too late. The spiritual works of the masters became a spectre of bygone childhood nightmares, an ogre that haunted them—and of whom they spoke with feigned respect in public, to propitiate him. Small wonder, then, that not too long ago, students of human behavior found the average mental age of adults to be little more than twelve years. The adult in our country was, in truth, an atrophied child!

This is a logical place at which I should make my closing comment about the current educational techniques used to prepare our youth for a full occupational and cultural adult life.

The formal transition to the youth stage is worth mentioning, for it marks the student's introduction to genuine productive activity. Pure play becomes alloyed with the element of service. The child enters, for the first time, the wondrous halls of production. Not that there follows a life of adult responsibility. Far from it! What actually happens is that the individual becomes initiated into his or her role as a member of one of our nation's rapidly expanding *Youth Communities*. Here the fledgling tries his wings. Childhood proficiencies begin to be tested and evaluated under conditions approximating adult society.

I think you will be fascinated by the activities in a Youth Community, when you visit one. It will disclose to you all the productive enterprises—both physical and mental—of adult concern. Self-governing, still under the supervision of the educational departments, the youth communities have their own manufactories, in which are produced not only the necessities of life, but, also, the tools, machines, houses and equipments, with which youth works. There, our young people create their own music, theater, games. The Youth Community is the great laboratory of productive service, in which they seek to find themselves.

I should point to a few more basics, of which you need to take note in your visit. Productivity, though remarkable in volume and quality, is still incidental. There are no quotas, no standard requirements; there is no pace, no established technique. The distinctive part is the latitude permitted to each student for making varied adjustments and readjustments. Early and pronounced vocational inclinations sometimes recede; latent ones develop. First loves are abandoned for new ones. Nonetheless, despite an occasional need for a re-evaluation of aptitudes and occupational goals, few instances present themself in adult life, in which the individual has not found his or her true stride.

Aside from this accomplishment, we cannot overlook the fine productive work that is done by the youth communities, in both the physical and mental (also the creative and aesthetic) productive services. The fact is, they are more than self-sufficient. In physical produce, alone, they manufacture considerably in excess of their young people's own needs. Of course, our youth takes great pride in its annual contribution to the aggregate social wealth.

Words fail altogether to give an adequate picture of a Youth Community's experimental achievements in aesthetic production. You must see for yourself, the creative works in art, music, mechanics, drama, to appreciate them, and to enjoy the freshness and thought-provoking originality of these ventures.

As our youth approach adult years, they require the aid of comparative and historical data. Theory and practice are analyzed, from the simplest methods of antiquity to the most modern ones. The natural and social sciences, and mathematics, are taken up in earnest. Planning, organizational and directive talents come upon the horizon. Performance acquires, at last, the finesse of maturity.

Somewhere between the twentieth and twenty-fifth years, the apprenticeship of youth has been completed. Personal inclinations have matured into multiple proficiencies. The formal inauguration of the young adult into his or her dual occupational position in adult society, is an event of highest meaning. It is an occasion that is never forgotten, both for the joyful festivities attending it and for the recognition of full adult status that it confers.

Now, along with the responsibility of daily psycho/physical productive services, starts the period of comprehensive cultural education. The full grown adult is ready to enter upon the study of history, economics, civics, literature, ethics, philosophy, etc. He begins an intensive study of human cultures because *they* are *a review*, an intriguing contemplation of the end-results of life itself. The adult is in need of and eager for this preoccupation. It has become a reality.

Finally, I have to confess that my closing commentary dealing with the adult stage of dual productive services, which our OCM chair has asked me to share with you, gives me more pleasure than I can possibly convey to you. I realize that this personal enjoyment stems from my reminiscences of the bygone struggles for psycho/physical education that started it all. I am happy that students now learn, from childhood on, and cherish the knowledge, that both common and individual well-being necessitates strict adherence to the mandatory performance of twofold productive service by *everybody*. The rest I can tell you in a few words.

You already know that one half of the mandate requires doing daily repetitive tasks, be they mental or physical or both; the other, engaging in more individualized, in-depth production. Please bear in mind that whatever the two sets of complementary mental and physical occupational services may be, they have been chosen by the students, in the course of their educational developement, because they express more effectively each student's inner psycho/physical urge.

It is, no doubt, clear to you at this point, that the whole complex implied by the above, embraces an innumerable host of productive activities; physical work as an assembly line producer in a diversity of agri-industrial operations; as a farm worker in the field, and in the manufacture of farm tools, machinery, equipments, supplies; as a clerical worker, doing filing, typing, stocking and shelving office materials; and doing all manner of daily chores, adinfinitum.

The *same people* who do these "menial tasks" also do the more "in-depth" work, for which they have been trained within their abilities, aptitudes, and limitations. The duties may be those of a business executive, scientific researcher, opera director, architect, construction engineer, sculpturer, public affairs official, and on and on in all societal functions.

This brings me to my closing comment. In short, it is about our peaceful Occupational Revolution that erupted a quarter of a century ago. It quickly made social upper, middle, and lower class stratification obsolete. The punch-press operator on the three-hour morning shift of a manufacturing plant, who later does his evening work as a history professor at the local university; or the truck driver who, on similar schedule, delivers farm produce to retail stores, then plays the tuba in the state symphony orchestra; or the sheet metal worker who helps produce water tanks and, in his other daily responsibilities, is a physician; and—but to get to the point: none of them has any need to be a member of an "upper class", or to fear being shoved down to a lower one. This panoramic flashback completes my assignment. You have been a wonderful audience, attentive, thoughtful, and patient to hear me out. I give you my heartfelt thanks.

Before our President of USOC had time to express her thanks, the entire assemblage, OCMs as well as VPs, rose to their feet, to give her a standing ovation. After the applause had subsided, the VP Chair was the first to speak:

It is we, my dear lady, who surely owe you our thanks. You have given us much food for thought, to take home to our own people. What you have told us will, moreover, help us greatly, to understand the many operations and institutions we shall be visiting. Again, our deep thanks to you.

The OCM Chair made the closing remarks, after reasssuring the VPs that it will be a pleasure to escort them to whatever and wherever they wish to visit:

I should like to ask you, before we adjourn, to remember the forces that have enabled us to fashion our present way of life. They are, of course, the two fundamentals, essential to human wellbeing: *reverence of life* and *enlightened frugality*. As a matter of fact, it is unlikely that we could have made much progress toward practicing those fundamentals, without the heritage of creative thinkers, who pleaded in vain, throughout the twentieth century, for mankind to stop violating them.

Since we in the United States were the most serious offenders, not only as killers of our own kind, and of our faunal and floral kin in unlike form, but, also, as atrocious polluters of the Earth's biosphere, we soon paid a heavy price on both counts. I urge you, as our thoughtful and well informed guests, to think back to the second half of that era, when our people had become accustomed, in alliance with the super-rich of our giant world corporations, to a profligate life-style. To reiterate, we had succumbed to this, at the cost, on the one hand, of gravely polluting our environment and, on the other, of needlessly denying the right to life of countless non-human sentient living creatures.

By the end of the century, came *our* time to pay and to suffer. I refer to the last decade of the century, when the super-rich ruthlessly displaced human labor with technological robots. You will recall our main speaker's observation that the resultant common suffering brought our people back to their common sense. They launched the ACP programs, and succeeded by means of peaceful political action at the ballot box, in transforming the large, money-mad private-profit corporations—some into non-profit cooperatives, others into social ownership. As sure as day follows night, this ended the greed for making money, which had been the prime cause of environmental pollution and death-dealing warfare; at least, it did so for our people.

Fortunately, for us—no, I should say for all mankind—this happened about the same time, as you well know, as did the great spiritual awakening. That made reverence of life, on a

The Ultimate Imperative

total ecological scope, the cardinal tenet of religious faith. Remember, we called it a Religious Revolution! From any social outlook, it was, certainly, the most significant sequel to those dark years at the close of the old century.

Together, these developments led us to a genuine dedication of reverence of life and enlightened frugality.

And now, I consider it a great privilege and honor, to have been asked to chair this important meeting, and to adjourn it by inviting you to join us in singing our national anthem, adopted by our nation shortly after the Occupational Revolution. The words are enclosed in the program notes each of you have.

We are proud of the excellent organ, and our fine organist, at your right. Let us, then, sing *America The Beautiful*.

THE END.

March 18, 1984
Clearwater, Florida.

Notes

The wide ecological and societal front on which the thrust of Natural Survival Through Human Selection must become operative, makes it impossible to confine our examination to anything less than a broadly integrated, sweeping exploration of many areas of human endeavor: Science, education, religion, industry, agriculture, philosophy and the arts, ecology, politics, for they are all inextricably interwoven.

By the same token, it would be impossible to touch upon more than a few essentials in so all-inclusive a realm of societal affairs; nor can we do more than draw sparingly, almost at random, upon supportive documentation from literally tens of thousands of relevant scholarly books, articles, tracts and treatises poured out monthly by commercial and academic printing presses. (From *The Endangered Human Animal* page 10).

Chapter 1

1. Toynbee, Arnold J.: In *The Observer*, London, January 3, 1973.
2. Kennan, George F.: *Address at Los Alamos*, 4/22/72. *New York Times*, L9, 4/24/72.

Chapter 2

1. Hey, Nigel: *How Will We Feed The Hungry Billions*, 13. Julian Messner, Division of Simon & Schuster, New York, 1971.
2. Montagu, Ashley: *Darwin Competition and Cooperation*, 15. Henry Schuman, New York, 1952.
3. Darwin, Charles: *The Origin of Species By Means Of Natural Selection*; first published in England, November 24, 1859; 78. Collier Books, Division of Macmillan Publishing Co., New York, 1962.
4. Ibid., 78.
5. Ibid., 78.
6. Ibid., 78.
7. Haeckel, Ernst Heinrich, a German biologist and philosopher (1834–1919); an early exponent of Darwinism. Wrote *The Evolution Of Man*, 1874, and *The History Of Creation*, 1864.
8. Keith, Sir Arthur: British anthropologist and anatomist. See his *Religion of a Darwinist*, 1925, and *A New Theory of Evolution*, 1948.
9. Thompson, Thomas: abstracted from author's conversations with him in the winter of 1977.
10. Darwin, Charles: *Origin Of Species*, 75.
11. Ibid., 89.
12. Montagu, Ashley, in aforementioned work, 15.

Chapter 3

1. Darwin, Charles: *Origin Of Species*, 97–98.
2. Ibid., 53, 60, 62, 69.
3. Lorenz, Konrad: *On Aggression*, 27. Harcourt, Brace & World, Inc., New York, 1963.
4. Ardrey, Robert: *African Genesis*, 23. Atheneum, New York, 1961.
5. Ibid., opening I.
6. Ibid., 29.

Chapter 4

1. Kropotkin, Petr: *Mutual Aid*, 11–12. Extending Horizon Books, with Introduction by Ashley Montagu, Boston, 1955.
2. Barnett, S. A.: *Instinct and Intelligence*, 120. Prentice-Hall, Englewood Cliff., N.J., 1967.
3. Ibid., 187–88.
4. Graven, Jacques: *Non-Human Thought*, 61. Translated from the French by Harold J. Salemson. Stein and Day, New York, 1967.
5. Ibid., 63.
6. Ibid., 63.
7. Limbaugh, Conrad: "Clearing Symbioses," *Science American*, 235, August 2, 1961.
8. Ardrey, Robert: *African Genesis*, 81. Atheneum, New York, 1961.
9. Lorenz, Konrad: *On Aggression*, 26–28. Harcourt, Brace & World, Inc., New York, 1963.
10. Ibid.

Chapter 5

1. Huxley, Thomas H.: *Life and Letters of Thomas Henry Huxley*, edited by Leonard Huxley. Vol. 2, 285. Appleton, New York, 1901.

Chapter 6

1. Lack, David: In *Science American*, April 1, 1953.
2. Carrighar, Sally: *Wild Heritage*, 66. Houghton Mifflin Co., Boston, 1965.
3. Asimov, Isaac: *Asimov's Biographical Encyclopedia of Science and Technology*. Doubleday & Co., Garden City, N.Y., 1964; new revised edition, 1972. For more information on great social and natural science researchers, from ancient times to the present, see other biographical encyclopedias available in most public libraries.

Chapter 7

1. Dreifuss, Kurt: *The Other Side Of The Universe*, 77–79. Twayne Publishers, New York, 1961.
2. Author's note: this study does not go into the specifics of the rapid technical development of the crystal radio device in the 1920's, or television in the 1940's. Our interest pertains only to the remarkable features of this new communications medium, which enabled the general public to witness the atrocities of the Vietnam War in the 1960's, via television in their living rooms.
3. Yankelovich, Daniel: In *Bulletin of Atomic Scientists*, January, 1970.
4. Ibid

Chapter 8

1. Udall, L. Stewart: *The Quiet Crisis*, 48–71. Holt-Rinehart and Winston, New York, 1963.

Notes   289

2. Borgstrom, George A.: "The Dual Challenge of Health and Hunger: A Global Crisis." *Bulletin Of Atomic Scientists*, 42, October, 1970.
3. Brown, Harrison: "Science, Technology and the Developing Countries." *Bulletin of Atomic Scientists*, 12, June, 1971.
4. Bculding, Kenneth: "Is Scarcity Dead?" *Public Interest*, 37, May, 1966.
5. In *Bulletin of Atomic Scientists* by Peter Andrews, Orie L. Loucks and Hugh H. Iltis, 2–6, January, 1970.
6. Ibid.
7. Boulding, Kenneth: ibid. as in n.4.
8. Ravel, Jean Francois: *Without Marx Or Jesus*, 1 and 19ff. Doubleday & Co., Inc., Garden City, N.Y. 1971.

Chapter 9

1. Parenti, Robert: Findings of his experiments at Kansas State Teachers College. See *St. Petersburg Times*, April 16, 1973.
2. Noss, John Boyer: *Man's Religions*, 4ff. Macmillan Co., New York, 1974 and 1980.
3. Ibid., 6ff.
4. Tylor, E. B.: *Primitive Culture*. Harper Torchbooks, 1872; re-issued in 1914, as *The Threshold Of Religion*.
5. Noss, John Boyer: *Man's Religions*, 208.
6. Ibid.
7. Stroup, Herbert: *Four Religions of Asia*, 32ff. Harper and Row, New York, 1968.

Chapter 10

1. Wolstenholme, Gorden E.: *Man and His Future*, 23ff. First American edition, dealing with the discussions at the 1963 Ciba Conference. Boston, Little, Brown. Boston, 1963.
2. Ibid., 71.
3. Ibid. Throughout this review of the Ciba Foundation's 1963 Convention, the author covers a wide range of scientific research, discussed by the conventioneers on the comparative data of single and multiple plant yield of protein-rich and amino acid-high food for humans.
4. Hey, Nigel: *How Will We Feed The Hungry Billions*. Editor's introductory statement. Julian Messner, Div. of Simon & Schuster, Inc., New York, 1971.
5. Ibid., 148–154.
6. Ibid., 154–178, and final chapter, "New Paths to Protein Plenty." Contents confirm our subsequent reference numbers 7, 8, and 9, re similar developments in other countries.

Chapter 11

1. Benner, James: See "Food and Population: The World Food Crisis," a group-study made under Benner at California Institute of Technology, 1956.
2. Ibid.
3. Joffe, Joyce: *Conservation*, 11, 23, 42–46, 54. Natural History Press, Garden City, N.Y., 1970. Published for American Museum of Natural History (Science Library).
4. Marsh, George Perkins: *Man and Nature*. See Introduction by David Lowenthal, XI. Cambridge, Belknap Press, in collaboration with Harvard University Press. First published by Charles Scribner, New York, 1864.
5. Huxley, Elizabeth (Elspeth). See Fitter, Richard S.: *Vanishing Wild Animals*, 18–19. Franklin Watts, Inc., New York, 1968.
6. McCoy, J.J.: *Saving Our Wildlife*: 210. Crowell-Collier Press (The Macmillan Co.), New York, 1970.
7. Fitter, Richard: *Vanishing Wild Animals of the World*, 17.

8. Perry, Bill: *Our Threatened Wildlife*, 16. Coward and McCann, Inc., New York, 1969.
9. Fitter, Richard: as above. Covers a wide range of endangered wildlife both in the United States and around the world. See, especially, 17–22, 28–32, and 89–107.
10. Sutten, Ann and Myron: *New Worlds for Wildlife*, 74–84, 173. Rand McNally & Co., Chicago, 1970.
11. Ibid.
12. Lindahl, Kai Curray: *Conservation For Survival*, 6ff and 204ff. William Morrow & Co., New York. See, also, Richard Fitter and John Leigh Pemberton, *Vanishing Wild Animals Of The World*.
13. Moore, J. Howard: *The Universality of Kinship*, Preface, VII. Charles A. Kerr & Co., Chicago, 1906.

Chapter 12

1. Singer, Peter: *Animal Liberation*, 31ff. Cites authentic data on the enormous number of domesticated and wildlife animals subjected to being injected with, and/or forced to take orally, toxic drugs and chemicals for experimental purposes. Avon Books; division of Hearst Corporation, New York, 1975. The study includes evidence of the appalling suffering endured by the animals for weeks and months, until death takes them.

    As to the enormity of the practice, the author refers to the following: "A 1971 survey carried out by Rutgers University College of Agriculture and Environmental Sciences, produced the following estimates of the number of animals used each year in U.S. laboratories: 85,000 primates, 500,000 dogs, 200,000 cats, 700,000 rabbits, 46,000 pigs, 23,000 sheep, 1.7 million birds, 45 million rodents, 15–20 million frogs, and 200,000 turtles, snakes and lizards; a total of more than 63,000,000 animals."

    In Chapter III, 93 titled "Down on the Factory Farm," he presents an equally startling picture of the "scientific" atrocities invented by angri-industrial corporations in raising and selling chickens, pigs and other farm animals.

    On 163–189, is presented a most interesting analysis of the pros and cons of becoming a vegetarian with/or without animal products like milk, cheese and eggs. The entire treatise warrants careful reading.
2. Celso-Ramon Garcia and Edward Wallach: *Biochemical Changes and Implications following long term use of oral contraceptives*, 253–275. Study made at the University of Pennsylvania, 1970.

    See also, Bernard J. Duffy, Jr. and Sister M. Jean Wallace: *Biological and Medical Aspects of Contraception*, 19, 21–22, 34, 60, 65–71, 87–96, and 109–113. University of Notre Dame Press, London, 1969.
3. Djerassi, Carl: *Birth Control After 1984*; a paper written by him at Stanford University, 122–229.
4. Ibid.
5. See Fitter, Richard: *Vanishing Wild Animals of the World*, 18–19.
6. Joffe, Joyce: *Conservation*, 23ff, 42, 46. For Natural Science Library, New York, 1970.

Chapter 13

1. Report of the President's Commission on Law Enforcement and Administration of Justice: The Challenge of Crime in a Free Society, 1, 4, 24. Washington, D.C., February 16, 1967.
2. *Newsweek*, 20. August 16, 1965.
3. Evans, Medford Stanton, and Margaret Moore: *The Law Breakers*, 22, 25–26. Also, see *Washington Star*, April 4, 1965; *Saturday Evening Post*, June 27 and July 4, 1964; *Wall Street Journal*, March 23, 1967; *Life Magazine*, December 3, 1965; *Look Magazine*, May 31, 1966.

4. Clark, Ramsey: *Crime In America.* Introduction by Tom Wicker, 11; also, 101–116, 189–238, 330–337; see, especially, Chapter XIII, titled "Prisons: Factories of Crime." Simon & Schuster, New York, 1970.
5. *Look* magazine, 21–27. May 31, 1966. Compares enormity of crime rate in the U.S. with much lower ones in other major nations around the world. See also, *Time* magazine, 76, November 6, 1978.
6. Banay, Ralph S.: *We Call Them Criminals*, 270–291. Appleton-Century-Crofts, New York, 1957.
7. Mitford, Jessica: *Kind and Usual Punishment*, 139–168. A.A. Knopf, New York, 1973; also see Robert E. Hodges and William B. Bean: "The Use of Prisoners for Medical Research," *Journal of the American Medical Association*, vol. 202, no. 6., November 6, 1967. Refers to "prison experiments in Alabama;" also to "report of U.S. Senate Subcommittee on Monopoly of the Select Committee on Small Business, Competitive Problems in the Pharmaceutical Industry. Part 14, hearings, 91st Cong., 1st session, June 19, August 7 & 12, 1969. Washington, D.C. Government Printing Office, 5689."
8. Banay, Ralph S.: same work and pages as above, under n.6.
9. Ibid.
10. Above mentioned Report of President Johnson's Commission on Law Enforcement, and The Challenge of Crime; see also the Commission's report in 1966.
11. *St. Petersburg Times*, 20A, March 10, 1979. See also Robert L. Heilbronner's, *In The Name of Profit.* Doubleday Co., New York, 1972. As Editor of the Book, Heilbronner presents a list of startling court cases, and other crime investigations, researched by a group of specialists, regarding so-called white collar "dark" crimes committed by large, well known agri-industrial corporations in the United States.

PART TWO
Chapter 14

1. Board, Joseph B.: *Government and Politics of Sweden*, 22. Houghton Mifflin Co., Boston, 1970.
2. Ibid., 23.
3. Ibid., 25, 178, 188.
4. Jenkins, David: *Sweden and the Price of Progress*, 38. Coward-McCann, Inc. New York, 1968.
5. Ibid., 39–42.
6. Ibid., 39–42.
7. Ibid., 39–42.
8. Ibid., 39–42.
9. Fleisher, Wilfred: *Sweden The Welfare State*, 240. John Day Co., New York, 1956.
10. Board, Joseph: ibid., 188.
11. Ibid., 21.
12. Ibid., 229.
13. Fleisher, Wilfred, ibid., 230.

Chapter 15

1. James, Daniel: *Mexico and the Americans*, 4. Frederick Praeger, New York. 1963. See also, Calvert, Peter: *Mexico*, 23–48. Details the growing power of big corporations in the USA, in a struggle with British, French, Spanish and native Mexican land owners, for possession and control of Mexico's natural resources in oil, minerals and metals. Cambridge University Press, London, 1968.
2. Cumberland, Charles: *Mexico, The Struggle for Modernity*, 3–11. Oxford University Press, New York, 1968.
3. James, Daniel: ibid. per n.1, 9–11.

4. Sundel, Alfred: *A History of the Aztecs and Mayas, and their Conquest*, 59ff. The Macmillan Co., New York, 1967.
5. Cumberland, Charles: ibid. per n.2, 41–62. Also see James, Daniel per above, 18ff.
6. Cumberland, Charles: ibid. 79.
7. James, Daniel: ibid., 20–21 re French and USA Revolutions; 23–29, re Miguel Hidalgo: 87–100, re victorious role played by Benito Jaurez.
8. Ibid.
9. Ibid., 34, 37, 40–43, 47–48. Also see Haley, Edward: *Revolution and Intervention*, 11–15. The M.I.T. Press, Cambridge, Mass., 1970.
10. Parkes, Henry Bunford: *A History of Mexico*, 306–10. Houghten Mifflin Co., 1960. Also, James, Daniel, ibid. 61–65.
11. James, Daniel: ibid., 117–19, 154ff; also, Parkes, ibid. per above.
12. Cumberland, Charles: ibid., 191–92, 224, 234.
13. Ibid., 207–08, 203.
14. Ibid., 241–242.
15. Parkes, Henry B.: 319–22, 401–10.
16. Cumberland, Charles: 288.
17. Ross, R. Stanley: *Is the Mexican Revolution Dead?*, 103–106. Alfred A. Knopf, New York, 1966.

Chapter 16

1. Olgin, Moissaye J.: *The Soul Of The Russian Revolution*, 13ff. Henry Holt and Co., New York, 1917. The author, a well known Russian journalist, produced this work during many years before and up to the outbreak of the Revolution. It is perhaps the finest, most comprehensive and compassionate treatise in existence, on the historical setting and causes of the Revolution. Olgin left to posterity an incredible overview of the suffering endured by the Russian people under the Tzars. As a journalist and scholar, he attended numerous sessions of the powerless national legislative body (the *Duma*), and made honest reports about the appalling social and economic conditions throughout the nation, revealed at those sessions and from his own findings. For this, he had to flee to the United States to avoid being exiled to Siberia, or assassinated by the Tzar's secret police. His work was published in New York at the very moment that the Revolution erupted and the Tzarist autocracy was overthrown. It is worth reading from cover to cover.
2. Ibid., 25–43.
3. Ibid., 50–55, 136ff, 169ff.
4. Ibid., 105–112.
5. Moorehead, Alan: *The Russian Revolution*, 10ff, 41ff, 44, 46, 80, 136, plus Editor's Foreword, VII–VIII. Harper and Brothers, New York, 1958. See also Reed, John: *Ten Days That Shook The World*, Author's Preface and 5–6; also, Introduction by Bertram D. Wolf. Random House, New York, 1960.
6. See Smulkstys, Julius: *Karl Marx*, 15–18. Twayne Publishers, New York, 1974; also, Karl Marx and Frederick Engels, *Selected Works*, a collection of works by Marx and Engels, 413–417. International Publishers, New York, 1968.
7. Karl Marx was a creative social philosopher and prolific writer. Through the years, so many publishers in the USA and other countries, have come out with books, letters, public addresses, magazine and newspaper articles—by both Marx and his most important collaborator, Frederick Engels—that present-day historians and students find themselves citing data on Marx's ideas and theories from a great variety of sources.

Marx was a political activist as well as a scholar. Since he expressed himself in a wide range of media, with little or no change in the wording of basic ideas that he voiced over and over, discussed first in Germany, then, around the world, it seems wise to supplement our limited citations with a list of his major writings. Interested readers can find published data on them in many public and/or private libraries, in just about all languages. The works of Karl Marx include:

Capital (six volumes); *The Communist Manifesto*, by Karl Marx and Frederick Engels; *Wage Labour and Capital* (in the Neue Rheinische Zeitung); *Preface To A Contribution To The Critique Of Political Economy*; *Theses On Feuerbach*; *Wages, Price and Profit*.

8. Karl Marx and Frederick Engels: *The Communist Manifesto*, 9, 18–19. International Publishers Co., Inc., New York, 1968.
9. Ibid., 19.
10. Ibid., 19, 21.
11. Ibid., 19.
12. Ibid., 30.
13. Ibid.
14. See John Reed, (re Lenin's character), 170; also, Alan Moorehead, 38–39, 40ff; also, Louise Bryant: *Six Red Months In Russia*, 137–139. George H. Doran Co., New York, 1918. It should be pointed out that the books by Reed and Bryant are of special importance. These two young people were journalists from the United States, who decided to be on location when the Revolution erupted in 1917. While there, they got to know many of the key leaders and met them personally, including Lenin and Trotsky.
15. Marx, Karl: *Neue Rheinische Zeitung*, September 14, 1848. Cologne, Germany.
16. International Publishers, re the peasants, 171ff; the Dictatorship of the Proletariat, 43, 46, 48, 52–53, 63, 326–327, 331.
17. Moorehead, Alan, 35.
18. Ibid., 41, 43.
19. Ibid., 44–45.
20. Ibid., 46ff.
21. Moorehead, 46–48.
22. Ibid., 80; see also, Louise Bryant, 139.

Chapter 17

1. Moorehead, 158–163.
2. Daniels, Robert V.: *Red October*, 4–7. Charles Scribner's Sons, New York, 1967; see Moorehead re Order No. 1, 153–154.
3. Reed, as above; explains names and roles played by numerous political groups, after the Tzar abdicated. See Notes and Explanations in opening pages of the book.
4. Trotsky, Leon: *The Russian Revolution*, 213, 261. (Lenin's call for revolutionary action); for aspects of the April Theses, 35, 36, 49, 61, 97–99, 209. Doubleday & Co., New York, 1959.
5. Moorehead, 187.
6. Trotsky, Leon, 48.
7. Schuman, Frederick L.: *Soviet Politics*, Alfred A. Knopf, New York, 1946.
8. Daniels, 109–111.
9. Ibid., 36–41.
10. Reed, 5.
11. Goldston, Robert: *The Road Between Wars, 1918–41*, 158–159. Dial Press, New York, 1918.
12. Ibid., 158.
13. Reed, John, 5–8; Lenin's appeal to Workers, Soldiers and Peasants, 148ff; re opposition by Mensheviks and propertied classes, 159, 165.
14. See Daniels, for description of the siege of Winter Palace, Chapter Nine, 165–199.
15. Bryant, Louise, as in Chapter XV for "on-location" report on the brighter side of the "siege;" see Chapter VIII, 79–89. See, also, Moorehead, Alan, Chapter XIV, 240–257.
16. Moorehead, 271–285, especially, 276.
17. Deutscher, Isaac: *Ironies of History—Essays on Contemporary Communism*. Oxford Press, New York, 1966.

294   Notes

18. Archer, Jules: *Trotsky, World Revolutionary*: covers in some detail Trotsky's remarkable military tactics that saved the emerging communist state from defeat by the allied armies of the Western European capitalist nations, plus Japan, and problematical aid from the United States. The major data are contained in pages 84–118, especially, 84, 98, 109–118. Julian Messner, New York. 1973.
    See, also, William Manchester: *The Last Lion*, 673–690. This section of the book, a biography of Winston Churchill, cites the desperate state of the Red Army "till one Leib Davidovich Bronstein, Leon Trotsky, became the Bolshevik's War Minister and proved himself to be a genius," 675ff; Churchill's intense hatred of the Bolsheviks, 676, 679, 681ff; "Lenin's and Trotsky's military supremacy, leading to the defeat of the Allied Invasion," 685–690.
19. Deutscher, Isaac: *Stalin, A Political Biography*. Gives excerpts from Lenin's Testament, 247ff, 250–251. Oxford University Press, New York and London, 1949. Footnote: "Lenin's Will" is quoted here from L. Trotsky's, *The Real Situation In Russia*, 320–321.
    Deutscher, as in n.17.

Chapter 18

1. Schuman, Frederick: His Speech at the Garrick Theater in Chicago; the author of this book heard it while at the meeting.
2. Goldston, Robert: *The Rise Of Red China*, 33, 34, 45–46; also, re the ancient aristocracies, Chapters II–III; re the suffering of Chinese peasants, 94–102. Bobbs-Merrill Co., New York, 1967.
3. Moorehead, Alan, 4.
4. Trotsky, Leon, 276.

Chapter 19

1. Snow, Edgar: *Red Star Over China*, 72, 97–99. Grove Press, Inc., New York, 1973.
2. Committee of Concerned Asian Scholars: *China! Inside The People's Republic*, 27. Bantam Books, Inc., a National General Co., New York, 1972.
3. Ibid., 25, 32–34.
4. Snow, Edgar, 160–161.
5. Note: For the rest of this chapter and all but a few pages toward the end of the next one, our reference data come from Edgar Snow's, *Red Star Over China*. The reason was stated in Snow's own words, in a conversation he had with Mao Tse-tung during a six month stay in the latter's "cave-office," after making a breakthrough into the Red Army's Northwest territory in 1936: "It seemed to me one of the amazing facts of our age that during the entire history of the soviets in South China, not a single 'outside' foreign observer had entered Red territory—the only Communist-ruled nation in the world besides the USSR. Everything written about the southern soviets by foreigners was therefore secondary material." 185.
    With this in mind, we shall simply list, in one sequence, data coming from Snow, after our reference number(s), followed by his book's page number(s).
6. 214–216. 7. 101. 8. 161ff. 9. 74–76.

Chapter 20

1. 165–171. 2. 172–177. 3. 178–179. 4. 180, 185–188.
5. Re the Evacuation for The Long March, 188–189.
6. Re The Long March, 190–199, 201–206.
7. Re The Yenan Period, 209–213, 336 (Red Army University at Pao An); BN 471 (Hsu Tehli); 465 (Chu Teh); 462 (Chou En-lai); 247, (Battles, to capture machinery and tools).

8. 373–383 (Anti-Japanese movement and the Sian Incident); see also, Allen, Steve: *Explaining China*, 150. Crown Publishers, Inc., New York, 1980.
9. Snow, Edgar, 108.
10. 360, re continued enormous financial and military aid to Chiang Kai-shek by the United States.
11. 397, 411–412.

Chapter 21

1. De Castro, Jesue: *The Black Book Of Hunger*, 21–25. Funk & Wagnalls, New York, 1967.
2. Ibid., 34–35.
3. Chesneaux, Jean: article in *Life* magazine, May 1, 1944.
4. Committee of Concerned Asian Scholars, 295–300. See also, *Bulletin of the Atomic Scientists*, 31, January, 1972; also, David Milton, Nancy Milton, and Franz Schurmann: *The China Reader*, Vol. 4, XXIX, 393–416. Vintage Books, New York, 1972.
    Note: From 1950 to 1958, the Soviet/Sino Friendship Treaty provided the PRC with crucially needed military and industrial aid. Then came the split, due not only to old clashing national interests over boundary territories between the two countries but, also, to new ideological clashes as to what a Communist society should be! This permits only fractionated documentation of cooperation between the PRC and USSR during the aforementioned short period.
5. Ibid., as under n.4 above.
6. Kirkpatrick, Clayton: *Understanding China*. Kirkpatrick's report was published daily from July 6 to the 13th. The excerpts were taken from the issues of July 6, 7, and 13. At the time, an attractively bound copy was available to the public, without charge. It contains excellent photographs and, coming from the Editor of a nationally influential, conservative newspaper, it is remarkably laudatory to China, as he saw it during his visit with other editors for nearly a month.
7. Committee Of Concerned Asian Scholars: a retrospective view of *The Spirit Of Yenan*, 35–45; also, the Committee's analysis of Mao's great success in establishing a "classless" society during the Yenan days versus the reappearance of class distinctions after peaceful, normal domestic life was resumed in the PRC. This led to bitter clashes between adherents to Mao's societal outlook and other old comrades-in-arms, who were in support of the way things were going, 46ff. The struggle was exacerbated by Mao Tse-tung's break with the leaders of the Soviet Union, over the same alleged restoration of a class society. It brought on the Cultural Revolution, 71–103.
8. Ibid., 72–73.
9. Ibid., 77–84.
10. The China Reader, as above: 30–31, 38.
    Note: At this point we conclude our "overview of the main events" of the Cultural Revolution. We have cited, only partially, what a number of competent and knowledgeable scholars have said about it in much greater detail. Some witnessed at first hand, the early development of the Revolution; others, at a later stage. They dealt in considerable detail with important aspects that we have only mentioned. We shall now refer to the pages and/or chapters of two of their works most pertinent to our own more limited coverage:
11. (a) *China! Inside The People's Republic*, by the Committee of Concerned Asian Scholars: Introduction, pp. 1–22. The 15-member Committee points out that they are all in their twenties, are students or teachers, and speak and read Chinese; also, that soon after they arrived they discovered their own stereotyped American notions about Chinese life during and since the Revolution. They then describe the background of each of the Committee's members, and how they made their initial adjustment to Chinese realities, supplemented by listing the groups's itinerary from June 23, 1971 to July 24, 1971.

The initial subject-matter of the report itself, focuses on background data under the headings *Years of Bitterness*, referring to past oppression and how the Chinese "keep the memory alive" for both children and adults, 23–34; *The Spirit of Yenan* that continued to inspire leaders and "the masses" alike during the early days of the People's Republic Of China, up to the beginning of great dissension among the leaders, which brought on the Cultural Revolution, 35–70.

By far the longest and most important part of the report pertains to the Cultural Revolution. That domestic struggle went on for ten years, from the time of Mao Tse-tung's disenchanting visit to Moscow in 1958 to celebrate the fortieth anniversary of the Bolshevik Revolution, to about 1968. The report starts with a review of the years before and shortly after the Cultural Revolution began. Then come the major Four Stages of the Revolution, entitled: *Mobilization of the Workers and Testing Public Opinion; Exposure and Criticism of the Capitalist Roaders; Seizure of Power and Formation of Revolutionary Committees;* and *Struggle, Criticism, and Transformation,* 70–90.

These discussions and assessments became the basics for a comprehensive sharing of what the young Concerned Asian Scholars had learned, 91 to end of report.

(b) *The China Reader: People's China.* The authors of Vol. IV—David Milton, Nancy Milton, and Franz Schurmann—confine their treatise to the period from 1966 to 1972, which is roughly concurrent with the beginning and end of the Cultural Revolution. Unlike the direct personal contact method of the Concerned Asian Scholars, from which to acquire their knowledge of the tumultuous events in the People's Republic of China, these scholars avoid completely the direct personal approach. Having written three previous volumes on China, the first covering the 18th and 19th Centuries, and the next two, the years 1911–1972, they choose to let prominent Chinese political leaders, journalists and scholars, as well as western top political leaders, journalists and writers, express their pro and con views on the Cultural Revolution and related subjects.

This largely impersonal technique enables the authors to give a remarkably intimate picture of the roles played by such key figures as Mao Tse-tung, Chou En-lai, Liu Shao-ch'i and Lin Piao, and by writers for the *People's Daily*, *Peking Review*, and *Red Flag*; by western journalists like James Reston of the *New York Times*, government heads like Julius Nyerere of Tanzania, Richard Nixon of the United States, and V. Pavlov of the USSR.

To give cohesion to this wide diversity of formal and authentic information, in a book of over 600 pages, the authors provide commentaries on the over-all settings, problems and objectives relevant to the subject to which the particular expressions address themselves. These explanatory statements begin with the *Introduction*, xix–xxx; with the sections on *Great Social Experiments*, 3–24; *The Cultural Revolution*, 217–237; and *China In The World*, 393–419.

Chapter 22

1. John Case and Rosemary C. R. Taylor: *Co-ops, Communes & Collectives*, 93. Pantheon Books, New York, 1979.
2. *Encyclopaedia Britannica*, Vol. 6, Cocker-Duis, 1969, 441–458; summarizes development of Rochdale Co-ops in Europe, Asia, Africa, and western hemisphere; has bibliography.
3. Zukin, Sharon: *Beyond Marx and Tito*, 48–49, 60ff, 187–188. An excellent study of the Yugoslavian system of property ownership, that merges worker self-management with the principle of Rochdale Cooperatives. Cambridge University Press, Cambridge, England, 1975. See, also, the periodical, *Northern Neighbors*, 16, April, 1981. Gravenhurst, Ontario, Canada. The article attributes "*absence* of unemployment, soaring prices and declining trade, to enormous development of co-ops in Soviet Union." See also, Encyclopaedia, as above.
4. *Co-ops, Communes & Collectives*, 106.

5. We should add to the standard practices of domestic and foreign—sometimes modified but basically sound—Rochdale Cooperatives, a current, ingeniously conceived and promising national coordinating project known as Co-op America. One of its co-founders and Director, Paul Freundlich, seeks to bring together producers and consumers who share the aspiration in a practical, economic manner, for cooperation toward community well-being and environmental conservation. Co-op America, he says, is a non-profit association of *individual* and *organization* members. Among the benefits it provides are a market-place for the exchange of the members' products and services—alternate health insurance—social investment information, a catalog of the products and services included, and a membership magazine. For more information, contact Co-op America, 2100 M Street NW, Suite 310, Washington, D.C. 20063.

Chapter 23

1. See *Columbia Encyclopedia*, 2084–2085. Columbia University Press, New York, 1959. Every standard encyclopaedia contains this information.
2. Graham, Shirley: *There Was Once A Slave*, Prologue, IX, Chapter One, 3ff. Julian Messsner, Inc., New York, 1947.
3. Scheinfeld, Amram: *Your Heredity and Environment*. J. P. Lippincott Co., 1965.
4. *Columbia Encyclopedia*, 1371.
5. With respect to the urgent need for effective occupational training and employment of the elderly and handicapped, it should be said here, that I, as the author of this book, have been employed from 1920 to 1971 by both private and governmental social agencies dealing with this problem. My experience for more than fifty years, and that of numerous colleagues, speaks in a strong, unanimous voice, that it is absolutely necessary to develop the proposed programs.
6. *Newsweek*, 74, June 1, 1981: Reports on the purchase by 2000 employees of the 90 year old Roth Packing Company of Waterloo, Iowa, to save the company from bankruptcy. Article points out the bona fide nature of the transfer of ownership, in contrast to the much publicized ESOPS being promoted by the owners of big corporations.
7. Lens, Sidney: "The Promise of Self-Management," in *The Progressive*, 43–45, October, 1981. See also, Landry, Wilbur G.: "The future as seen in Japan—it works." This is a series of articles in the *St. Petersburg Times*, September 27 to October 3, 1980, that attribute success to a Japanese modified version of ESOPS.
8. Hochschild, Adam: "Shuttling Manhattans To The Sky." Article in *Mother Jones*, 37–39, May, 1978.
9. See *Toward Freedom*, a monthly newsletter published in Chicago. It contains an article on "the 77," now the Non-Aligned Nations, by Homer A. Jack: *Bandung Influence Continues Down The Decades*; makes a brief statement on the origin and development of this international organization, 2, June, 1980.
10. See *The New Yorker*, 145ff., October 22, 1979, which gives an anti-Soviet Union opinion of the then ongoing conference of the Non-Aligned Nations in Cuba; see also, *Maclean's*, 31, September 10, 1979, published in Toronto, Canada, for a less one-sided appraisal.
11. See *The Case for a United Nation's System of Bicameral World Federation*, a 43-page booklet published in 1974, by the Society for a World Federation. The closing pages of this chapter are based, largely, on this document.

Chapter 24

1. Basic information on Buddhism, including bibliography, is available in every standard encyclopaedia.
2. Spoken by the Reverend John E. Burciaga, Minister of The Unitarian Universalist Church of Clearwater, Florida.

3. The basics of the ensuing discussion at the *presumed* conference, held in the United States in the year 2023, and attended by the visiting National Delegation of a small nation, and the national representatives of our own country—those basics were set forth, as already stated, in *The Other Side Of The Universe*, published in 1961 by Twayne Publishers, New York. It was again published in 1979 by Pomurska Zalozba, Belgrade, Yugoslavia, where it made the best seller list.
4. See *USA Today*, August 9, 1983; reports a study—and prediction—made by the AFL-CIO on the enormity of unemployment to be expected by 1990, due to the use of technological robots instead of human labor.